THE FRUGAL GOURMET COOKS AMERICAN

JEFF SMITH

"Smith is hotter
than his Hunan Bean Curd with Peppers
and the ingredients of his success
are as varied and exotic."
People

"The Frugal Gourmet
is known as the Leo Buscaglia of cooking...
but he is invariably true to his title—and frugal,
he likes to point out, doesn't mean cheap;
it means not wasting anything."
Newsweek

THE FRUGAL GOURMET COOKS AMERICAN

JEFF SMITH

Illustrations by Chris Cart

AVON BOOKS ◣ NEW YORK

Other **FRUGAL GOURMET** *Books by*
Jeff Smith
from Avon Books

THE FRUGAL GOURMET COOKS WITH WINE
THE FRUGAL GOURMET COOKS THREE ANCIENT CUISINES

Permissions, constituting a continuation of the copyright page, are listed on pages 527-529.

AVON BOOKS
A division of
The Hearst Corporation
1350 Avenue of the Americas
New York, New York 10019

Copyright © 1987 by Frugal Gourmet, Inc.
Illustrations copyright © 1987 by Chris Cart
Front cover photograph copyright © 1987 by Dale Wittner
Published by arrangement with William Morrow and Company, Inc.
Library of Congress Catalog Card Number: 87-28163
ISBN: 0-380-70672-5

First Avon Books Printing: July 1990

AVON TRADEMARK REG. U.S. PAT. OFF. AND IN OTHER COUNTRIES, MARCA REGISTRADA, HECHO EN U.S.A.

Printed in the U.S.A.

OPM 10 9 8 7 6

To Patty Smith
my wife, and a true American patriot,
with the patience of Martha Washington,
the insight of Eleanor Roosevelt,
and a serious commitment to
a Coney Island hot dog

Acknowledgments

Trying to thank the people behind my efforts in this book is like trying to thank my history teacher in high school. You never know what you owe that giving person until long after the gift is given.

I am fortunate to be able to thank most of the people that have caused me to think about food and American history . . . and for me the two are tied together so closely that I now have trouble separating a turkey from a history lesson!

The most important contributor to this book is the Native American. We Europeans were met on the shores by a gracious people who taught us how to survive in *their* land, and now they must certainly wonder about what they have done.

I thank the American farmer. He has fed us well for two hundred years and now wonders what will become of his own farm and family.

And I raise a pork sparerib to James Beard. He was the first to begin trying to teach us that there is such a thing as American cuisine.

Ivar Haglund, the Clam Impresario of Seattle, is dead now, so I cannot tell him what an effect he had upon my youth in Seattle. I expect he is now offering the Holy Spirit some new ideas for clam dishes.

This whole binge on food and American history began with the President's Council, a group of very busy women in Tacoma, Washington. They asked me to write a short talk for the Bicentennial celebration some years ago . . . and I have not been able to stop the research. This book is their fault!

Bless the people who have helped me dig about through kitchens and monuments and memories. My lady friends in New Hampshire, the historians at Mount Vernon, Monticello, and Colonial Williamsburg. I thought these places were tourist joints . . . and now I know they are places of serious historical insight and education.

My own office staff has been more help than I could have believed. Here's a big turkey to Dawn, Mark, Craig, Tracy, and Vinita. Thanks, gang. Now, pass the dressing. Give Craig an extra-large helping for his skill in testing so many of these recipes.

Here is a pumpkin pie for my special friends at Fante's in Philadelphia, and to those gracious people in Albuquerque. Save a slice for Lillian in Atlanta and for Harriet Fields in Tacoma.

The great farmers' markets of this country remain an inspiration to me. May we long appreciate the Pike Place Farmer's Market in Seattle, the Reading Terminal Market in Philadelphia, the South Water Street Market in Chicago, the Open Market at Faneuil Hall in Boston, the Italian Market in Philadelphia, the Central Market, Los Angeles, the French Market in New Orleans, and the Indianapolis City Market. These places are genuine American institutions.

The beautiful illustrations in this book were created by a young man named Chris Cart. The pictures will be an inspiration to you as he has been an inspiration to me. I am still amazed that he understands my feelings on this subject so completely.

I love the cover photograph on this American book, and, as you can see, the jacket is the work of many people. The dear lady sitting next to me is Pasqualina Verdi. She has been selling her homegrown produce in the Pike Place Farmer's Market for decades, and she has become a dear friend. The stall that we are sitting in is the Pure Food Fish Company, one of Seattle's food institutions. Solly is owner and friend. The Boy Scouts of America, of which I was a member for years in my youth, have provided the color and enthusiasm for the picture. David McNeil, the taller Scout, is a gracious young man, and he hopes some gorgeous young lady will see this picture and call me for his number. The other Scout, Geoff Emerson, is the youngest Eagle Scout in the entire Seattle Council. I am proud of him. And, I am proud of Lucille, the turkey. She is a pro and was willing to sit in my lap for this picture. Did you ever try to teach a turkey to sit in your lap? Don't.

I offer up a cranberry pie to Mom. (You thought that I was going to say apple pie, didn't you? She would prefer cranberry pie.) She has continued to offer me support, guidance, and confidence through the years . . . and several recipes for this book.

Pour a good California dry sherry and drink it to our American restaurants. We eat so well in this country and we really do not give the restaurateurs enough credit. So, here's to some of my favorite *American* restaurants. To Place Pigalle and Ivar's Indian Salmon House in Seattle. To Sauerken's and Star's Delicatessen in New York. To Jake's Crawfish House in Portland, Oregon, and to The Rattlesnake Club in Denver. To the Union Oyster House and Durgin-Park, Boston, and to Joe's Stone Crab in Miami Beach. To Naw'lins Cookery, the Bon Ton, and Commander's Palace in New Orleans. To Café American and Tadich's Grill in San Francisco and to Arthur Bryant's in Kansas City. To Carson's Ribs, Pizzeria Uno, and Byron's Hot Dog Stand in Chicago. And to La Tertulia in Santa Fe, New Mexico, and Harbor Lights in Tacoma, Washington. These are great places for a real American meal.

Bill Adler, my book agent, and Maria Guarnaschelli, my editor, have continued to amaze me with their protective and insightful support. And here's a bowl of corn chowder for the bunch at William Morrow. What good Americans!

In the end I have to thank my family for the time to

do this book. They have been quietly patient while I have been writing about the necessity of eating with your family each evening, and I have missed too many dinners ever to expect them to enjoy another of my cookbooks in the future. Cheer up, Channing and Jason, and we will all go eat in New Orleans! And to Patty, my wife, to whom this book is dedicated. Thank you. You have more patience than I deserve . . . a great Brooklyn trait.

Contents

"Sweet land of liberty,
Of thee I sing!"

INTRODUCTION

We Americans have had a bad image of ourselves and our food for a long time, and I am done with it. I am so tired of people from the New World bowing to Europe, particularly France, when it comes to fine eating. We seem to think that if it comes from Europe it will be good, and if it comes from America it will be inferior. Enough! We really do not understand our own food history, and I think that means we do not actually understand our own culture.

Most Americans do not think of themselves as an ethnic group, but we are an ethnic body, all of us put together. The word *ethnic* comes from the Greek *ethnos,* meaning "nation." It refers not necessarily to a bloodline but to a group of persons distinguished by singular customs, characteristics, and language. While we are a nation populated for the most part by immigrants, we are nevertheless an ethnic group, a strange mixture, perhaps, but an ethnic group. We share a common language, but more importantly, we share a common memory. And there certainly is such a thing as American ethnic cooking. It is cooking that helps us remember and restore that common cultural memory.

A favorite philosopher of mine, Lin Yutang, once asked this question: "What is patriotism except memories of that which we ate as a child?" This cookbook is a collection of memories that can be recalled and celebrated by everyone who calls himself/herself an American. It has nothing to do with the fact that your blood is not Native American, but it has much to do with the fact that even though you speak fluent Chinese, and learned same from your grandmother in San Francisco, you will be marked in China as an American. We are a special group with a very special memory.

All ethnic groups have foods that help them continue to identify themselves. Most of us Americans are not aware of the wonderfully complex history of our own

2

foods . . . since most of us still think that everything there came over from Europe or some other part of the world. The following is a list of food products that are ours, coming from one of the Americas, and these products were unknown in Europe prior to the discovery of the New World:

corn	cocoa
turkey	vanilla beans
peanuts	potatoes
black walnuts	sweet potatoes
tomatoes	avocados
kidney beans	pimentos
lima beans	allspice
navy beans	bell peppers
string beans	cranberries
squashes	wild rice
pumpkins	

So there! These foods belong to us, and they actually do help define us. You enjoy turkey at Christmas even though your grandmother was born in Sicily. And the influence that these foods have had upon the rest of the world should never be overlooked. Italy had no tomatoes, Ireland no potatoes, and Switzerland had no vanilla or chocolate. Spain had no bell peppers or pimentos and China had no corn, peanuts, or sweet potatoes. These last three edibles kept most of China alive at the beginning of this century. American foods have influenced the diet of the world.

When thinking about who we are we must remember that America was discovered by the Europeans while on a search for food. Columbus was not after property for housing developments, he was after trade routes for valuable spices! And ever since the Europeans began moving about between the New World and the Old there has been such a thing as American ethnic food, food that is ours and is foreign to the rest of the planet. You see, I am not talking about hamburgers and hot dogs, though these are the delicacies that most Americans use in answering the question about "real American food."

Our real American foods have come from our soil and have been used by many groups—those who already lived here and those who have come here to live. The Native Americans already had developed an interesting cuisine using the abundant foods that were so prevalent. You will enjoy the recipes that I have found from various peoples and tribes.

The influence that the English had upon our national eating habits is easy to see in the Colonial section. They were a tough lot, those English, and they ate in a tough manner. They wiped their mouths on the tablecloth, if there happened to be one, and ate until you would expect them to burst. European travelers to this country in those days were most often shocked by American eating habits, which included too much fat and too much salt and too much liquor. Not much has changed! And, the Revolutionists refused to use the fork since it marked them as Europeans. The fork was not absolutely common on the American dinner table until about the time of the Civil War, the 1860s. Those English were a tough lot.

Other immigrant groups added their own touches to the preparation of our New World food products. The groups that came still have a special sense of self-identity through their ancestral heritage, but they see themselves as Americans. This special self-identity through your ancestors who came from other lands was supposed to disappear in this country. The term *melting pot* was first used in reference to America in the late 1700s, so this belief that we would all become the same has been with us for a long time. Thank goodness it has never worked. The various immigrant groups continue to add flavor to the pot, all right, but you can pick out the individual flavors very easily.

The largest ancestry group in America is the English. There are more people in America who claim to have come from English blood than there are in England.

But is their food English? Thanks be to God, it is not! It is American. The second largest group is the Germans, then the Irish, the Afro-Americans, the French, the Italians, the Scottish, and the Polish. The Mexican and American Indian groups are all smaller than any of the above, though they were the original cooks in this country.

Some unusually creative cooking has come about in this nation because of all those persons that have come here. Out of destitution comes either creativity or starvation, and some of the solutions that the new Americans have come up with are just grand. Only in America would you find an Italian housewife sharing recipes with her neighbor from Ireland. It has always been this way. The Native Americans were gracious enough to teach the first Europeans how to cook what was here, and we have been trading favorite dishes with one another ever since.

I am talking about American food—food that has come to us from the early days, using American products, and that continues to provide one of the best diets on earth. I am not talking contemporary artsy plates, nor am I talking about *nouvelle gauche*. And, I am not talking about meat loaf and lumpy mashed potatoes. Even at the time of the writing of the Declaration of Independence we were celebrating one of the most varied, and probably the best, cuisines in the world. It has not changed.

The following chapters will help you better understand your roots in terms of true American cooking, from the Native American gifts to the wonderful regional dishes that we can celebrate regularly.

Pour a glass of sherry and run through these recipes and stories. Think of your own childhood . . . the house and the front room. Think of the kitchen and how it smelled, and who was seated at the dining-room table. Lin Yutang is right: The memories of what we ate as a child form a sort of patriotism that lasts throughout our life. We are a special group of citizens who eat special foods in order to recall who we are. I stand with my young friend Alexandra, my editor's daughter, who said, upon hearing of this book, "Mom, it's about time. Instead of saying, 'Let's eat Northern Chinese tonight, or Thai, or Armenian,' we can say, 'Let's eat American,' and mean it. I think he's got something here!" Thank you, Alexandra, this whole country has got something, and it is wonderful.

Now, call your grandmother and ask for those recipes you have been meaning to get, and we can get started on eating our own history lessons, on tasting our spirit of patriotism.

I wish you well.

—JEFF SMITH

September 1987
On the 200th anniversary of
the Constitutional Convention of
These United States

". . . in order to form a more perfect union . . ."

"O'er the land of the free
And the home of the brave..."

GLOSSARY

Hints

Kitchen Equipment

KNIVES

Be careful of the knife that looks modern or contemporary but simply doesn't cut properly. I am conservative when it comes to knives because they are your most important kitchen tools. I choose the old standard French-style knives. When you purchase knives be sure to choose those that fit your hand and can be sharpened easily. The stainless-steel knives that you buy in the dime store or department store are generally difficult to work with because they are made to go into dishwashers. They are not made for cooks. Buy good knives that are made of high carbon steel, and then keep them sharp with a sharpening steel. Most will not stain.

I use the following constantly:

10-inch chef's knife
Boning knife
Paring knife
Long slicing knife (thin)
Sharpening steel

·Keep your knives very sharp. A dull knife will force you to work too hard, and it will slip and cut you. Better to have a very sharp knife that will work for you with little effort. Use your sharpening steel often, and carefully.

I am particularly fond of Henckels knives from Germany. They are expensive, but I have never had to replace one. You will also be happy with Elephant

Brand Sabatier knives from France. They are good quality and not quite so costly.

Chinese Cleaver: I could not cook without my Chinese cleaver. Cleavers are not expensive, and once you learn to use one you will find yourself depending upon it for many kitchen jobs. There are two basic styles. The thinner one is for vegetables and the thicker one for meats and light bone cutting or "hacking." Either will cost between $15 and $20. Do not buy stainless-steel cleavers. Go to a Chinese or Oriental market, where you will find a cleaver of carbon steel.

POTS AND PANS
Good pans will make good cooking easy. Pans that are thin and flimsy can offer only burning, sticking, and lumps. Buy good equipment that is heavy. You will not be sorry.

Tips for Buying Good Equipment
1. Don't buy pots and pans with wooden or plastic handles. You can't put them in the oven or under a broiler.
2. Buy pans that fit your life-style, that are appropriate for the way you cook. They should be able to perform a variety of purposes in the kitchen. Avoid pans that can be used only for one dish or one particular style of cooking. I am thinking of such things as upside-down crepe pans. What for? They have no other use and are, therefore, not a frugal investment.
3. Choosing the material for pans:

   Aluminum is fine for cooking. Buy heavy restaurant-quality. Keep it clean with a 3M green scrubbing cloth and do not store food in it. The old scare about getting aluminum poisoning from such pans need not concern you. As long as you are cleaning your pans and you do not store foods high in acid (such as tomatoes or lemon juice) in the pans you will have a good time with them. As a matter of fact, I store no food in aluminum. Many now come coated with SilverStone and are a joy to use.

I am not particularly fond of anodized, or blackened, aluminum pans. The advantages are few and the cost is almost doubled.

Copper pans are a joy. The heat always stays even during cooking and the pans look great on your wall. Buy good heavy weight with tin lining, as thin decorative pans are not functional. Don't worry if it is not French. Chile and Korea are now making good pans, and my favorite copper pieces come from Brooklyn. The brand is Waldo Copper and their price is more reasonable than European brands.

Stainless-steel pans used to have no place in my kitchen because they were so cheaply made and were so thin: plastic handles, the works. You know the brands. Several companies, however, are now making heavy stainless ware with metal handles and an aluminum core sandwiched inside the bottom. These are great. Plan to spend some money, but you will probably be giving them to your grandchildren someday. Restaurant-supply houses carry several brands. You should be able to find these in both restaurant-supply houses and large department stores. Be ready for a big bill for very good equipment.

Cast iron with porcelain enamel pans are heavy but wonderfully versatile. You can cook in them, serve in them, and they are easy to keep clean. I have a whole collection of the stuff. Le Creuset is probably the best-known brand. French made, it is of high durable quality.
4. The pots and pans I use the most:

20-quart aluminum stockpot, with lid
12-quart aluminum stockpot, with lid

4-quart aluminum sauteuse, with lid
10-inch aluminum frying pan, lined with SilverStone, with lid
Several cast-iron casseroles, with lids; varying sizes (I like Le Creuset)
Copper baking pans and saucepans; varying sizes

CASSEROLES AND BAKING PANS
I have a good selection of porcelain casseroles with lids. They are easy to clean, very attractive, and useful. I both cook and serve in them. You can find many from France, but Hall China, here in America, is now offering wonderful porcelain casseroles and bowls of all sizes and of heavy construction.

Glass casseroles are also attractive and work well. Corning has brought in a great selection from France.

MACHINES AND APPLIANCES
Please do not fill your kitchen with appliances that you rarely use. I do not have a deep fryer or a Crockpot or an electric hamburger fryer or an electric egg cooker or . . . well, you get the point. I would rather spend my money on good equipment that I can use in many different ways.

I do regularly use the following:

Food Mixer: Choose a heavy machine, one that will sit in one spot and make bread dough, grind meat, mix cake batters, etc. I prefer a KitchenAid.

Food Processor: I use my food processor less than my mixer, but a processor is great for special chopping and mincing jobs. It is also a must for a good pâté. I find a medium-sized machine to be the most helpful.

Food Blender: There are many good ones on the market. Just remember to find a brand that you can trust, from a company that will stand behind what it sells.

Electric Coffee Grinder: This small German gadget is great for grinding spices and herbs. I rarely use mine for coffee.

HINT: **To Cure or Season Your Pans.**
Remember the rule: *Hot pan, cold oil, foods won't stick*. That means that you never put the oil in the pan and then heat the pan. You heat the pan first; add the oil and then, immediately, the food. You will have much less sticking that way.

An aluminum frying pan is cured, or seasoned, by this simple method: First, wash the pan with soap and water, using a cloth or sponge, never a steel soap pad or steel-wool pad. Rinse the pan and dry it. Never put soap in your frying pan again! Heat the pan on a burner until quite hot, and then add 2 or 3 tablespoons of peanut oil. Gently swirl the oil about the pan and allow the pan to cool. Heat the pan again, add more oil, cool, and repeat once more. Your pan is now ready for use. If foods should stick or if you have trouble getting the pan clean, do not resort to soap. Instead, rub the pan with a green scouring cloth or try a bit of peanut oil and salt; rub with a paper towel to clean.

SilverStone frying pan: This excellent product from Du Pont is easy to care for. Wash once with soapy water, and cure just as you cure aluminum frying pans (see above). Care for the pan in precisely the same way.

SPECIAL EQUIPMENT

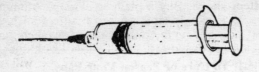

Flavor Injector: This is a strange-looking plastic and metal device that resembles a hypodermic needle and is used for injecting flavors and juices into meats. You can find it in any gourmet shop.

Garlic Press: I cannot abide garlic in any form except the form that the Creator intended. Buy a Susi garlic press, also labeled Zyliss. It looks expensive to start with, but it remains the best on the market.

Lemon Reamer, Wooden: Any good gourmet shop should have one of these for you. It works better at extracting lemon juice than any juicer I have ever seen. You can now find it in plastic and it works well.

Heat Diffuser or Tamer: This is an inexpensive gadget that you place on your burners to even out and reduce the heat. It will save you from a lot of burned sauces. Any gourmet shop or hardware store should have this item.

Wooden Spoons and Spatulas: I never put metal spoons or gadgets into my frying pans or saucepans. Metal will scratch the surface, causing food to stick. Buy wooden gadgets and avoid that problem. Yes, they will be clean if you wash them in soap and water and allow them to dry before putting them away. Never soak your wooden cooking gear.

Wok: I use my Chinese wok constantly. It is an ingenious device that is actually much larger than it appears because of its shape. Buy a plain steel wok. Aluminum woks heat too evenly, and the advantage of a Chinese wok is a "hot spot" in the center of the pan where juices and liquids can evaporate; an aluminum wok does not have the necessary hot spot. A copper wok will have the same problem. A stainless-steel wok cannot be seasoned properly, and food always will stick. Finally, an electric wok generally heats too slowly and cooks too slowly, so the advantage of the wok—quick heat and rapid cooking—is lost.

Bamboo Steamers from China: These stackable steamers, usually three or four in a set, allow you to steam several dishes at once. The advantage that these have over metal steamers stems from the fact that bamboo will not cause moisture to condense and drip on your food. Metal steamers drip, always. I use bamboo steamers for Chinese cooking and for warming up leftover dishes. Find them in Oriental markets or in any good gourmet shop.

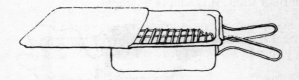

Stove-top Smoker: This is a wonderful device put out by Cameron and it is made entirely of stainless steel. The idea is to place it on the top of your stove with a bit of sawdust in the bottom and you can smoke things in just a moment in your kitchen. Instructions for use are found on page 386, along with the recipe for Stove-Top Smoked Trout.

Kamado Smoker: This is the most wonderful barbecue device I have ever found. Originally designed in China, it became very popular in Japan. It is now being made in Taiwan due to heavy production costs in Japan. The Kamado cooker is available through some gourmet outlets, and I think it is the greatest thing.

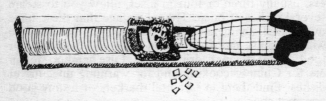

Corn Creamer/Grater: This wonderful device is made by Mrs. Lees, and you should be able to find one in a local gourmet shop. It is simply a delight.

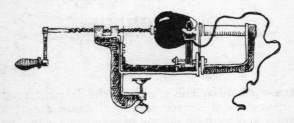

Apple Parer/Corer/Slicer: I think that this device was originally invented by the Shakers, but I am not sure. In any case, the best version is currently being produced by NorPro. You should be able to find it easily.

Apple Parer/Wedger: This German device is made of metal and is easy to use and easy to clean. It will core and pare an apple in nothing flat and it is not expensive. You can find it in most department stores or good gourmet shops.

Whisk: I have been very nervous about using metal whips or whisks in my pans since they tend to scratch and damage the surfaces. The new wooden or plastic whips are far superior. I have found one from Denmark that does an exceptional job and will not become deformed with use. I am very happy with mine.

Pastry Blender: The shape of the pastry blender illustrated here is a bit different. It is a Scandinavian device and it works just beautifully. I have become a great biscuit and pastry maker because of it. You can find it in most gourmet shops.

Pepper Mill: I love the flavor of freshly ground black pepper. You cannot get that kind of flavor in something preground. I have three good mills: one for the dining-room table, one for the kitchen stove, and one for my traveling cooking kit. Buy pepper mills made in France; they last much longer than the Japanese versions. I also love my Greek coffee grinder for pepper.

Flour Dredger: This looks like a big salt shaker. Fill it with flour and have it ready to help you flour things with much less waste and time.

Meat Pounder: A heavy disk of metal with a handle that will help you prepare thin slices of meat. You can also use a short length of two-by-four wood.

Plastic Sheeting: Sheeting is very helpful when you are pounding meat thin or when you need another piping bag. It is inexpensive and available at most large lumberyards. Ask for clear vinyl sheeting 8 millimeters thick.

Fire Extinguisher: A must for your kitchen. Buy one that will work on electrical fires as well as stove fires. Talk to the salesperson. You will sleep better at night.

Marble Pastry Board: This can be purchased in many sizes. I could not make bread or pastry without one.

Wine Bottles: Save old ones for oils, soy sauce, vinegars, and of course, wine.

Oil Can: I keep near the stove a tiny spouted little can filled with peanut oil. The little spout means that I use less oil in my cooking. It can be found at any gourmet shop.

Kitchen Scale: Buy something that is fairly accurate. It will be helpful in baking perfect French bread and in judging the size of meats. You will be able to buy things in bulk and save some money.

Stainless-Steel Steamer Basket: This is a great help. It will fit any size pan and is readily available and very cheap.

Ice Cream Maker: Sherbets and ice cream will be much easier if you purchase a Donvier Ice Cream machine. It is inexpensive and foolproof, and can be found in any department store or gourmet shop.

Mandoline: This is a most wonderful device for cutting vegetables into thin slices or into julienne-style matchstick cuts. The French model is very expensive, but the Zyliss people have brought one in from Germany that is plastic with steel cutters. It works better than any I have seen on the market. The brand name is Moha.

THINGS I LOVE BUT COULD PROBABLY DO WITHOUT

When I buy a new piece of cooking equipment I must always ask myself, "Do you really need this to be creative?" Often the answer is no, but I buy it anyway. I have few electric gadgets like hot dog cookers or electric egg poachers or upside-down chicken cookers. These I can do without. But the following items are in my kitchen because I love them:

Glass Plates, Dessert Size: These are cheap, and I use them for salads, pastas, and desserts. They make the food look attractive.

Big Dinner Plates: I hate eating a nice dinner that has been squeezed onto a regular plate. Buy big ones, 12 inches in diameter. You may have to go to a restaurant-supply house. Loneoak Company in California makes wonderful plates.

Good Wineglasses: I do not enjoy drinking wine from a glass with a lip or heavy rim. Shop carefully and you will find good wineglasses without lips, and they are not expensive. I own several dozen big ones, glasses big enough to make even a medium-class wine look and taste fine. You can get carried away with wineglasses because there are many different kinds for several different wines. Start with a 10-ounce clear tulip glass; it will do fine for any wine. Your collection can grow as your wine cellar grows.

Big Serving Platters: I find these in antique stores and junk shops—serving platters from a time gone by. It is great fun to put an entire main course on a gigantic platter and bring it to your friends and family.

Big Wooden Salad Bowls: I don't really believe that you can make a good salad in glass or metal. Metal is harsh in its appearance, and glass is too fragile for a proper mixing or tossing of the salad. A wooden bowl can be seasoned with a clove of fresh garlic and thus impart a most delicate flavor to your greens.

Pitchers and Serving Jugs: My sons never put a container of milk on the table, and every liquid is served in a pitcher of some sort. It makes the event of the meal seem a little more important to all of us.

Piping Bags and Tips: These will help you add some class to your efforts in the kitchen. I use three sizes the most—10, 12, and 14 inches. Choose several tips that will be helpful in cake icing, in piping cheese, mayonnaise, or potatoes.

Cooking Terms

AL DENTE

This is a wonderful Italian term that means to cook "to the teeth." It means nobody wants soggy pasta. Cook pasta to the teeth, or until it is barely tender, still a bit firm. It is much better that way . . . and the way Italians intended same to be eaten.

BLANCHING

Plunging food into boiling water for a very few minutes (the time varies and will be explained in each recipe). The food is then removed and generally placed in cold water to stop the cooking process. The purpose is to loosen the skin of a vegetable or fruit, to set the color of a vegetable, or to cook a food partially in preparation for later completion of the dish.

BROWNING MEAT

When preparing stews and cassoulets, I usually do not flour the meat. You end up with browned flour instead of browning the natural sugars that are in the meat itself. Use a hot pan, and do not crowd the meat or cook it slowly. The meat should be seared or browned very rapidly, thus giving color to the stew and sealing the meat cubes.

CHOW (STIR-FRY)

A basic cooking method in the Chinese kitchen. Generally a wok is used, but you can also do this in a frying pan. The food is tossed about in a hot pan with very little oil, in a process not unlike sautéing.

CORRECT THE SEASONING

When a dish is completed, a cook should always taste before serving. To correct the seasoning simply means to check for salt, pepper, or herbs to make sure that the dish has turned out as expected. A little correction at the last minute may be necessary.

DASH

Generally means "to taste." Start with less than 1/16 teaspoon.

DEGLAZING A PAN

After meats or vegetables have been browned, wine or stock is added to the pan over high heat, and the rich coloring that remains in the pan is gently scraped with a wooden spoon and combined with the wine or stock. If there is excess fat in the pan, you may wish to pour it out before deglazing.

DEVELOP

Developing a food product means that you have allowed it to sit for a time before serving so that the flavors might have a chance to blend or brighten.

DICE

This means to cut into small cubes; the size of the cube is generally stated in the recipe. For instance, a 1/4-inch dice means a cube of that size. It is accomplished very quickly and easily with a good vegetable knife.

DREDGING IN FLOUR

Meats or fish, generally sliced thin, are rolled about in flour in preparation for frying or sautéing. The flour is usually seasoned.

HACK
When cutting up chickens or thin-boned meats, one "hacks" with a cleaver, thus cutting the meat into large but bite-size pieces and retaining the bone. The presence of the bone will help keep the meat moist during cooking. Do this hacking carefully.

MARINATING
Meats or vegetables are soaked for a time in a flavoring liquid, such as soy sauce, wine, oil, or vinegar. The time of the marinating varies with the recipe.

MATCHSTICK OR JULIENNE CUT
Cut vegetables into thin slices, stack the slices, and then cut the slices into thin sticks, like matchsticks.

MINCE
A minced vegetable or herb is one that is chopped very fine. It is fine enough to be of a very coarse, granular nature. This pertains especially to garlic, onion, and herbs. The process is done by hand with a knife or a food processor.

MIREPOIX
A blend of vegetables and herbs sautéed together and used to flavor other dishes.

PINCH OF HERBS OR SPICES
Usually means "to taste." Start with less than 1/16 teaspoon, and then increase if you wish.

POACHING
Gently cooking fish, meat, or eggs in stock or water at just below a simmer. The liquid should just barely move during the poaching process. When fish or eggs are poached, a little vinegar or lemon juice is added to the liquid to help keep the food firm.

PURÉE
When you wish to make a sauce or soup that is free of all lumps of any sort, purée the stock. This means that you put it in a food processor and mill it until it is free of all lumps, or run it through a strainer or sieve.

REDUCING
Boiling a sauce or liquid over high heat until it decreases in volume, generally by half. The result is a very rich concentration of flavors.

ROUX
A blend of oil or butter and flour used to thicken sauces and gravies. The fat and flour are mixed together in equal amounts over heat. If a white roux is desired, the melting and blending are done over low heat for a few minutes. If a brown roux is desired, the flour is cooked in the fat until it is lightly browned.

RUBBED
When whole-leaf herbs, such as sage or bay leaves, are crushed in the hands so that their oils are released, the herbs are then referred to as having been rubbed.

SAUTÉ
This term comes from a French word that means "to jump." In cooking, sauté means to place food in a very hot pan with a bit of butter or oil and to shake the pan during the cooking process so that the food jumps about. Thus one can cook very quickly over high heat without burning the food. It is not unlike Chinese chowing, or stir-frying.

SCALDED
Generally this term applies to milk in recipes and it simply means to heat the milk to just under simmering. The milk is scalded when it becomes very hot. It is not a boil at all.

SHOT
A liquid measurement that amounts to very little, or to taste. A shot of wine is about an ounce, but a shot of Tabasco is less than 1/16 teaspoon.

STIR-FRY
See Chow.

TERRINE
A dish used for the cooking and molding of coarse-ground meat loaves or pâtés. Also the meat itself. The dishes can be found in many styles and materials.

Ingredients and Food Definitions

ANCHO CHILES
Find in any Mexican market or large delicatessen. Remove seeds and soak before using.

ANCHOVIES (flat, canned)
Used for salads and Italian and French cooking. Buy in cans from Portugal or Spain. Very salty.

BALSAMIC VINEGAR
Italian wine vinegar that has been aged for years. This is wonderful, and no other vinegar can quite compare. From Modena, Italy. Find in any Italian market. The fancy food shops will charge you much too much money for this item.

BÉCHAMÉL SAUCE
See Cream Sauce.

BEEF STOCK
Please make your own. Canned consommé or bouillon is little more than salt. Real beef stock is rich in flavor and inexpensive to make from fresh bones. My recipe follows:

BASIC BROWN SOUP STOCK

MAKES 5 QUARTS OF STOCK

This is one of those things that you prepare on your one major cooking day each week. It takes some time to concoct, but this soup stock is just basic to a properly and frugally run kitchen. It is used for soups, sauces, and gravies.

Bare rendering bones, sawed into 2-inch pieces	**Yellow onions, unpeeled and chopped**
Carrots, unpeeled and chopped	**Celery, chopped**

Tell your butcher that you need bare rendering bones. They should not have any meat on them at all, so they should be cheap. Have him saw them up into 2-inch pieces.

Roast the bones in an uncovered pan at 400° for 2 hours. Be careful with this, because your oven may be a bit too hot. Watch the bones, which you want to be toasty brown, not black.

Place the roasted bones in a soup pot and add 1 quart water for each pound of bones. For 5 pounds bones, add 1 bunch carrots, 1 head celery, and 3 yellow onions, chopped with peel and all. (The peel will give lovely color to the stock.)

Bring to a simmer, uncovered, and cook, for 12 hours. You may need to add water to keep soup up to same level. Do not salt the stock.

Strain the stock, and store in the refrigerator. Allow the fat to stay on the top of the stock when you refrigerate it; the fat will seal the stock and allow you to keep it for several days.

CAPERS
Pickled buds used in salads and dressing. Found in any good supermarket.

CHEESE
This list is offered simply because I use all these in my recipes, though I rarely have them all on hand at once. Buy fresh cheeses, and grind or grate your own. Find a good delicatessen or cheese store, and you should find each of the following:

Parmesan (imported, aged Italian, if you can afford it)
Romano
Asiago (my favorite Italian pasta cheese for grating)
Swiss (Wisconsin fine for baking, imported for snacking)
Monterey Jack
Cheddar
Bleu (imported Danish excellent for cooking)
Feta (Greek)
Ricotta
Brie

CHICKEN STOCK
A chicken soup or stock made from chicken backs and necks, carrots, yellow onions, celery, and a bit of salt and pepper, and is allowed to simmer for a good hour. It is then strained and served. My recipe follows:

CHICKEN SOUP STOCK

MAKES ABOUT 4 QUARTS OF STOCK

Chicken stock, or soup, is used for soups and sauces that have a lighter touch than the heavier beef versions. The stock is not expensive to make nor does it take much time. The result, however, is so far superior to the canned stuff or the salty chicken bouillon cubes that you won't believe it.

3 pounds chicken
 necks and backs
4 stalks celery,
 chopped into
 large pieces
6 carrots, chopped
 into large pieces

2 yellow onions,
 peeled and
 chopped into
 large pieces
Salt and pepper to
 taste

Boil the chicken necks and backs in water to cover. Add the celery, carrots and yellow onions. Add salt and pepper. Simmer for 2 hours. Strain and refrigerate.

CHICOS
This is a dried corn product from New Mexico. They can be found in Latin American or Mexican markets. They can also be purchased from the Casados Farms. See page 60.

CHILE PODS
See Red Chile Pods.

CHILI SAUCE
Bottled product found in the catsup section of the supermarket.

CREAM
When the term is used in this book, I mean half-and-half or whipping cream. Either may be used, or you may dilute whipping cream with milk.

CREAM SAUCE
Basic white sauce made with cream or milk and thickened with a roux of flour and butter; very rich. Also called Béchamél Sauce. See page 303 for recipe.

DIJON MUSTARD
A style of mustard from France. A good American brand is Grey Poupon.

FILBERTS
Sometimes called hazelnuts, these are delicious in many ways in the kitchen. If you use them a lot, buy in bulk from food co-ops or from health food stores. They are cheaper that way.

FISH STOCK/SOUP
It is made from the skin, bones, backs, tails, and heads of any fresh fish, which is simmered in water along with carrots, celery, yellow onions, and salt and pepper. It is cooked for about an hour and then used as the basis for other recipes. My recipe follows:

FISH STOCK

Fish skin, bones, heads, and tails	4 stalks celery, chopped
2 carrots, cut up	Salt to taste
2 small yellow onions, peeled and chopped	

Cover all ingredients with water, and simmer until the vegetables are soft. Strain, and use the liquid for cooking.

HAZELNUTS
See Filberts.

HERBS AND SPICES
See pages 36 to 41.

HOMINY
This corn product can be found canned in most super-markets and dried in Latin American markets. It also can be purchased in bulk in many health food stores. See page 438 for full discussion.

HOT SAUCE
Tabasco or Trappey's Red Devil will do well. They are found in any supermarket.

IMITATION MAYONNAISE
This is low-fat mayonnaise, and it is called imitation because it does not have all the fat of ordinary mayo. Good for low-fat diets.

KITCHEN BOUQUET
This is a vegetable extract used for coloring sauces and gravies. It can be found in any supermarket.

LEEKS
These look like very large onions. Wash carefully because they are usually full of mud. Found in the produce section of your supermarket.

LIQUID SMOKE
For use in barbecue sauce. I like Wright's. Find it in the condiment section of the supermarket.

MAGGI SEASONING
This vegetable extract is used for flavoring soups and gravies. I think it is excellent and buy it in any super-market.

MAPLEINE
An artificial maple extract manufactured by the Cres-cent Company of Seattle. Supermarkets in other areas of the nation should carry a similar product. Look in the spice section.

OILS

Butter
Olive Oil
Peanut Oil
Sesame Oil

These are the common oils that I use in my kitchen. I use little butter, but I enjoy the flavor; I dislike margarine.

ORANGE FLOWER WATER
This orange blossom extract can be found in fancy food shops. It was common in Colonial cooking.

ORZO
Pasta shaped like rice. Great for pilaf. Find it in Middle Eastern, or Italian, or other good delicatessens as well as the supermarket.

PASILLA CHILES
Find in any Mexican market or large delicatessen. Remove seeds and soak before using.

PESOLE
Native American name for hominy. See Hominy.

POTATO FLOUR
This item can be found in most delicatessens and Scandinavian shops.

PICKLING SALT
Used in pickled meat dishes. Find in any supermarket.

PINE NUTS
Expensive little treasures that actually do come from large Italian pinecones. Find in Italian markets, or substitute slivered almonds.

POLENTA
Coarse cornmeal used in Italy. You can find this in any Italian market, or use ordinary cornmeal.

QUICK-RISING YEAST
There are a couple of brands on the market now that will cause the dough to rise in half the time. Both Red Star and Fleischmann's manufacture such a thing. You can find these in any supermarket.

RED CHILE PODS
These are from New Mexico and can be found in any Latin American or Mexican market. Many supermarkets carry these as well. Please see the discussion on pages 59 and 60.

SALTPETER
A common kitchen chemical used in preserving meat or preparing corned beef or pork. May be purchased at a drugstore.

SEMOLINA
A very coarse-ground flour made from hard durum wheat. Buy in an Italian grocery. Its flavor is far superior to farina, which may be used as a substitute in a pinch.

SESAME SEEDS
Buy in bulk, and then roast them by stirring them in a frying pan until lightly browned.

SHALLOTS
A cross between garlic and onion that are a classic ingredient in French cuisine. Find them in the produce section or substitute a blend of onion and garlic.

SHORT-GRAINED RICE
This is a Japanese variety grown in this country. Used in Italian dishes as well as Japanese dishes, it should be readily available.

SOURDOUGH STARTER
This necessary item for sourdough baking can be purchased in most delicatessens and fancy food shops.

VINEGARS
These are the vinegars that I use most in my cooking. They are all readily obtainable in most markets:

Red Wine Vinegar
White Wine Vinegar
White Cider Vinegar
Tarragon Wine Vinegar
Rice Wine Vinegar

WHITE SAUCE
See Cream Sauce.

WINES FOR COOKING
All of the wines below are readily obtainable, with the exception of the Chinese rice wine. That you can find in any Chinatown. Please do not buy wines that have salt added; they are labeled "cooking wine" but really should not be used at all. My rule is simple: If you can't drink it, don't cook with it.

The wines are arranged in the order of their importance in my kitchen:

Dry Red Wine	Sweet Vermouth
Dry White Wine	Brandy
Dry Cocktail Sherry	Tawny Port
Dry Marsala	Ruby Port
Sweet Marsala	Champagne
Madeira	Chinese Rice Wine
Dry Vermouth	Sake

Herbs and Spices

> ### HINT: Buying, Storing, and Grinding Herbs and Spices.
>
> Herbs and spices are some of the most important ingredients in your kitchen. Try to keep them as fresh as possible, so don't buy them in large amounts. Keep them in tightly sealed jars. Try to buy most herbs and spices whole or in whole-leaf form; they have much more flavor that way. Crush the leaf forms as you add them to the pot. Or use a wooden or porcelain mortar and pestle. For seeds that are hard to grind, I use a small German electric coffee grinder. I have one that I use just for spices; it works very well.
>
> Try to buy the herbs and spices that you use most frequently in bulk, and then put them in your own spice bottles. The saving realized here is about 70 percent. Hard to believe, but it is true. Find a market that has big jars of spices, and you will also be amazed at the difference in flavor.

ALLSPICE
Not a blend of spices at all, but a single one. Basic to the kitchen. Buy it ground because it is hard to grind.

BASIL
Common in French and Italian cooking. Grow it fresh or buy it dried, whole.

BAY LEAVES
Basic to the kitchen for good soups, stews, etc. Buy whole, dried, or if your area is not too cold, grow a bay laurel tree. I have one in Tacoma.

BOUQUET GARNI
A bouquet of fresh herbs, generally tied in a bundle or in a cheesecloth sack. Usual ingredients include parsley, thyme, and bay leaves. You can use all these dried.

CARAWAY
Whole seed, dried.

CARDAMOM
Common in Scandinavian and Middle Eastern dishes. Rather sweet flavor. Expensive. Buy whole seed, and grind as you need it.

CAYENNE PEPPER
Fine-ground red pepper; very hot.

CHERVIL
Mild French herb that resembles parsley in flavor. Buy dried, whole. Use in soups and sauces.

CHILI POWDER
Actually a blend of chile peppers. Buy in the can, ground. Usually I use the hot blend. Or make your own (page 363).

CILANTRO
This fresh form of the coriander plant looks very much like parsley. It can be found in many supermarkets and Oriental groceries.

CINNAMON
Hard to grind your own. Buy it powdered.

CLOVES
I use both the powdered and the whole.

CORIANDER
The dry, whole seed is common in Mediterranean cooking. The fresh plant, which looks like parsley, is common in Chinese, Indian, and Mexican cuisines. You may see the fresh form in your supermarkets listed as cilantro or Chinese parsley.

CUMIN
Used in Mexican, Middle Eastern, and Indian cooking a great deal. Buy powdered in the can, or buy the whole seed and grind it. The flavor is much brighter with the whole seed.

CURRY POWDER
An English blend of many spices. Many brands are on the market, so choose one that seems to fit your family. I like Sun from India. Or a much more powerful one may be made at home. Find a recipe in any good Indian cookbook.

DILLWEED
Dried, whole. Great for salad dressings and dips. Common in Middle Eastern cuisine.

FENNEL
A seed that resembles anise or licorice in flavor. Produces that special flavor in Italian sausage. Buy it whole, and grind it as you need it.

FILÉ
Ground sassafras leaves, along with a bit of thyme. Essential in New Orleans cooking. Also called gumbo filé.

FINES HERBES
A blend of parsley, chervil, tarragon, and chives. Very mild and very French. Used in everything from salads to soups and stews.

GARLIC
The bulb, of course. Use only fresh. And buy a good garlic press!

GINGER, FRESH
Very common in Chinese dishes. Buy by the "hand," or whole stem, at the supermarket. Keep in the refrigerator, uncovered and unwrapped. Grate when needed.

JUNIPER BERRIES
These are to be found dried in good spice shops. They will remind you of the flavor of English gin. There is no substitute.

MACE
The outer covering of the nutmeg. Not as strong as nutmeg, but rich in flavor. Buy ground. Common in Early American cooking.

MARJORAM
Common kitchen herb, light in flavor. Buy whole, dried.

MINT, DRIED
Common in Middle Eastern dishes. Buy whole. Also makes a great tea.

MINT, FRESH
Grow this in the backyard if you can. Great for salads, mint juleps, Middle Eastern dishes.

MUSTARD, DRY
Absolute necessity if you love salad dressings. I buy Colman's, from Britain.

NUTMEG
Basic to the kitchen. Buy it in bulk, and grate your own with an old-fashioned nutmeg grater.

ORANGE PEEL, DRIED
Great for Italian tomato sauces for pasta. Dry your own by saving the peelings and letting them sit on top of the refrigerator.

OREGANO
Basic to the kitchen for salads, meats, sauces, etc. You can grow your own, but the best comes from Greece. Buy whole, dried.

PAPRIKA
Light, lovely flavor and color. Buy ground, imported from Hungary.

PARSLEY, FRESH
Buy in the supermarket produce section, or grow your own. I like the Italian variety, which has flat leaves and a bright flavor.

PEPPERCORNS, BLACK
Buy whole, and always grind fresh. See page 18.

PEPPERCORNS, GREEN
These delicious peppercorns are literally green and come packed in water in a tin. Find them in any gourmet shop or good delicatessen.

RED PEPPER FLAKES, HOT, CRUSHED
Also labeled "crushed red pepper flakes." Buy in bulk, and use sparingly. The seeds make this a very hot product.

RED PEPPERS, HOT, DRIED
Buy whole. Necessary for many Chinese dishes and in southern cooking.

ROSEMARY
Basic to the cooking of Italy and southern France. Grow your own, or buy whole, dried.

SAFFRON
Real saffron is from Spain and is the dried stamens from the saffron crocus . . . and costs $2,000 a pound. Buy it by the pinch or use Mexican saffron, which includes the whole flower and is very cheap. Works well, just remember to use much more.

SAGE
Basic kitchen herb. Grow your own, or buy it whole, dried.

SAVORY
Close to thyme in flavor. Common in French cooking. Buy it whole, dried.

THYME
Necessary to good French cooking—soups to stews to meat dishes. Buy it whole, dried, or grow your own.

TURMERIC
Bitter orange-colored spice that gives the flavor and color to pilafs, curry powders, and Indian braised dishes. Buy it ground. Cheaper in Middle Eastern and Indian stores.

The Television Shows
and Recipes for Each

SHOW 412 ◊ Crabs
Crab Cakes Maryland ◊ *406*
Fried Crab Legs ◊ *407*
Steamed Blue Crabs ◊ *408*
Crab and Shrimp Seasoning ◊ *408*
Fried Soft-Shell Crabs ◊ *409*
Joe's Florida Stone Crab Mustard Sauce ◊ *411*
Crab Louis Seattle ◊ *410*
Crab Cocktail ◊ *411*

SHOW 413 ◊ Clams
Steamed Clams ◊ *416*
Fried Razor Clams ◊ *418*
Fried Clams ◊ *420*
Pasta with White Clam Sauce ◊ *418*
Stuffed Clams ◊ *421*
Corn Chowder with Clams and Chicken ◊ *437*
Geoduck Steak ◊ *418*
Turner's Boston Clam Chowder ◊ *422*

SHOW 414 ◊ Crawfish
Boiled Crawfish ◊ *275*
Crawfish Bourbon Orleans ◊ *274*
Crawfish Etouffée ◊ *277*
Crawfish Newburg ◊ *276*

SHOW 415 ◊ George Washington
Cream of Peanut Soup ◊ *111*
Oyster Sauce for Virginia Ham ◊ *114*
Virginia Spoon Bread ◊ *115*
Fried Tripe ◊ *112*
Cabbage and Salt Pork ◊ *114*
Ragoo of Onions ◊ *113*

SHOW 420 ◇ Pot Pies
Basic Easy Crust ◇ *311*
Steak and Kidney Pie ◇ *313*
Pork, Ham, and Sausage Pie ◇ *312*
Cold Pork Pie ◇ *315*
Chicken Pot Pie with Onions and Salt Pork ◇ *316*
Chicken Pie with Biscuit Topping ◇ *318*

SHOW 421 ◇ Thomas Jefferson
Monticello Muffins ◇ *123*
Pea Soup ◇ *122*
Peas and Salt Pork ◇ *122*
Jefferson Fried Chicken ◇ *127*
Boiled Pork ◇ *131*
Baked Polenta ◇ *128*
Macaroni Pie ◇ *130*
Stewed Tomatoes ◇ *125*
Baked Ice Cream ◇ *133*
Apple Pudding ◇ *133*

SHOW 422 ◇ Catfish
Fried Catfish ◇ *263*
Hushpuppies ◇ *264*
Grilled Catfish ◇ *265*
Blackened Catfish ◇ *266*
Poached Catfish ◇ *267*
Creamed Catfish ◇ *269*

SHOW 423 ◇ Chicago
Deep-Dish Pizza ◇ *356*
The Chicago Hot Dog ◇ *358*
Steak in a Hot Pan ◇ *359*

SHOW 433 ◇ Cranberry
Cranberry Fool ◇ *201*
Cranberry Cheddar Sandwich ◇ *202*
Cranberry Ice ◇ *205*
Cranberry Roast Pork ◇ *207*
Chicken with Cranberries ◇ *206*
Cranberry Dumplings ◇ *205*

SHOW 434 ◇ Northwest Indians
Indian Salmon Bake ◇ *70*
Salmon Jerky ◇ *71*
Salmon Soup ◇ *72*
Steamed Fiddlehead Fern Tops ◇ *72*
Bannock Bread ◇ *73*
Whipped Raspberry Soup ◇ *76*

SHOW 435 ◇ Oregon Trail
Bacon Corn Bread ◇ *475*
Soda Bread or Skillet Bread ◇ *476*
Buffalo Stew ◇ *478*
Buffalo Jerky ◇ *479*
Chicken-Fried Steak with Cream Gravy ◇ *480*

SHOW 436 ◇ Plains Indians
Berry Soup ◇ *79*
Indian Blueberry Pudding ◇ *80*
Was-Nah Corn and Cherry Snack ◇ *81*
Jerky Stew ◇ *82*

SHOW 437 ◇ Chocolate
Chocolatl Drink ◇ *333*
Mexican Chocolate Drink ◇ *334*
Cocoa Black-Bean Soup ◇ *335*
Cocoa Rye Bread ◇ *336*

"O beautiful for patriot dream
That sees beyond the years..."

THE RECIPES

"My native country, thee,
Land of the Noble Free..."

THE NATIVE

AMERICANS

It has been a long time since our Native Americans were the "Noble Free." They have been robbed and kept captive on tiny remnants of the lands that were formerly owned by all of the Native Free. No longer. The line from the preceding song does not even refer to them . . . but rather to immigrants that arrived on these shores long after a profound group of creative cultures had already been founded. Even the name "Indian" is wrong . . . very wrong. It adds to the insult that we have already offered these giving people. They have never even been to India and I suppose it is just too late to call them simply Americans. "Native Americans" seems to be best.

When the European settlers landed on these wonderful shores they were graciously met by "the Red Man." He was not red then, and he is not red now. He was giving, however. The English could not have lasted even that first winter had it not been for the kindness of the Native American. He gave us corn, pumpkins, cranberries, salmon, oysters, clams, turkeys, herbs, kidney beans, lima beans, squashes, and wild rice. He gave us all of these foods, and kept us alive. He even taught us how to grow these blessings.

The Native American kept us Europeans alive because he felt it was his duty. Tribal thinking is very different from Puritan thinking in that the tribal mindset sees value in a person simply because he is a person. He is a member of the tribe and therefore everything is shared with that member. Puritan and European thinking stems from the belief that the only value a person has is connected with his ability to produce or manufacture, and that which is gained in production belongs to the individual, not the tribe or family. For those of us who are white and decide to share, it is a matter of decision, not of custom or mores or ethical laws. No, the Native American gave us food and taught us how to use these foods because he felt he should . . . and now he is very sorry. He is tragically sorry.

It has been a long time since our native country has been the land of the original noble free.

SOUTHWEST INDIANS

I have finally realized that it is just about impossible to understand a people and their art forms if you have not seen their lands. I had no particular appreciation for the art of the Southwest Native American tribes until I finally visited their lands, the deserts. I live in an area surrounded by evergreen trees and mountains and the sea is at my front porch. I was not prepared to absorb the quiet and calming beauty of the desert of New Mexico. I did not understand that the sands and hills, the clouds and sky, offer colors that you cannot see in any other place. I arrived in Albuquerque and drove across the desert to Santa Fe . . . and I know that I will never look at the art of this region in the same way again. It was a most beautiful experience, one that you *must* enjoy.

The original art and culture of this region is still very much alive and available, especially the food. The tribes that created these wonderful gifts include the Navajo, Apache, Pima, Papago, and Pueblo. The famous Zuni and Hopi peoples are part of the great Pueblo tribes. Their lands cover all of New Mexico and Arizona, the southwest corner of Colorado, southern Utah, southwestern Nevada, and the California border of the Colorado River. The white man's division of the states certainly was not based on any concern for the unity of these tribal lands.

The diets of various tribes were very similar. The staples were corn, squash, beans, and pumpkins. These foods were integral to the rituals and religion of these peoples, a religion based on mutual respect for one another and a common sharing of all food products and cultural opportunities. Food was cooked in pottery, or baked in ashes. A great deal of the diet was dried for winter use and then boiled to reconstitute the food product. It is difficult to imagine how precious water was in the desert, and how carefully you had to cook so that you were not wasting this precious commodity.

Additional foods entered the Native American diet with the arrival of the Spanish around 1540. Wheat, oats, onions, and chick-peas were rapidly adopted by the Pueblo and Pima tribes, which had cultivated crops for hundreds of years. Their favorite addition to the diet was the watermelon.

One of the foods that belongs to the Americas and was taken back to Europe was the chile pepper. The varieties of dried red chiles are numerous, and in New Mexico you must never speak to an old timer about California chiles. New Mexico citizens claim theirs are the finest . . . and I tend to agree. However, bringing them home on the airplane is a bit of a task. I got on a flight back to Seattle/Tacoma armed with a three-foot-long strand of beautiful chiles that had just been harvested. They were not even dry yet and the fragrance was rich and heavy. I was terribly popular with many of the passengers . . . and others moved their seats! It was their loss.

When you are looking for dried red peppers, you may have difficulty finding New Mexico peppers. Use California peppers instead. They are delicious and available. Look for them in Mexican or Latin American food stores and be sure to ask about the hotness of the pepper. They run from mild to murder, so you can suit your taste. Common varieties of these large, red, dried treasures are Chile Ancho, Chile Pasilla, Chile Mulato, Chile Negro, Chile de Ristra, New Mexico Chile, and Anaheim Chile.

Please do not confuse chiles with American chili powder. Our commercial chili powder is already blended with sugar, garlic powder, salt, oregano, cumin, and who knows what else.

One more thing: You must go to Santa Fe and visit the old city. It is a wonderful place and you can load up on chiles. Try a meal at a wonderful restaurant called La Tertulia. Oh, boy!

NOTE: All of the food products in this section may be ordered through the mail from:

Casados Farms
P.O. Box 1269B
San Juan Pueblo, NM 87566

They are very nice people and they offer fine-quality dried foodstuffs.

HINT: On Cleaning Dried Red Chiles.
Please understand that the oil in the dried peppers will stick to your hands. So, if you should rub your face, or worse yet your eyes, while cleaning these peppers, you are going to hurt for a while. Use rubber gloves when cleaning the peppers and tell your children to do the same. Better yet, don't let younger people handle the pods at all.

CARNE ADOVADO

SERVES 6

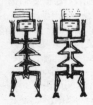

When I saw this dish, ready to cook, in the meat shops of Albuquerque I was almost afraid to try it. The dried red peppers make the marinated pork look as if it's hot enough to remove paint from walls! Actually, it's not as hot as you might think. You can vary the spiciness of this basic New Mexico dish simply by choosing hotter or milder dried chile pods. I now make this dish often and I never cease to enjoy it. The flavors are just superb!

I believe that the American Indians of the Southwest have one of the richest food backgrounds in America.

BLENDED RED CHILE PODS

7–8 whole dried chile pods, seeded and deveined	2 cloves garlic 1 teaspoon oregano 1 teaspoon salt

Choose the dried chiles for your dish. They range in "heat" from mild to very hot . . . so ask your merchant to point the way.

Prepare the chiles by slitting or cracking them open and removing the seeds and veins. The seeds and veins are what make the chiles hot, so you should clean the peppers according to how hot you wish them to be. Place the chile skins in a bowl and add enough hot tap water to cover. Allow them to sit for 1 hour and then drain, reserving the liquid. Place the pepper skins in a blender and add enough of the water to bring the total amount in your machine to 1 pint. Add the garlic, oregano, and salt. Blend until thick and smooth.

THE MEAT

2 pounds boneless
    pork butt or
    shoulder, sliced
    thin

Place the sliced pork in a stainless steel bowl and pour in the chili sauce. Mix the meat and marinade and cover. Refrigerate overnight.

When ready to cook, heat oven to 350°. Place meat and marinade in a covered casserole and bake at 350° for 1 hour. Wonderful, and not as hot as it looks.

I like this with Corn Bread (page 430) and Sweet Potatoes and Onions (page 352). This should sound a little heavy to you, so add a green salad. See what I care!

BEANS WITH CHICOS AND PORK

SERVES 6–8 AS MAIN DISH

Chicos are a wonderful and very rich corn product. They consist of a rich sweet corn that is sun- or kiln-dried and then removed from the cob. They are a basic treat in the diet of the Southwest Indians, and I have come to just love the stuff. The use of corn and beans together should certainly tell you that this dish is legitimate. Remember the East Coast Indians made a similar dish called Misacquetash or succotash (page 435). This dish is *much* better.

You will find *chicos* in any Mexican or Latin American market. They come in little 6-ounce bags and appear to be expensive, but you must remember that they swell up more than rice. They are rich in flavor and great in food value. If you cannot find them in your area it is worth sending away for them (page 60).

6 ounces *chicos* (page 30)	3 cloves garlic, peeled and chopped
2 cups dried pinto beans	½ red chile pod, seeded and chopped
2 tablespoons olive oil	½ pound lean pork, cubed (¼-inch pieces)
1 large yellow onion, peeled and coarsely chopped	Salt to taste

Soak the *chicos* and beans together in ample water overnight.

Put the oil in a medium-hot frying pan and sauté the onion, garlic, and red pepper flakes until the onion is transparent. Remove from the pan and place in a 2-quart covered saucepan. Sauté the pork in the same frying pan just until the meat begins to brown. Drain the *chicos* and beans and add all of the ingredients to the saucepan and then add enough water to just barely cover. Add salt to taste and simmer, covered, until the beans and *chicos* are tender, about 1 hour.

This is a very rich dish. It can be served as a side dish or as a main course. Add a vegetable dish and you have a complete meal.

NOTE: Bacon can be substituted for the pork and the dish is very good that way. Use about 6 thick slices.

GREEN CHILE STEW WITH PORK
(Pueblo)

SERVES 6–8

Patty and I began eating green chile stew, made with pork, long before the boys were born. A fellow named Mingo ran a fine restaurant out near the military base in Tacoma, and the Spanish-speaking troops loved his green chile stew. Was it hot? Was it hot! I have looked for it ever since and have found nothing but cold green pap. This recipe, from Santa Fe, is just terrific, and you can adjust the hotness very easily. Patty gave me an A+ on this one. (Do you know how hard it is to get an A+ from Patty?)

3 **pounds boneless pork, cubed (½-inch pieces)**	4 **cloves garlic, peeled and crushed**
3 **tablespoons peanut oil**	**Chicken Soup Stock (page 29) or canned chicken broth or water to cover (not bouillon)**
3 **stalks celery, chopped**	
2 **medium tomatoes, diced**	
7 **green chiles, roasted, peeled, seeded, and chopped**	**Salt to taste**
	La Victoria brand *salsa jalapeño* **(if you dare)**

Brown the pork in the oil, doing so in 2 or 3 batches. Use a large black frying pan so that the meat will brown quickly.

Place the meat in a 3- or 4-quart covered oven casserole and add the next ingredients. Deglaze the frying pan with the chicken broth or water and add to the pot. Barely cover the ingredients with chicken broth or water. Chicken broth may make this too rich for you, so you might try just water or half of each.

Cover and simmer until the stew is thick and the meat very tender, about 1½ hours.

Add salt to taste before serving.

If the stew is not hot enough for you, add a bit of La Victoria *salsa jalapeño*. This is wonderful, but be careful. It's hot!

Pueblo tradition calls for the addition of corn or potatoes to this dish. I prefer it without. It makes a wonderful filling for enchiladas.

Patty and I simply serve a big green salad with this dish . . . and a pile of wheat tortillas. Then we take the telephone off the hook!

PESOLE WITH PORK

SERVES 6–8 AS MAIN DISH

Pesole is a whole form of hominy (page 32) and it can be found in any Latin American or Mexican shop. Or, you can use regular hominy and will enjoy the dish, I know. This is another basic food product of the Southwest. I suspect that you will come to think of it as a staple in your pantry.

2 cups dry *pesole* or hominy
6 cups water
1 pound pork, cubed (½-inch pieces)

Red chili powder to taste
Oregano to taste
Salt to taste

Soak the *pesole* in the water overnight. Then, place the *pesole* and water in a 3-quart cooking kettle and add the remaining ingredients. Simmer, covered, until the kernels burst, about 2 hours.

This is really a complete meal. But since most of us are not used to thinking that way, I suggest you add some Cabbage and Salt Pork (page 114), along with bread and a salad.

Northwest Indians

One of the great things about living in the Pacific Northwest is the ability to see the art and culture of the Northwest tribes. The Native Americans here reached an artistic level that rivals that of the Incas and the Aztecs. All early tribes used local natural resources for their artistic creations, and that meant stone in South America and in Central America. In the Pacific Northwest wood was used, so the greatest treasures of the culture are gone. However, many wonderful things can still be seen in fine museums in Seattle and Vancouver, British Columbia. And I am pleased to tell you that young people have taken a new interest in the art of their ancestors.

The original inhabitants of the Pacific Northwest are believed to have migrated from Asia via Siberia. Their route was probably a narrow isthmus of land that in later times became submerged beneath the waters of the Bering Strait. By the time the first Europeans sailed into the area, the Northwest was already settled by a diverse people, speaking many different languages and dialects, and with a rich culture of its own.

The Northwest provided an ideal environment for the early inhabitants. The coastal regions yielded an abundance of seafood, and a wide variety of wild fruits and vegetables was also available. Inland, the natives had access to salmon and other fish in the rivers, and there was plenty of game to be hunted. The land was so rich with foods that the Indians were able to live comfortably during the winter months on what they had preserved from the spring and summer. The luxury of having enough to eat meant having leisure time, during which the Northwest tribes built a rich culture. The importance of the necessity of having ample food in the midst of a developing culture cannot be overemphasized. Whole societies have not developed any artistic culture at all simply because all of their time is spent searching for and growing food.

The Northwest Indians certainly did not lack food, and they celebrated accordingly. The development of the potlatch, an extravagant feast held during the winter months, points to the sense of class-consciousness that grew up among these peoples. A great feast was held by tribal leaders in which so much food was offered the visiting guests that the meal could not possibly be consumed. In order to prove the wealth of the tribal leader, and thus the social status of the tribe, valuable objects were destroyed to show that the group could certainly afford to do so. Canoes would be ripped up, reserves of oil burned, and precious sheets of decorated copper, which were used as money, were damaged so as to make them useless.

The number of gifts that was given away to the guests defined the success and impressiveness of the party. The term "potlatch" comes from the Nootka word "patshatl," meaning to give, and give they did. We have record of a Kwakiutl potlatch at which the guests came away with eight canoes, six slaves, forty-four elk skins, two thousand silver bracelets, seven thousand brass bracelets, and thousands of blankets. Can you imagine guests walking home, and the husband turns to his wife and asks the same question that you and I ask after a party? "Well, honey, did you have a good time?"

The coastal peoples lived together in permanent villages during the winter months, but in the spring they broke up into smaller family units to begin searching for food. Their diet consisted mainly of fish and shellfish, but they did gather various roots, bulbs, and many kinds of berries. Much of the find was dried for winter use.

Catching salmon, which was the most important food for the coastal Indians, was urgent. When the salmon began to run, the very first fish caught was greeted with elaborate and wonderful ceremonies that reminded everyone of their ties to nature and their place in the whole ecological scheme. The fish would be brought to the shore and the whole village would stop and sing to it. The children carried the fish to a bed of fresh ferns,

and it was the children who would be given the honor
of tasting the first salmon.

The gifts given the white man by the Pacific Northwest natives are endless. Are you impressed by a *nouvelle cuisine* meal of thinly sliced fish served on a leaf
with a side of fresh berries? That was lunch in the old
days in Puget Sound. The use of common seafoods to
create great delicacies is a part of the heritage of the
region.

The most valuable gift is that of the Northwest native
belief that all things have been created to exist together
in mutual goodwill, sharing and intertwining their lives.
The great totem poles of the region point to that very
understanding of our place in nature, an insight and gift
that the rest of us have still not accepted.

INDIAN SALMON BAKE

There is no food that is more typical of the Northwest
Indian diet than salmon. The oldtimers claim that they
can remember days in which the "waters were silver"
with salmon during the spawning period. Salmon was
so plentiful that its name simply meant "fish" in several
Indian dialects. And the fish was treated with respect.
When the first one of the season was caught, it was
greeted with a profound ceremony in which everyone
was reminded again that life among the tribes was dependent to a large extent upon the salmon. It is still
the most popular fish in the Pacific Northwest.

One of the dishes that was always served at large
gatherings in the old tribal days was salmon cooked
over alder-wood fires. The head and tail of the fish were

cut off and saved for another use. There was little waste
to this process. The salmon was then opened and but-
terflied, or the belly was cut from one end to the other
so that the fish was entirely open. It was cleaned and
the bones were removed. Then the meat was cleverly
laced with alder branches and stuck in the ground alongside the fire. Salmon is still prepared in this way at
Indian festivals; or you can travel to Blake Island, in
Puget Sound, and feast on Indian-style cooked salmon.
You must do this when you travel to Seattle.

I prepare a salmon fillet and cook it in my Kamado
(page 16) with alder chips over the coals. And then, as
we are about to eat, we remember the prayer of thanksgiving to the Great One. It is a prayer in which you
address the salmon and thank him for coming to your
table, and then thank the Great One for offering such
wonders.

SALMON JERKY

This is a wonderful treat, though now expensive to
make. Strips of salmon fillet were left in the sun to dry
and become jerky. Now it is easy to do if you have a
constant pilot light in your gas stove. Stretch or "jerk"
the thin salmon strips and place them on a rack in the
oven. Within 12 hours you will have jerky, or "squaw
candy."

OOLICHAN GREASE

This does not sound very appetizing, I know, but it is
really very interesting. The Quilicum restaurant, in
Vancouver, British Columbia, offers it on the menu
every day. In earlier times it was used as a cooking oil
as well as to add richness to food.

The oolichan, or what whites call the "little candle-

light fish," is allowed to ferment a bit and then the oil
is drained from the batch of fish. Boiling the fish produces additional oil. Some tribes would allow the fish
to ferment for some time, thus giving the oil a darker
color and deeper flavor. This oil was mixed with dried
meats to freshen them, or even used with raspberries
to make a kind of ice cream dessert.

STEAMED FIDDLEHEAD FERN TOPS

I was very surprised the first time that I tasted this
wonderful dish. The tops of the ferns, which do resemble the head of a fiddle, were snipped off and steamed
until tender. They were then served with a bit of oolichan grease. I prefer mine with butter. They taste a
bit like asparagus and I don't want you ever to pass
them up if you see them. You can feast on them at the
Quilicum restaurant year round. (They freeze them!)

SALMON SOUP

SERVES 4

You can make this soup with smoked salmon or with
fresh. Salmon was smoked as a means of preservation,
not just for flavor. I have added a bit of richness to the
soup by using chicken stock as a base. In the old days
one would use plain water.

1 quart Chicken Soup
   Stock (page 29) or
   canned chicken
   broth
1 pound very fresh or
   smoked salmon,
   sliced
   (I prefer smoked
   salmon for this
   dish.)

1 medium yellow
   onion, peeled
   and sliced thin
⅛ teaspoon freshly
   ground black
   pepper
   Salt to taste
1 bunch spinach
   leaves, well
   washed and
   chopped

Bring everything to a boil except the spinach. Turn the heat down to a simmer and cook, covered, for about 15 minutes. Add the spinach and cook 5 minutes longer.

BANNOCK BREAD

SERVES 4–6 AT A NORMAL MEAL

The name of this dish, one which I believe comes from Scotland and therefore is not the proper Indian name at all, refers to the fact that the bread is turned. This bread has a nice flavor and it is not complicated to make.

2 cups flour
½ teaspoon salt
4 teaspoons baking
   powder
½ cup Crisco (You
   could use bear
   grease or
   oolichan grease.)

½ cup water to make
   a thick dough
   Additional
   shortening to
   grease the pan

Mix the dry ingredients together well. Cut in the shortening using a pastry blender (page 17). Mix in the water and knead until the dough is very smooth, about 15 minutes. You can do this in much less time with a powerful electric mixer such as a KitchenAid.

Grease a black frying pan, including the sides, and press the dough into the pan. Bake on top of the stove over low heat. Watch carefully so that the bread does not brown or burn before the center is cooked. When the bread is free from the pan, turn the loaf over and continue to cook. The total cooking time will be about 10 minutes on each side.

HINT: **On Getting the Gamy Flavor Out of Wild Game.**
To get some of the gamy flavor out of wild game, soak overnight in water and baking soda, refrigerated, of course. Rinse well and then proceed with the cooking.

ROAST DUCK

Duck was common among the Northwest Indians. For that matter, so were clams and oysters. But because the ducks lived on salt water and ate saltwater fish, they had a rather fishy taste.

Duck with a fishy flavor does not appeal to the white man . . . at least, not to very many. My mother, Emily, was raised on the Lummi Indian reservation on Lummi Island, near Bellingham, Washington. As a child, she ate fishy duck all the time and learned to love it. Northwest fishermen still come to her door to give her fishy ducks that they have caught and will not eat. But my mother relishes them. She also used to eat the skin off my salmon when I was a boy. She had Lummi tastes, and now years later I eat the salmon skin myself and plead for a fishy duck. She has me hooked too!

This is as close as I can come to what went on in the old days here in the Northwest. I don't expect you to build a fire and roast your duck slowly for a long time. But if you ever get any wild duck from around saltwater, this is what you do . . . and it is very close to what the Northwest Indians still do.

Rub each bird with salt and pepper, inside and out. Brown the birds in a big black frying pan with just a bit of oil. Turn so that each side is browned a bit. Stuff a medium-sized peeled onion inside each bird (the Northwest Indians used wild onions), and place the birds in a covered oven-proof pot. Deglaze the frying pan with a bit of water and add that to the pot. Cover and bake at 325° for about 1 hour. (Wild ducks are rather small, so don't overcook them.) No, wild birds will never be as tender as domesticated birds, but the flavor is something else!

WHIPPED RASPBERRY SOUP

SERVES 4–6

One of my Northwest Indian friends tells me that his grandmother used to make this dish for him when he was tiny, but she used oolichan grease or fish oil with the raspberries rather than honey. I expect that you would prefer this dessert with honey. No, I have not tried it with fish oil either.

1 quart raspberries, washed and drained	**½ cup honey**

Place the berries in an electric mixing bowl along with the honey. Mash the berries and then whip them until they are light. Chill well before serving. This is a very delicious conclusion to your Northwest Indian dinner.

PLAINS INDIANS

Most of us take for granted the things in history that have really changed our eating habits. The refrigerator, for instance, is rarely mentioned as a life-altering event, but it was, of course. For the Plains Indians the coming of the horse was such an event, completely changing their life-style, their eating habits, and thus their mind-set.

Previously most of the Plains Indians had lived on the fringes of the Great Plains or along rivers. They constructed permanent villages and were semiagricultural. Buffalo were hunted on foot when nearby, but since the natives had no means of transportation they were unable to follow the herds. They grew corn, melons, squash, and beans, and supplemented these foods with wild berries and greens, as well as the scarce buffalo meat. When the horse came up from Mexico during the 1700s and was adopted by the Plains Indian culture, a great change came about. The natives no longer had to wait for migrating buffalo to come to them and the tribes became much more nomadic and their culture flourished.

With this change in traveling habits buffalo became more of a regular part of the diet. Antelope, elk, deer, and rabbits were also hunted, though the buffalo remained the chief source of food. It was dried for winter use as jerky or made into pemmican, a mixture of dried meat, fat, marrow, and a paste made of wild cherries (probably chokecherries).

The following recipes will give you a taste of the culture. I have also suggested a place where you might buy buffalo meat (page 478). The meat is really quite good and is now provided by buffalo farms so that the mighty bison is protected from extinction.

BERRY SOUP
(Sioux)

SERVES 4–5

This unusual dish would have been quite familiar to a
Sioux family. It is actually a buffalo-and-blackberry
stew, though good results can be obtained with a beef
steak. I have tried to eliminate the heavy animal fat
that would have been used in this dish by substituting
peanut oil.

1½ pounds 1-inch-thick
   chuck steak,
   boned and
   trimmed of excess
   fat
3 tablespoons peanut
   oil
1 medium white
   onion, peeled and
   sliced

2 to 3 cups Basic Brown
   Soup Stock
   (page 28) or
   canned beef
   broth
1 cup blackberries,
   fresh or frozen
1 tablespoon light
   honey
Salt to taste

Broil the chuck steak in the oven until brown on both
sides. In the old days this would have been done over
the fire, so you might wish to quickly barbecue the meat
in order to increase the flavor. Set the meat aside to
cool.

In a Dutch oven heat the oil and brown the onions.
Cut the meat into bite-size pieces and add to the pot.
Add the blackberries and enough beef stock to barely
cover the meat. Stir in the honey and simmer the meat,

covered, until it is very tender, about 1 hour. If the berries are too tart add more honey to taste. Add salt and serve in bowls.

This is great with Bacon Corn Bread (page 475) and Hominy Baked with Cheese (page 440).

INDIAN BLUEBERRY PUDDING

SERVES 6–8

This dish was originally also made with chokecherries. I had no idea what a chokecherry was since they are not found in the Pacific Northwest. However, my artist, Chris Cart, sent me some chokecherries from Maine. These tiny cherries are bitter enough to surprise you, and the pit is the biggest part of the fruit. The whole cherry, pit and all, was pounded up and used to preserve meat, and they are certainly sour enough to do just that. When they were made into a pudding it must have taken the family's entire stock of honey to provide enough sweetening. Wild blueberries, which could not be preserved so easily, were also used for this dish. You can use frozen and have an Indian meal at any time of the year.

1 pound blueberries, fresh or frozen	½ cup flour
4 cups water	1 cup sugar or honey, to taste

Boil the berries in the water. Drain the juice and set aside. Mash the berries and mix with the flour. Combine the sugar or honey with the juice and add to the berry/flour mix. Stir well. If lumps are present add a little more water and continue to stir. Bring to a simmer and stir constantly until thick. Check for sweetness. Cool and serve.

WAS-NAH CORN AND CHERRY SNACK

SERVES 8–10 AT SNACK TIME

I think it is important to let our children know that not all Americans have enjoyed sweet things in the forms that are so common today. This is such a treat . . . a treat from the Indian community. It is made with truly American food products, though we will substitute Bing cherries for the chokecherries and butter for the buffalo kidney fat. We still have a dish that is close to a wonderful Indian snack. The toasted cornmeal winds up tasting something like popcorn.

2 cups cornmeal
1 cup seeded Bing
    cherries, fresh,
    frozen, or canned

½ pound soft butter
2 cups brown sugar

Place the cornmeal on a cookie sheet and toast it in a 325° oven until it begins to brown. Careful—this will not take long.

Drain the cherries well and chop coarsely. Mix all ingredients together well and chill in the refrigerator. To serve, simply dish out by the tablespoonful. It is eaten like candy.

JERKY STEW

SERVES 6

When the tribes moved about one had to carry food that weighed little and would offer as much nourishment as possible. This was a common solution. I have substituted regular potatoes for the prairie potatoes that the Indians would have used.

1 pound jerky, beef or
   buffalo (page 479)
2 cups whole dried
   hominy, soaked
   overnight in ample
   water (page 438)
1 large yellow onion,
   peeled and
   chopped

1 pound unpeeled
   potatoes, diced
Salt and freshly
   ground black
   pepper to taste

If you are not inclined to make your own jerky for this dish you will have no trouble finding commercial sources. Ask in any good delicatessen. German sausage makers produce a fine jerky.

Break the jerky up into 1-inch pieces and place in a heavy, lidded kettle. Drain the hominy and add to the jerky, along with the onion. Cover with water and bring to a boil. Simmer, covered, until the hominy is tender, about 2 hours. You will have to watch this closely, as more water will have to be added as you go along. Add the potatoes and cook for an additional 20 minutes. Season with salt and pepper.

"Land where my fathers died..."

THE IMMIGRANTS

THE COLONIES

The history of American food is made very much alive in Colonial Williamsburg, in Virginia. Here you can see the coming together of traditions from England with the foods offered the English explorers by the Native Americans.

The English settled Jamestown in 1607, but realized after a few years that they had chosen a most difficult place in which to live. The capital of Virginia was moved from Jamestown to Williamsburg and from 1699 until about 1780 Williamsburg was a most important center for the birth of the new nation. It was there that the likes of George Washington, Patrick Henry, George Wythe, George Mason, and Thomas Jefferson gathered to shape the foundations of the coming new republic. Jefferson went to school in Williamsburg at the College of William and Mary, and he later returned to occupy the Governor's Palace after the resident English governor was forced to flee during the night.

The town of Williamsburg has been beautifully restored and it is surely one of the best places in the country for a lesson in Colonial living. Two kitchens have been restored and are in working order. The first is at the Governor's Palace and I entered expecting a Colonial kitchen. What I found was an English kitchen straight from the old country. Of course, the governor had brought his staff and equipment with him . . . and both had to stay when the Colonial rebellion began to heat up and he was forced to flee.

The difference between an English kitchen at the time and a Colonial kitchen was the fireplace. In Colonial America we cooked over several fires of varying temperatures in the middle of a great fireplace. Pots were hung over the fires or placed on trivets within the fires, while cooking temperatures were controlled by moving the pots about in the fireplace. Colonial cooks spent a great deal of time stooped over the fires. The English kitchen that the governor had imported had no such fire, but rather a grill network. The grill was a series of thin iron bars about four feet long and three feet high.

Two of these grills were placed about eight inches apart so that you could heap wood and embers in the center space and turn and roast meat in front of the upright fire. Pots and pans were placed on a rack on top of the grill when cooking, thus eliminating the need for bending over.

You must go see these kitchens. Your children will never forget the experience, I promise. And you will never forget it either. When you return from the pilgrimage to these two kitchens, your own culinary center is going to look so good to you. Cooking in Colonial times was sheer drudgery. Since you had no refrigeration, you had to start from scratch each morning. Since you had no running water, you had to tromp to the well. Since you didn't have a KitchenAid mixer, you had to do everything by hand. Don't you dare ask again why your great-great-great-grandmother never became a famous oil painter. She had time for one thing and one thing only . . . cooking.

We do have some interesting cookbooks from that period. Food in the colonies was not bad, but remember cookbooks were very expensive. Generally they had been brought from England. Therefore, rather than take the book into the kitchen where it might be soiled, the instructions were copied in another room in the house and the "receipts" were taken into the kitchen.

You can probably find the two following books in facsimile reprints in any large city library. I own both now, but the price of $40 might be a bit much unless you are a serious collector. Find a wonderful book called *The Art of Cookery Made Plain and Easy* by "A Lady," Mrs. Hannah Glasse, published in London in 1747. We know that Martha Washington was particularly fond of this book. A reproduction of it is distributed in this country by the University of Virginia Press. The second book from England was published in 1730 and is called *The Complete Practical Cook,* by Charles Carter. It is also distributed by the University of Virginia Press. These books are just great fun to read through; the "receipts" will take a bit of doing as the

instructions are not as complete as they must be in a
contemporary cookbook.

When you visit Colonial Williamsburg you will find
a book for sale that is very practical and well designed.
It is a compilation of Colonial "receipts," some from
the books above, called *The Williamsburg Art of Cookery*, by Mrs. Helen Bullock. You will also have a good
time with the first real American cookbook, published
in Hartford in 1796. It is called *American Cookery*, by
Amelia Simmons. These last two books are not all that
expensive and should be in your collection.

SYLLABUB

SERVES 10

The recipe for this dish appeared in Virginia in 1742,
but it obviously goes back to England. It is called syllabub, I suppose, because it divides itself into a couple
of layers. Syllables are parts of a word. So it is with this
dessert. Since the wine acts to preserve the cream a bit,
the dish was often made up to 3 days before a party,
and it would stand well. I suggest that you make it the
day before serving and store it overnight in the refrigerator. It will separate and provide a great deal of conversation at the table, as well as a great dessert.

1½ lemons	1 cup Rhine wine
2½ cups whipping cream, very cold	½ cup dry sherry
½ pound (2 cups) powdered sugar	

Grate the rind from the lemons and set aside. Squeeze the juice from the lemons and set aside.

Be sure that the cream is cold. I even chill my electric mixing bowl. Begin whipping the cream on your machine and then add the sugar and lemon rind. While it whips, blend the wine and sherry together with the lemon juice. Add the wine and lemon juice, along with the lemon rind, to the cream. Gradually add the sugar and whip until the mixture is very thick, about 15 minutes on a machine such as a KitchenAid. It will not be quite as thick as regular whipped cream, but it will thicken if the cream is cold. (In the old days it thickened because the cream was high in butterfat. Cream in our time has a much lower butterfat content and therefore must be very cold to whip.)

Spoon into wineglasses. It will separate and provide a wonderful dessert. Store in the refrigerator until serving.

CARROT PUDDING

SERVES 8–10

This is a very interesting dessert based on a recipe from Hannah Glasse's cookbook. The book was not uncommon in the colonies but it was very expensive, of course. Copies were brought from England along with remembrances of English meals that were the common heritage of the colonists in the early days.

You will need to use your scale for this one.

1 pound grated carrots	3 tablespoons orange juice *or* 3 tablespoons orange flower water (found in most delicatessens, gourmet stores, and Middle Eastern markets)
1 pound fresh bread slices, crusts removed	
1½ cups sugar	
1 stick (4 ounces) butter, very soft	
8 eggs	
1 cup whipping cream or half-and-half	
1 cup dry sherry	¼ teaspoon freshly grated nutmeg

Grate the carrots and remove the crusts from the bread. Process the fresh bread slices with the metal blade in your food processor, a few slices at a time. We want fresh, moist bread crumbs.

Cream the sugar and butter together and then add the eggs. Whip until smooth. Add the cream, sherry, orange juice or orange flower water, and nutmeg. Blend with your KitchenAid until smooth and stir in the carrots. Finally, gently fold in the fresh bread crumbs.

Bake this in a preheated 350° oven in a 2-quart pudding mold set in about 2 inches of water. Bake uncovered for about 1 hour 15 minutes, or until the top is a light brown and a table knife, stuck into the center of the pudding, comes out clean.

The original recipe calls for baking this in a large pie shell or puff paste. I think it is just a little too heavy for that.

FRICASSEE OF RABBIT (OR CHICKEN)

SERVES 4–6

When the English hit the New World, they were not very well prepared to deal with the wild. Had the real Native Americans, the Indians, not taught the English how to live in the wilderness, all would have died, we are sure. Enough died as it was, but those who survived learned to use the woods and wild foods carefully. The rabbits that were running loose in the New England woods were probably pretty tough creatures, but this old English method of cooking them could soften up the most stubborn critter. (Chicken may be substituted.)

2 **rabbits, about 3 pounds each, skinned and cut up, or similar amount of chicken**	2 **cups brown gravy**
4 **egg yolks, beaten**	1 **glass (1 cup) red wine**
2 **cups bread crumbs**	½ **pound fresh mushrooms, sliced**
⅛ **teaspoon mace**	**Salt to taste**
⅛ **teaspoon nutmeg**	2 **tablespoons *each* butter and flour, cooked together to form a roux (page 25)**
¼ **cup butter or olive oil for frying**	

Rub the rabbit pieces with the egg yolks and roll in bread crumbs to which you have added the mace and nutmeg. Fry in butter or oil in a black frying pan or Dutch oven until well browned. Add the remaining ingredients and stir until thick. Cover and simmer until tender.

This is great along with a Carrot Pudding (page 89) and a nice garden salad.

RICH CAKE

MAKES 2 LARGE CAKES

The name of this recipe is correct. This is a wonderful cake and it is certainly rich, both in flavor and in cost. I first tasted it at Colonial Williamsburg, where the cooks actually work in the kitchen of the old Governor's Palace. They use only those pieces of equipment that were typical of the area in the late 1700s and cookbooks that barely explain the dish. You must go there and watch their efforts. You might even get a slice of this cake!

I have cut the recipe down just a bit. The original writer of the recipe, Mrs. Hannah Glasse, specified 4 pounds of flour, 6 pounds of butter, and so on. You could feed an entire elementary school with her recipe.

1 pound currants
½ pound blanched almonds
2 tablespoons orange flower water (found in most delicatessens, gourmet stores, and Middle Eastern markets)
2 tablespoons dry sherry for almonds
3 egg yolks
4 whole eggs
¾ pound (3 cups) powdered sugar

1½ pounds butter, at room temperature
Pinch *each* of mace, cinnamon, cloves, nutmeg, and ginger
¼ cup dry sherry
¼ cup brandy
1 pound all-purpose flour
1 cup candied orange and lemon peel, diced to your liking

Soak the currants in hot water for 15 minutes. Drain well.

Grind the almonds along with the orange flower water and the 2 tablespoons of sherry in a medium-size food processor until fine. Set aside.

Beat the 3 yolks and the 4 whole eggs together.

Cream the sugar and butter together. Stir in the almonds and add the eggs. Beat until white and thick and then add the spices, the ¼ cup sherry, and brandy. Stir in the flour. Finally, mix in the soaked and drained currants along with the citrus peel.

Bake in two 10-inch round turban cake molds or two 12-inch ring molds. Grease them well or spray with Pam.

Bake in a preheated 350° oven for 70 minutes, or until a table knife stuck into the middle of the cake comes out clean.

SALLY LUNN BREAD

MAKES 2 LOAVES

This old Colonial favorite is still being served in the restaurants and bakeries in Colonial Williamsburg . . . although I like this recipe better than theirs. It is close to an egg bread in texture and makes just delicious sandwiches and positively smashing toast!

Don't worry about having to work with yeast doughs . . . kneading, and all of that. This is a batter bread and your KitchenAid mixer will do all of the work. This comes from a basic old southern cookbook.

2 cups milk	1 package dry quick-rising yeast
2 tablespoons butter	
2 tablespoons sugar	3 eggs
2 teaspoons salt	4 cups flour

Scald the milk, or bring it almost to a simmer, and add the butter, sugar, and salt. Let cool until tepid or just warm (95°). Dissolve the yeast in ¼ cup of tepid water. Using your electric mixer, if you have a powerful one, beat the eggs and then add the milk mixture, the yeast water, and finally the flour. Beat until very smooth, about 5 minutes.

Leave the dough in the mixing bowl and allow it to rise for one half hour. Beat it down with the mixer just for a moment and then allow it to rise again. Do this a total of 3 times and then put the dough in 2 large greased bread pans. Allow to rise to double in bulk and then bake in a preheated 375° oven for 45 minutes to 1 hour. The bread should be light and have a nice crust.

NOTE: You can also use this recipe with cast-iron muffin pans. The rolls are just delicious.

MUSHROOM CATSUP

MAKES 2 CUPS

This wonderful sauce is from Hannah Glasse's *The Art of Cookery Made Plain and Easy*. However, plain and easy those recipes are not! Mrs. Glasse gives the measurements for everything but the mushrooms themselves. Typical of old cookbooks! I worked out the following recipe for this delicious sauce to be used for meats and added to gravies.

1 tablespoon salt
3 pounds mushrooms
(Buy them when
you can get them
on sale . . . when
they are a bit
brown or bruised.)
2 cups beer
1 tablespoon
horseradish
2 bay leaves
1 yellow onion, peeled
and stuck with 2
cloves

Pinch of mace
Pinch of nutmeg
⅛ teaspoon black
pepper, coarsely
ground
Pinch of allspice
Pinch of fresh
ginger
Garlic (optional)
(Mrs. Glasse
didn't like garlic
in this.)

Put the salt over the mushrooms in a large stainless container. Set overnight. Break up the mushrooms with your hands and simmer them, covered, for a few minutes so that the liquor can come out. Wring the liquid out of the mushrooms using a coarse cloth such as cheesecloth or a potato ricer. Reserve the liquid. Return the mushrooms to the pan and add the beer. Simmer, covered, for 15 minutes. Strain the fluid from the mushrooms again, just as before. Reserve the liquid. Discard the mushrooms and combine the 2 fluids in the pan.

Add remaining ingredients and bring to a simmer, covered. Reduce by one third. Strain through several layers of cheesecloth and place in bottles. Cool and cork. Keeps in the refrigerator for 2 months.

PHILADELPHIA

One of the most fascinating "food cities" in America is Philadelphia. William Penn, an English Quaker, established it in 1682 as the City of Brotherly Love and intended to use the land as a refuge for Quakers and others who shared his vision of a free and peaceful community. Since he needed more settlers to celebrate his "holy experiment," he invited people from England, Holland, and Germany. Each group brought with them their Old World customs, and, of course, their wonderful and diverse foods.

During the 1600s the Swedes, Dutch, English, and Germans came to the city, with more English arriving during the 1700s. During the 1800s the Irish and more Germans arrived and finally, during the 1920s, the Italians, Eastern European Jews, Poles, and Slavs made Philadelphia their home. The Hispanic groups and blacks arrived as well. Of course, many blacks were already in Philadelphia in Penn's time, some of them as slaves at Quaker Penn's country mansion. In any case, the food traditions that were brought with each group have given the city of the "holy experiment" a culinary history that is hard to match anywhere in America.

It was in Philadelphia that the Declaration of Independence was adopted, printed, and first read publicly to the people. It remains the city of Ben Franklin, of wonderful museums and markets, and of restaurants that still serve dishes common to Philadelphia history.

The background of Philadelphia cooking is that of the Colonial period and the British Quakers. The other very strong influence has come from the Pennsylvania Dutch or Germans who settled in rural areas not far from the city. One of the most famous dishes from the German settlers is Scrapple (page 100). It is still eaten at breakfast in all hotels and in many homes. Pepper Pot Soup (page 105) is another dish that came from the Pennsylvania Dutch.

Ice cream seems to have a long tradition in the city.

Although it was not invented there, the Philadelphians claim it was introduced to their city in July of 1782 and served at a party given by the French envoy at which General George Washington happened to be present. Washington was hooked and began making ice cream himself. This story edges out the claim by Jefferson scholars that Thomas brought an ice cream maker with him from France in 1789 and introduced the product to the colonies. The ice cream soda was invented in Philadelphia at the Centennial Exposition of 1876, and the city still has the nation's largest ice-cream factory, Breyers.

The Walter Wilson company developed a special cookie for the opening of the Philadelphia Zoo in 1870. It was the birth of the animal cracker! And the wonderful Philly steak sandwich came about in 1930, but I have given you the recipe for that in an earlier book.

The restaurants in the city are just wonderful. And you must go to the Reading Terminal Market, where you can purchase foods from the Amish people of the Pennsylvania Dutch tradition. The sausages and pretzels will make you cry, they are so good. The pretzel belongs to the city as well, as it came with the German immigrants.

The Italian market in South Philadelphia is one of the few remaining open-air food markets in this country. You will have a grand time buying Italian foods and vegetables. For cooking equipment, stop at Fante's, one of the best cooking-supply houses in America.

The following recipes will give you a taste of my Philadelphia, but to really understand it you must go visit yourself.

STEWED PRETZELS

You must understand that the dried, salty, skinny pretzel that is known in most of this country does not stand a chance in Philadelphia, or in most of Pennsylvania. The Philadelphia pretzel is a soft pretzel, and is a wonderful warm snack. Some of the best pretzels that you can imagine can be purchased just after baking in the Reading Terminal Market. Or you can order them through a very popular Philadelphia bakery called Federal Pretzel Baking Company.

A very common but delicious dish for breakfast is made in the following manner. Heat a bowl of milk for each person. Put a dot of butter into each bowl and break in a soft pretzel. This is often topped with "pork pudding." The closest thing I know to this pudding is lightly browned, bulk pork breakfast sausage. Be sure to drain the fat from the pork sausage before putting it on top of the stewed pretzels.

SCRAPPLE

SERVES A SMALL ARMY

The term *scrapple* literally means "scraps." It was made during the hog-butchering season, thus utilizing the remnants of the pig. The dish was served for late Sunday evening meals or for breakfast. It still is, and it's delicious! The word is not found in early cookbooks because it was taken for granted that readers knew how to make this popular but inexpensive farmer's food. I suppose that it was not considered something that one would put into a polite cookbook. It finally appeared as a recipe in the second quarter of the nineteenth century.

3 pounds pork neck
  bones
4 quarts water
2 teaspoons salt
1 teaspoon pepper

2 teaspoons whole sage
  leaves, rubbed
1 teaspoon savory
3 cups cornmeal

Simmer the pork neck bones, covered, in the water for 1½ hours. Remove the bones and cool, reserving the stock. Remove the meat from the bones and chop coarsely. You will need 2 to 3 cups of meat. Discard the bones.

Heat 3 quarts of the stock and add the salt, pepper, sage, and savory. Bring to a rolling boil and gradually stir in the cornmeal, stirring all the time in order to avoid lumps. When thickened like a mush, about 15 minutes, add the meat and continue to cook over low heat for 20 more minutes, stirring occasionally.

Pour into loaf pans and refrigerate.

To serve, slice ¼-inch thick and pan-fry in hot fat along with a bit of butter.

Traditionally this was served with hot maple syrup. I like it just as well plain.

MOCK SNAPPER SOUP

MAKES 5–6 QUARTS

Most of us have trouble getting turtle. Besides, the poor terrapin, which was originally used in this recipe, is now on the endangered species list. So I have given you a mock version that is really very good. Terrapin was a very popular and inexpensive dish in the old days among Philadelphians, so popular that they ate up an otherwise very frugal source of food. A very good version of this soup, using a different variety of turtle, is still available at Bookbinder's restaurant in Philadelphia.

I have developed a soup that has no turtle in it at all, but I think you will like the flavor. It takes a little doing, but this recipe is worth it.

3 pounds beef neck bones

¼ pound salt pork

1 cup chopped celery

1 cup chopped, but not peeled, yellow onions

1 cup chopped carrots

½ chicken (3½-pound size) in 1 piece

1 tablespoon whole basil leaves

1 teaspoon whole marjoram leaves

1 tablespoon whole thyme leaves

3 whole bay leaves

20 whole peppercorns

1 teaspoon cayenne pepper

1 bunch whole parsley leaves

6 cloves garlic, chopped, peel and all

1 can (28 ounces) tomatoes, puréed in blender or food processor

2 sticks margarine

1 cup flour

½ pound halibut (cheeks or boneless filet)

½ pound crabmeat

2 teaspoons salt, or to taste

Juice of 1 lemon

½ tablespoon Tabasco, or to taste

3 tablespoons Worcestershire sauce, or to taste

¼ teaspoon ground cloves, optional

1 cup dry cocktail sherry

8 hard-boiled eggs, grated

Place the beef neck bones in a roasting pan and roast, uncovered, for 45 minutes at 400° or until lightly browned.

Dice the salt pork and pan-fry in a large frying pan. When the fat has been rendered, add the celery, onions, and carrots. Sauté until tender.

Place the roasted bones and the sautéed vegetables in a large kettle and cover with water. (This should take about 6 quarts.) Bring to a simmer and add the half chicken, the next 6 seasonings, the parsley (just throw it in), the garlic, and the tomatoes. Cook at a good simmer for ½ hour. Remove the chicken to cool, and allow the stock to continue to cook. Debone the chicken and save the meat, covered. Return the bones and skin to the pot. Continue cooking the stock and bones for a total of 2 hours, from start to finish.

Remove the beef bones from the pot and allow them to cool.

In the meantime, prepare the roux. Melt 2 sticks of margarine in a frying pan and add the flour. Stir over medium heat until the roux is the color of peanut butter. Set aside.

Remove the meat from the beef bones and chop into very small dice. Discard the bones.

Strain the stock and discard all solids. To remove fat from the top of soup stock, use a plastic tube. Plastic tubing about ⅓ inch in diameter can be purchased at hardware stores. Strain the stock, and then remove the stock from beneath the fat by siphoning with the plastic tube. Tip the kettle holding the stock so that you can always keep the siphoning tube beneath the level of the fat.

Return the stock to the kettle and add the chopped beef. Thicken the soup with the roux, stirring the whole time that the *hot* roux is added. Add the halibut and simmer 10 minutes. Remove the fish and "flake" or tear into strings. Return the fish to the pot, along with the crab and precooked chicken. Add salt to taste, along with the lemon juice, Tabasco, Worcestershire, and optional cloves.

Keep the pot at a very low simmer as you add the dry sherry and the grated eggs.

Serve very hot with toast squares on the side.

CHICKEN CORN SOUP WITH RIVELS

SERVES 8–10

This dish is terribly popular with the Pennsylvania Dutch, who form a major food influence in Philadelphia. Your kids will get a kick out of making "rivels," very quick soup noodles that are common in Pennsylvania. The word *rivel* means "lump," and that is what you are going to get in this delicious soup.

Please do not confuse this with normal chicken noodle soup. This thick, rich, early American soup will bring them back to the farm!

1 chicken (3–3½ pounds), cut in half	Salt and pepper to taste
3 quarts water	6 ears corn, scraped from the cob (page 16) *or* 1 bag (20 ounces) frozen corn kernels and 1 can (17 ounces) creamed corn
1 small yellow onion, peeled and chopped	
1 bay leaf	
2 sprigs parsley, whole	

RIVELS

2 eggs, beaten	4 hard-boiled eggs, peeled and sliced
2 cups flour	1 tablespoon chopped parsley, for garnish
Pinch of salt	

Rinse the chicken halves and place them in a 6-quart soup pot. Add the water, onion, bay leaf, parsley sprigs, and a bit of salt and pepper. Bring the chicken to a boil, turn the heat down to a good simmer, and cover the pot. Cook for 1 hour. Remove the chicken from the soup and allow to cool. Save the soup stock. Debone the chicken, discarding the skin and bones, and coarsely chop the meat. Set the chicken meat aside, covered.

Scrape the corn from the ears or, if using frozen corn, run it through your food processor for a very short time to chop up the kernels. Remove the fat from the chicken soup and bring the pot to a light boil.

To make the rivels, mix the beaten eggs with the flour and salt, using a fork. Stir this until it turns into large grains of dough. Rub this mixture through your hands over the soup pot, so that very small lumps of dough fall slowly into the pot. Stir gently and simmer the soup and rivels for about 10 minutes or until tender. Check the soup for salt and pepper. Add the corn and chicken and cook for an additional 5 minutes. Serve with hard-boiled egg slices and parsley garnish.

NOTE: I have seen recipes that substitute popcorn for the rivels. Yes, you read me correctly. How would your children react to popcorn soup?

PEPPER POT SOUP

MAKES 2 QUARTS AND SERVES 8

The common story is that George Washington told his cook to treat the boys at Valley Forge. Having only tripe and a few other odds and ends, he developed this soup. I love that story but the dish was probably developed in Philadelphia long before the war. During the late 1700s and early 1800s it was common to hear a black woman singing out this description of her wares: "Pepper pot, smokin' hot!"

You can put as much pepper in this soup as you can stand! (Freshly cracked, of course.)

1 pound honeycomb
tripe

5 slices bacon, diced

½ cup peeled, chopped
yellow onion

2 green sweet bell
peppers, seeded
and chopped

2 quarts Basic Brown
Soup Stock (page
28) or canned
beef broth

1 teaspoon whole
thyme leaves, or
more to taste

½ teaspoon marjoram

½ teaspoon ground
cloves

½ cup chopped celery

3 leeks, cleaned and
chopped

1 bunch parsley,
chopped

¼ teaspoon crushed
red pepper flakes

1 bay leaf

1 teaspoon freshly
ground black
pepper (more if
desired)

1 large potato, peeled
and diced

4 tablespoons *each*
butter and flour,
cooked together
to form a roux
(page 25)

Place the tripe in a saucepan and cover with water. Bring to a boil and turn off the heat. Allow the tripe to cool a bit in the water and then drain and rinse. Cut into ¼-inch dice.

In a large heavy kettle, sauté the bacon until clear. Add the onion, celery, leeks, parsley, and green peppers; sauté until tender. Add the remaining ingredients *except* the potato, flour, and butter. Bring the kettle to a boil and turn down to a simmer. Cook, covered, until the tripe is very tender, about 2 hours. Add the diced potato and cook for an additional 20 minutes.

Prepare the roux by stirring the flour into the melted butter and cooking for a moment on the stove. When the soup is done to your liking, stir in the roux and simmer, stirring all the while, until the soup thickens a bit. Correct the seasonings.

It is common in Philadelphia, and among the Pennsylvania Dutch, to serve this dish with dumplings (page 469). It makes a full meal and it is just a wonderful blend of flavors.

GEORGE WASHINGTON

The Washingtons were great entertainers. I suppose they had to be, since Mount Vernon, where the general really loved to reside, was a great distance from any city, so visitors simply came to stay. We have a record of one fellow who came to the front door and offered the gracious Washingtons a letter of introduction. They had never met the man, nor had they known that he was coming. He stayed three weeks!

Plantation life consisted of living off the farm itself, as much as possible. The plantation provided most of the food for the table, food that would feed dinner parties of fifty regularly. The crops at Mount Vernon were varied, ranging from Martha Washington's wonderful vegetable gardens to the rye that the General grew for his whiskey still. Of course they grew their own wheat and corn and made their own bread. Mrs. Washington, the former Mrs. Curtis, had arrived at Mount Vernon already an accomplished cook, so she saw over the kitchen for the whole of the household. She had a full staff, of course, but she personally monitored the bread baking and she was terribly proud of her hams. She cured four hundred each year and cooked one a day since she never knew who was going to show up at the dinner table. Toward the end of his life, General Washington, who was short on cash, complained that his beloved Mount Vernon was becoming "a well resorted tavern!"

Washington owned some eight thousand acres, and by our standards he would have been considered a wealthy man. However, owning land did not mean that you had any cash flow. Everything was tied up in the plantation, and while you did a great deal of trading with foodstuffs there was seldom any money in the bank. He once had to travel into Alexandria in order to float a loan so that he could afford to go to New York by horse and coach . . . for his inauguration as the first President of these United States!

The meals at Mount Vernon must have been wonderful. Many courses were served and guests were often quite surprised that the hospitable Mrs. Washington would make tea herself. Breakfast was served on the great front porch, overlooking the Potomac, at about seven in the morning. The general preferred corn pancakes swimming in honey for his first meal of the day. He would then ride the plantation. The main meal of the day was served at three with several meat courses, many vegetables, and one of Mrs. Washington's hams. Supper, a lighter meal, was served at nine in the evening, though General Washington seldom participated. He was a plantation owner and arose early for work, so he went to bed before nine each evening. He was also a punctual man and refused to wait for more than five minutes for a late dinner guest. My kind of man!

It is hard to believe that the Washingtons entertained so many people . . . and so regularly. From the last twenty years of their lives together, we have a record of two evenings, only two, in which the couple ate together by themselves.

It took a large staff to run such a plantation, and most of them were slaves. While this is repulsive to us now, it was a normal economic practice for any large farm owner. However, it is interesting to note that General Washington disliked the practice and was one of the first to desire that the legislature of Virginia look to the abolition of slavery. He refused to break up families and records indicate that he treated his slaves quite well. Upon his death in 1799 all of his slaves were set free. Many continued to work at Mount Vernon as free citizens. This was not the case with Washington's acquaintance Thomas Jefferson, who passed his slaves along with the estate when he died in 1826.

Though George Washington became our first President, he was never called by that title since what he had done for the colonies as a military leader during the Revolution was so much more important. Nor was he called Mr. He was always addressed as General Washington.

You must go to Mount Vernon and see the mansion and the kitchen. I hope they will restore the wonderful cooking room so that demonstrations might be put on showing what the Washingtons ate. They do this sort of thing at Colonial Williamsburg. I urge the Mount Vernon Ladies Association of the Union, the caretakers of the estate, to do the same.

This supposedly was Washington's favorite menu:

Cream of Peanut Soup (page 111)
Virginia Ham with Oyster Sauce (page 114)
mashed sweet potatoes with coconut
string beans with mushrooms
Virginia Spoon Bread (page 115)
Martha's Virginia Cake (page 116)

Other dishes that regularly appeared on the table:
Hominy (page 438)
roasted fowl
Boiled Pork (page 131)
cabbage, fried with salt pork
Peas and Salt Pork (page 122)
cucumbers, cooked or fresh
artichokes
pickles

CREAM OF PEANUT SOUP

SERVES 6

General Washington's step-granddaughter, Martha Curtis, lists this dish among the first President's favorites. It is very simple to make and quite delicious. Your children will get two things out of this dish. First, they will learn that peanuts really are one of the most versatile food products imaginable, and, second, they will taste a dish that appeared often on the table of the father of our country.

1 quart Chicken Soup
  Stock (page 29) or
  canned chicken
  broth
2 carrots, chopped
1 yellow onion, peeled
  and chopped
1 cup smooth-style
  peanut butter

1 cup whipping
  cream or half-
  and-half
½ cup dry-roasted
  peanuts
Salt and pepper to
  taste
Tabasco to taste

Place the stock in a 2-quart pot and add the carrots and onion. Bring to a boil and turn down to a simmer. Cook, covered, until the vegetables are very tender. Purée in a food processor and return to the pan. Stir in the remaining ingredients, bring to a simmer, and serve. Be careful with the salt!

FRIED TRIPE

SERVES 6–8

This may not sound like a great dinner dish to you, but it was popular with the Washingtons. Actually, if you take the time to cook the tripe until it is very tender, the dish is quite enjoyable.

2 pounds honeycomb tripe, cut into 2 × 3-inch pieces
1 carrot, chopped
1 yellow onion, peeled and chopped
1 bay leaf
Salt and pepper to taste

3 egg yolks
2 cups bread crumbs
3 tablespoons butter for pan-frying
3 tablespoons olive oil for pan-frying

SAUCE

½ stick melted butter
2 tablespoons Dijon-style mustard (Grey Poupon)

Place the tripe in a saucepan and cover with water. Bring to a boil, drain, and rinse the tripe. Cover the meat with water again and add the carrot, onion, bay leaf, and salt and pepper. Bring to a simmer and cover. Cook until tender, about 2 hours.

Drain and cool the tripe. Whip the egg yolks; dip the tripe into them and then into the bread crumbs. Pan-fry in the butter and olive oil until golden brown on both sides.

Serve with the butter/mustard sauce on the side.

RAGOO OF ONIONS

SERVES 4–6 AS A VEGETABLE DISH

This easy dish is typical of English cooking. I sometimes forget that General Washington was born in England and knew this kind of food very well. While he broke with England politically, he certainly did not give up his favorite dishes from the Old Empire. On the other hand, his menus always offered a wide selection of American food products such as turkey, pumpkin, and corn. (*Ragoo,* rather than *ragout,* was the Colonial spelling.)

1 cup bread crumbs	2 tablespoons flour
½ stick (2 ounces) butter for the bread crumbs	½ teaspoon salt Black pepper, freshly ground, to taste
1 stick (4 ounces) butter for the onions	½ cup good brown gravy
2 cups very small onions, blanched and peeled	1 teaspoon Dijon-style mustard (Grey Poupon)
4 large yellow onions, peeled and chopped	

Fry the bread crumbs in a pan with the butter. Cook just until they are golden brown, stirring all the while.

Melt the butter in a large skillet and add the onions, both kinds. When they are a light brown, add the flour and stir until the flour thickens the dish a bit. Add the salt, pepper, brown gravy, and mustard. Bring to a simmer and serve with the bread crumbs on top.

CABBAGE AND SALT PORK

SERVES 6–8 AS A VEGETABLE DISH

Martha Washington said, "Vegetables are the nicest thing about living in the country!" The Mount Vernon table was always covered with vegetables from the vast gardens to be found on the plantation, some of the seeds having been brought from England many years before. This dish appeared often on the table since cabbage kept well through the winter. I had to guess at the recipe, but I am sure the General and Mrs. Washington would nod approvingly.

½ **pound salt pork,
   cut into ¼-inch
   dice**
1 **yellow onion,
   peeled and
   chopped**

2 **heads cabbage,
   cored and sliced
   Salt and pepper to
   taste**

Rinse the diced salt pork under hot water and place in a large Dutch oven. Render or "try out" the pork: Simply brown it a bit in the pan. Add the onions and cook until clear. Add the cabbage and cook over medium-high heat, stirring occasionally, until the cabbage is wilted and tender, but not soggy. Add salt and pepper to taste.

OYSTER SAUCE FOR VIRGINIA HAM

MAKES 1 PINT OF SAUCE

The General was very fond of Virginia ham. Mrs. Washington took great pride in curing some 400 hams a year, and she cooked almost every day since she never really quite knew who was going to show up for dinner. Her husband preferred his ham with this sauce.

The recipe comes from a collection attributed to Mrs. Hannah Glasse, "A Lady," published in London in 1747. We know that Mrs. Washington had a copy and used it often. This is the most likely source for the General's favorite sauce for ham.

1 pint oysters with their liquor	3 tablespoons *each* flour and butter, cooked together to form a roux (page 25)
1/8 teaspoon ground mace	
1 cup dry white wine	

Place the oysters in a saucepan, along with their own liquor. Add the mace and bring to a simmer. When the oysters are plump (a very short time), remove them from the pan. Add the wine to the juices and reduce a bit. Add the roux and thicken the sauce. Return the oysters to the sauce and serve.

VIRGINIA SPOON BREAD

SERVES 8

Spoon bread is simply a very rich and dense corn bread, a dish so dense that it must be served up with a spoon. General Washington loved this dish and it was apparently served quite often at Mount Vernon.

1 cup cornmeal, either white or yellow	2 cups milk, scalded
1 1/2 teaspoons salt	2 1/2 teaspoons baking powder
	2 eggs, separated

Mix the cornmeal and salt together and stir them into the hot milk. Cook over very low heat, stirring all the time, until thick and smooth. Continue cooking for 15 more minutes, stirring occasionally. Cool slightly. Stir in the baking powder and well-beaten yolks, and fold in the stiffly beaten egg whites. Turn into a greased casserole or 8-inch-square pan. Bake in a moderate oven (375°) about 35 minutes, or until the bread is firm and the crust is brown. Serve from the baking dish.

MARTHA'S VIRGINIA CAKE

MAKES 2 CAKES

The General had a special fondness for this cake. The family referred to it as "Virginia whiskey cake," but the only recipes that I could find used red wine and brandy . . . not whiskey. This recipe came from the hand of Mrs. Washington's granddaughter and it did not mention whiskey at all. I expect that Ms. Curtis, the stepgranddaughter of General Washington, was not too keen on the fact that the old boy had a large rye whiskey still and traded whiskey in the West Indies for special food products that he loved to eat at Mount Vernon, products such as bananas and coconut. He also drank the rye whiskey. So, in a fit of questionable historical research, I have restored the whiskey to this cake. I believe that the father of our land would approve.

This is an unusual type of fruit cake and it keeps for a good time, thus offering Mrs. Washington another course for those unexpected visitors who constantly appeared at her front door. It *should* have lasted; her recipe calls for 40 eggs, 4 pounds of butter, 5 pounds of flour, and an equal amount of fruit.

1 stick soft butter	1 cup sweet port wine
½ cup sugar	¼ cup brandy
3 cups flour	1½ cups diced dried mixed fruit (for fruitcake)
2 teaspoons baking powder	
⅛ teaspoon freshly grated nutmeg	6 eggs, separated
¼ teaspoon mace	1 cup whiskey

Cream the butter and sugar until smooth. Mix in the yolks.

Mix the flour, baking powder, and spices together. Stir the flour mixture into the egg/sugar mixture. Mix in the port and the brandy. Stir in the dried fruit.

Whip the egg whites until they form very soft peaks. Stir in about a quarter of them to lighten the batter. Fold in the remaining egg whites very gently.

Bake in a preheated 325° oven in 2 loaf pans for 1 hour, or until a toothpick stuck into the middle of the cake comes out clean.

Cool the cakes and pour half of the whiskey over each. Cover each pan with aluminum foil and allow to sit for a day before serving.

THOMAS JEFFERSON

Europe had great Renaissance men. Benvenuto Cellini called himself the greatest goldsmith, the greatest gunsmith, the greatest lover. Well, we have our own Renaissance man and he was and remains Thomas Jefferson.

Mr. Jefferson was an architect, statesman, a great agriculturalist, the author of the Declaration of Independence, and a president of these United States. And he was a great gourmet and a well-known ladies' man.

In 1784 we sent Jefferson to France as our American diplomat. He was very open-minded about Europe, contrary to the likes of Ben Franklin, and he traveled about the Continent among the peasants, looking "into their kettles and eating their bread." In 1789 he returned home to his beloved Monticello, and with him came a pasta machine from Italy. He was the first to serve pasta at a Colonial dinner party. He brought back a waffle iron and French fries. He literally stole a new strain of rice while in Italy and he popularized ice cream with clever coatings, something that we now call Baked Alaska. And wine. He brought back a knowledge of wine that was beyond that of anyone else in America.

He was more than a gardener, he was an agricultural genius. He tried growing everything imaginable on his Virginia plantation. His efforts included some failures, such as sesame seed and olives for olive oil, but many more successes. He had 250 varieties of vegetables and herbs growing in his garden and he loved to experiment with peas, some 50 varieties, and tomatoes. The master of Monticello was enjoying tomatoes when the rest of the country thought they were poison!

His critics, such as Patrick Henry, complained that Mr. Jefferson had become some sort of Francophile dandy. No matter to Jefferson. He served lavish meals with up to thirteen dessert courses. And his meals were carefully planned so that few servants ever appeared on the scene. He didn't want the flow of conversation interrupted. Some letters indicate that he did much of the talking, but all was planned so that the guests would be comfortable. His critics claimed that Thomas had too much fun eating with his guests, and it was probably true. He wanted to "mitigate business with dinner," and to that end he insisted on "No Healths [toasts], No Politics, No Restraints." This last admonition to his guests resulted in their having to find their own places at the table and then seat themselves, a practice one Englishman thought totally insulting. Jefferson actually served his guests himself and rarely allowed anyone else to pour the wine.

His desire for "mitigating business with dinner" caused him to invent the dumbwaiter and the lazy Susan so that guests could be cared for by the fewest possible servants.

I visited the kitchen at wonderful Monticello (you really must go) and I was disappointed to hear that Jefferson's black servant, Isaac, claimed that the only time his master was in the kitchen was to wind the clock. He loved machines and his clocks were a source of great pride. But he did watch over the whole of the plantation, including his smokehouse, fishpond, and endless gardens. He had help from his daughter, Martha Jefferson Randolph, in running the house. Mrs. Jefferson had died very young so Martha spent a great deal of time taking care of the head of Monticello. The two were so close that Thomas Randolph, Martha's husband, was incensed with the relationship and seldom came near the house. Now, that is probably all gossip, but it is interesting!

Jefferson's dinner menus for guests were elaborate, with several meats being served. He preferred vegetables to meats and used meats as a flavoring in his own diet rather than as a course. Interesting to note that he was way ahead of his time on this point as well.

He loved his Monticello and intended to die there. He did. He went into a coma that lasted for several days. The doctors were sure each day that he would be dead within a few hours, but he hung on. Finally, on

July 4, 1826, he awoke from his coma and asked, "Is it today?" They replied that it was indeed Independence Day. Thomas Jefferson said, "Thank you," and he died.

PEAS AND SALT PORK

SERVES 4–5

It was Mr. Jefferson who really got us into peas. He was so fascinated by this legume that at one point he experimented with some fifty varieties. This must have been a typical way of cooking them since it is a method of cooking many vegetables in Virginia. In any case, when you have peas be sure and remember Mr. Jefferson. He would love to be at your table with you!

¼ pound salt pork, cut into ¼-inch dice
1 yellow onion, peeled and sliced thin
1 bag (20 ounces) frozen peas, defrosted
Freshly ground black pepper, to taste

The simplicity of this dish is what makes it so good. Salt pork was used for richness, much the same way we would use butter now.

Dice the salt pork and blanch it for 1 minute in boiling water. Drain. Heat a large frying pan and sauté the salt pork just until clear. Add the onion and cook until the onion is clear. Add the peas and stir all well. Cover and cook until the peas are tender, about 8 minutes. Season with pepper and serve.

PEA SOUP

SERVES 4

This soup is based on a common recipe of the day, and it is very close to what Mr. Jefferson used to enjoy after riding about the plantation in Monticello.

1 cup fresh or frozen
   peas
2½ cups water
   Salt to taste
¼ cup sugar
1½ tablespoons *each*
   butter and flour,
   cooked together
   to form a roux
   (page 25)

2 egg yolks, beaten
½ tablespoon
   chopped parsley
2 tablespoons butter

Bring peas to a boil in salted water. Simmer until tender
and drain, saving the water. Purée in a food processor
with a bit of the water. Return to the pan and add the
rest of the water, the sugar and the roux. Stir constantly
over heat until the mixture thickens a bit. Add ¼ cup
of the soup to the beaten yolks, stirring constantly, and
then stir the yolks into the soup. Top with the parsley
and the butter.

MONTICELLO MUFFINS

MAKES 24 "MUFFINS"

We have the recipe. It was described by Jefferson's
daughter . . . but the explanation makes little sense to
me. Further, ingredients were omitted because the
writer assumed that we knew how the dish would ba-
sically be prepared. The following recipe is for breakfast
yeast rolls with sesame. The dish that is described in
the original called for yeast and "setting aside." So this
should not be called a muffin at all. I have also included
sesame seeds because Mr. Jefferson was very fond of

them. The slaves brought the seeds with them from Africa and Jefferson did his very best to get them to grow at Monticello.

2 **packages quick-rising yeast**	5½ **cups flour**
½ **cup tepid water (85–90°)**	5 **tablespoons roasted sesame seeds (See note below)**
2 **cups milk**	2 **tablespoons raw sesame seeds**
3 **tablespoons sugar**	
1 **teaspoon salt**	
2 **tablespoons salad oil**	

Dissolve the yeast in the water. Stir into the milk. Add the sugar, salt, oil, and 2 cups of the flour. Mix with an electric mixer for about 5 minutes. Add the roasted sesame seeds and work in the remaining flour. If you have a KitchenAid, do this with the dough hook. If you need to do this by hand, use a wooden spoon. After all of the flour is incorporated or mixed in, knead the dough until smooth. Using the machine, this will take about 5 minutes.

Let the dough rise under a large stainless bowl on a plastic counter. When it is double in bulk, after 1 hour, punch down and divide into 2 pieces. Divide each half into 12 pieces and place in greased muffin pans. Top with the raw sesame seeds and allow to rise until double in bulk. Bake at 400° for 20 minutes or until light brown.

NOTE: Sesame seeds can be found raw in any health-food store and many fancy markets or nut shops. Roast them by placing in a frying pan over medium heat and cook, stirring, until they are golden brown.

TOMATO SALAD

SERVES 6–8

A vine-ripened tomato remains, for me, one of the greatest things in the food world. Mr. Jefferson seemed to feel the same way, though not everyone shared his enthusiasm. Up until the beginning of this century, there were still people about who thought the tomato was poison. We know that there were a few in Jefferson's time who thought him eccentric, and surely his love for this "poisonous fruit" must have added to their silly criticisms.

5 ripe large tomatoes
2 white onions, either
    Vidalia (Georgia)
    or Walla Walla
    (Washington
    State) Bermudas
    are good too.

1 cup Vinaigrette
    Dressing (page
    384)
Salt and pepper to
    taste
Parsley, chopped,
    for garnish

Slice the tomatoes and onions thin. Layer in a bowl and add the dressing and the salt and pepper. Allow to marinate in the refrigerator for 2 hours before serving. Top with the parsley garnish.

STEWED TOMATOES

SERVES 6

I think of doing this very seldom. When I was a child my mother used to heat up canned tomatoes with some old bread cubes. It was not my favorite. However, fresh stewed tomatoes are something else. Mr. Jefferson thought of many ways to serve this delight, and I think he certainly would have enjoyed this version. We know that he kept a large herb garden going all of the time, so the herbs would have found their way into his beloved tomatoes. He also loved olive oil and tried to grow olives at Monticello.

3 tablespoons butter	Basil or oregano to
1 yellow onion, peeled and sliced	taste (Fresh would be best, but dried
6 very ripe large tomatoes, cored and quartered	will certainly do.)
	¼ cup dry white wine
	Salt and pepper to taste

In a heavy saucepan melt the butter and sauté the onion until clear. Add the remaining ingredients and simmer until the tomatoes are very tender, or to your liking.

COOKED GREENS WITH GARLIC AND TOMATO

The name of this dish also gives the recipe. I wish recipe names were all this simple, as you would then know what is going on the minute you read the name of the dish. That is generally what the Chinese do, but we are inclined to use strange names for simple food. Mr. Jefferson got into the habit of using many French names for dishes at his table. But then, the recipes were very much influenced by his time in France.

Simply sauté some garlic and tomato slices together in olive oil. Add any greens you wish and "cook them down" over high heat stirring often. Kale, spinach, savoy cabbage, mustard greens or collard greens would all be good. You might wish to start the pot with diced bacon instead of olive oil. Season with salt and pepper.

VIRGINIA HAM

Mr. Jefferson, a great entertainer, very often had his own hams on the table for guests. While he did not eat much meat himself, he did put out a lavish spread. Hams were cured on the plantation and finished in a smokehouse very near the kitchen. Most hams on the

American market bear no resemblance whatsoever to the old dry-cured hams of the days of General Washington and Mr. Jefferson. With a bit of detective work you can find a ham from Smithfield, Virginia. These are still prepared very much as in Colonial times... and they will keep for months without refrigeration. They are loaded with salt so they must be soaked for a good time before cooking. The result is worth the effort, I promise.

A recipe for cooking one of these wonderful hams is found on page 215.

JEFFERSON FRIED CHICKEN

SERVES 5–6

It is true that Mr. Jefferson became very fond of French cuisine and imported many foods and wines from France. His archcritic, Patrick Henry, once complained that Jefferson had become so fond of the French that he "abjured his native victuals." Oh, nonsense! This recipe comes from his daughter, Martha Randolph, and must have been used at the mansion often. You can't get more Virginia than fried chicken! This is a delicious version with old-fashioned cream gravy. Wonderful!

2 cups cold cornmeal mush (page 430)
2 cups flour
Salt and pepper to taste
2 chickens, 3 pounds each, cut up
½ cup fat for pan-frying (She would have used lard. I prefer peanut oil.)

1 tablespoon chopped parsley
1 cup whipping cream
1 tablespoon butter
6 sprigs parsley, for garnish

Slice the cold cornmeal mush and cut into small decorative circles using a cookie cutter or small glass. Panfry until golden brown on both sides and keep in warm oven until serving time.

Season the flour with salt and pepper and dredge the chicken in it. Heat a large black frying pan and add the oil. Pan-fry the chicken until golden brown and done to your taste. Turn several times during cooking. You will have to do this in 2 or 3 batches.

Remove the chicken from the pan and keep warm in the oven. Drain the oil and add the parsley, cream, and butter. Cook for a moment while stirring and scraping the bits of brown in the pan. Arrange the chicken on a platter and surround with the cornmeal circles. Check the cream gravy for salt and pepper and pour over the chicken. Top with parsley sprigs.

Begin the meal with Pea Soup (page 122) and add Mr. Jefferson's Macaroni Pie (page 130).

BAKED POLENTA

SERVES 4

This recipe illustrates an interesting bit of history. Corn came from the New World and was taken to Italy. Our beloved cornmeal mush became known as polenta in Italy, and while in Italy Mr. Jefferson learned a new trick. He brought this recipe back with him and evidently served it often at the plantation.

1 quart water	½ stick, ⅛ pound,
1 teaspoon salt	butter, melted,
1 cup polenta	or ¼ cup olive
1 cup grated Parmesan	oil
or Romano cheese	

Bring the water to a boil. Add the salt and slowly stir in the polenta. Stir constantly to avoid lumps. After the mixture begins to thicken you can stir less frequently.

Simmer for about 20 minutes or until very thick. Pour into a greased loaf mold or bread pan. Allow to cool in the refrigerator overnight.

Cut into ¼-inch slices and layer like tiles in a baking dish. Pour the butter or oil over the top and then the cheese. Bake in 375° ovens for about 20 minutes, or until the cheese is melted and all begins to brown just a bit.

FISH WITH POTATOES

SERVES 6

This is one of the dishes that Mr. Jefferson's daughter, Martha, recorded from the original Monticello cookbook. At least we think it is from that original book. It looks like New England codfish-ball mix baked in a pie crust. Rather heavy but interesting. I would not try to serve this to the kids very often. However, when you have a Tom Jefferson party this will be just the thing.

1 pound any whitefish fillet, quickly poached and shredded (Cod is good with this dish. Even catfish will work.)
2 cups mashed cooked potatoes
2 tablespoons butter
¼ cup whipping cream
⅛ teaspoon grated nutmeg (She used ¼ teaspoon.)
⅛ teaspoon black pepper
½ teaspoon salt
2 tablespoons brandy
1 recipe Basic Easy Crust (page 311)

Cook the fish just until it flakes and shred it, being careful to remove the bones. Drain it very well. Mix all ingredients, except the crust, together with an electric mixer. Beat it until it is light. (Wouldn't Mr. Jefferson get a kick out of a good kitchen mixer? He loved gadgets, clocks, etc.) You may need a bit more milk or cream in order to get this very light.

Bake in a 9-inch pie crust at 375° until the crust is light brown and flaky, about 35 to 40 minutes.

MACARONI PIE

SERVES 5–6

This one comes from the original Monticello cookbook. Mr. Jefferson became fond of this dish while in Italy and brought it with him to the colonies. Since he used "white or yellow cheese," and since yellow cheese is very uncommon in Italy but common in the colonies, we can almost say that Jefferson designed what we call macaroni and cheese. This is the dish, and he served it at formal parties.

Do you remember the line from the Yankee Doodle song about sticking a feather in your hat and calling it macaroni? This was originally an English song making fun of the colonists, who were eating well and becoming very arrogant with King George of England. The "doodles" of the colonies were now taking to eating macaroni. Just who did they think they were, eating Italian foods and arguing with the King? So the song refers to the Yankees getting a little fancy with feathers in their hats . . . and calling it macaroni. The colonists thought it was funny and began singing the song themselves. I credit Mr. Jefferson with this whole episode! When you serve this to your children, be sure and tell them the story.

2 cups uncooked
macaroni
Salt
¼ pound grated white
or yellow cheese

¼ pound butter, melted
(Use microwave.)

Boil the pasta in salted water until barely tender. Drain.
Mix with the cheese and butter and place in a baking
dish. Bake at 350° until the cheese is melted and bubbly,
about 15 minutes.

BOILED PORK

SERVES 6–8

Since plantation owners like Washington and Jefferson
cured so many hams each year, we may assume that
there was a lot of pork around to be eaten. Some could
be cured in the form of sausage and kept for a time but
large cuts were often boiled. This is a very delicious
way to enjoy pork. I think Mr. Jefferson would approve
of my recipe.

4 pounds boneless
pork roast,
trimmed of as
much fat as
possible
1 yellow onion, peeled
and sliced
2 carrots, chopped
2 bay leaves

2 teaspoons whole
thyme leaves
1 teaspoon whole
sage leaves
6 sprigs parsley,
whole
10 whole black
peppercorns
½ tablespoon salt

Place the pork in a Dutch oven or kettle just barely large enough to hold the meat. Add water to halfway up the side of the meat. Add remaining ingredients. Cover and bring to a boil. Turn to simmer and cook the meat until tender, about 1¼ hours. Remove the meat from the broth and slice at the table.

This is great with Cooked Greens with Garlic and Tomato (page 126) and some Monticello Muffins (page 123).

CHEESE CURD PUDDING

SERVES 4

This is an interesting and a rather fun dish to make. The kids should get a kick out of this as it is a very old dish and something they have certainly never seen. It comes from the hand of Jefferson's daughter, Martha, and we assume it was in the original Monticello cookbook.

2 quarts milk	Sugar to taste
2 cups white wine	Pinch of salt
½ cup unsalted butter, melted and cooled	2 tablespoons butter, melted for topping
2 eggs	¼ cup white wine for topping
1 additional egg yolk	
½ cup fine cake or cookie crumbs	3 tablespoons sugar for topping

Pour the milk and wine into a stainless-steel pan and heat gently. Do not stir. After a few minutes a curd will form. Put a double piece of cheesecloth in a colander and drain the whey from the curd. Discard the whey.

Mix the curd with the butter. Beat the eggs and add to the curd. Stir in the crumbs and sweeten to taste, adding a pinch of salt. Butter a one-quart baking dish and turn the mixture into it. Bake in a 325° oven until set, about 30 minutes. Serve with melted butter, wine, and sugar sprinkled over the top.

APPLE PUDDING

SERVES 4–6

This is a quick and delicious bit of Virginia history. Jefferson planted several varieties of apples and they can be seen in the daily cooking of the plantation. We assume that this recipe came from the old original Monticello cookbook.

1 cup applesauce (They made theirs fresh at Monticello.)	3 tablespoons butter, melted
½ cup whipping cream	3 eggs, beaten
	½ cup powdered sugar
	Rind of 1 lemon, grated

Mix all of the above together well and put in a pie shell or a baking dish. I prefer a small baking dish. Bake 35–40 minutes at 350° or until set.

BAKED ICE CREAM

SERVES 8

This is the result of Jefferson's ingenious mind as an engineer, architect, and cook. He developed methods of putting a dough or meringue on a bit of ice cream and then baking it. His guests must have been fascinated with the things the man of Monticello would develop. He actually invented what we now call Baked Alaska.

You can bake this in an oven or you can use a small acetylene torch. Don't let the kids try this or you may lose the house!

1 quart brick ice cream or molded ice cream, very cold	**MERINGUE**
	2 egg whites
	¼ teaspoon cream of tartar
	4 tablespoons powdered sugar
	½ teaspoon vanilla extract

Have the egg whites at room temperature. Whip in your electric mixer along with the cream of tartar. When they form stiff peaks, fold in the sugar and vanilla. Frost the ice cream form and bake in a preheated 350° oven for 10–15 minutes, or until the meringue is lightly browned.

I have much better luck browning the meringue with a hand-held acetylene torch.

SESAME COOKIES

Try this one in memory of Mr. Jefferson. He would have loved it because he loved sesame seeds. For all I know, he ate these often.

Mix raw sesame seeds into your favorite sugar-cookie recipe and bake as usual. The flavor is delightful and makes a pleasant change for the children. You can also give them a quick lesson on American history. Read the recipe for Monticello Muffins on page 123 before giving the lecture.

PHILADELPHIA RICE PUDDING

SERVES 6–8

This one comes from the hand of Mr. Jefferson's grand-daughter, Virginia Randolph Trist. Her instructions are a little vague, as are all cookbook instructions from that time, so I have developed the following recipe. It is very tasty and again points to Thomas Jefferson's fondness for rice.

1 cup long-grain rice, rinsed and drained well	½ teaspoon salt Dash of freshly grated nutmeg
1½ quarts milk	1 teaspoon vanilla extract
1 cup sugar	

Mix all of the above together and place in a 3-quart covered saucepan. Bring to a simmer on the top of the stove and then place, covered, in a 300° oven. Bake without disturbing or stirring for 2 hours and 45 minutes. The pudding will almost caramelize and become a pale golden color. It is just terrific.

Mrs. Trist used to cook this in a slow fireplace for 5 or 6 hours. I suggest you try the above method since your fireplace is not really ready for a cooking fire that will gently smolder for 5 to 6 hours.

PENNSYLVANIA DUTCH

From the late 1600s onward, thousands of German Protestants fled their homeland and immigrated to Pennsylvania. Most were suffering religious persecution. Although they had no connection with Holland, they were referred to as Pennsylvania Dutch due to a corruption of the word *Deutsch,* meaning "German." Many of these people came from the Rhine Valley, which had been ravaged, first by the Thirty Years' War and then by the armies of Louis XIV. First came the Mennonites, and then many others—the Crefelders, Amish, Dunkards, Shwenkfelders, Seventh-Day Adventists, Moravians, and others. By 1763 there were approximately 280,000 Germans in Pennsylvania. Enormous communities of these hearty people still exist in and around centers like Lancaster, Allentown, and just outside Philadelphia.

It is wonderful to note that the self-denial that marks the religious precepts of the Pennsylvania Dutch does not apply to cooking and eating. Their own phrase for themselves is *feinschmeckers,* which crudely translated means "Those who know how good food should taste and who eat plenty of it." Many of them had been persecuted in Germany by having their crops and farms destroyed, so food in the New World became particularly important. My Pennsylvania Dutch friends, one of whom is a Schwenkfelder, put out meals that are heavy and simply wonderful.

The religious meals that come from this tradition are beautiful, and somewhat involved. Christian holidays have many special dishes that are celebrated and the Pennsylvania Dutch must be credited with bringing the Easter egg to this country. The extravagance of holiday meals is met with a genuine and pious bit of frugality the rest of the time. It seems to me to be a very healthy system. You will enjoy these recipes, especially the Duck and Kraut and the Potato Soup with Rivels.

138

SALT PORK, BEANS, AND HOMINY

SERVES 6 AS A HEARTY MAIN DISH, TWICE THAT AS A VEGETABLE DISH

This dish shows how fully the German immigrants used American food products, from the very beginning. It is a tasty dish, and it will certainly "stick to your ribs." My cook, Craig, after tasting this, said, "Stick to your ribs indeed. This stuff would swamp a water buffalo!" I will admit that this is heavy fare, but then you must remember that this is food for very hard-working German farmers.

½ pound white navy beans
½ pound dry hominy (page 32)
½ pound salt pork, sliced and rinsed

⅛ teaspoon marjoram
Black pepper, freshly ground, to taste (I like plenty of pepper in this dish.)

In separate bowls soak the beans and the hominy in ample water overnight. Drain and place both in a 4-quart heavy pot or Dutch oven. Add the remaining ingredients and cover with water. Bring to a boil, turn down to a very low simmer, and cover. Cook until the dish is thick and the hominy tender, about 4 hours. You will have to keep adding water to this dish as you go. When the hominy is about tender, remove the lid and cook until the excess water has been absorbed or evaporated. Do not drown this dish!

DUCK AND KRAUT

SERVES 4

I love this dish, and the thought of it simmering away on the stove makes me feel comfortable and cared for and wealthy, in a very basic sort of way. That is how I really feel about Pennsylvania Dutch cooking.

1 duck, about 3 pounds, fully defrosted if frozen

2 quarts sauerkraut (I prefer kraut packed in glass rather than cans.)

2 small yellow onions, peeled

3 tablespoons brown sugar

Black pepper, freshly ground, to taste

Place the duck in a roasting pan and roast in a 400° oven until lightly browned, about 25 minutes. Remove and cool a bit. Disregard the fat in the pan.

Place the duck in a very close-fitting casserole and pack the sauerkraut around and under the duck. Put the remaining kraut, along with the juice, on top. Add the onions to the pot. Add 1 cup of water and top with the sugar and black pepper.

Cover and bake at 325° until the duck is very tender, about 1½ hours.

It is traditional to serve this dish with rich mashed potatoes.

This very rich dish needs a green salad and a big bowl of creamy mashed potatoes.

SCHNITZ UND KNEPP

SERVES 10

The name of this dish, literally translated, means "Apples and Buttons." It is a soup-ham-and-apple-stew-dumpling–type dish that could only have come from the kitchen of a woman who had to keep her menfolk heavy and healthy. It worked!

1 quart dried apples (health food store)	4 teaspoons baking powder
1 3-pound piece smoked ham, bone in	¼ teaspoon freshly ground black pepper
2 cups flour	1 egg, beaten
½ teaspoon salt	3 tablespoons salad oil
	4 tablespoons milk

Soak the dried apple slices in water to cover overnight.

Place a 12-quart covered stockpot on the stove and add the ham piece. Barely cover with water and bring to a boil. Reduce heat, cover, and simmer for 2 hours. Then add the apples along with the water in which they soaked. Cover and simmer for 40 minutes.

In the meantime, make the dumpling batter. Mix all the dry ingredients together in a mixing bowl. Mix the liquids together and stir into the flour. Drop by small spoonful into the boiling ham and apple broth. Cover and simmer, without lifting the lid, for 20 minutes. You will have better luck if you make these dumplings very small. A measuring teaspoonful should be ample.

Serve on a very large platter so that each person may have a little ham along with their "Apples and Buttons."

Serve with pickles, Cabbage and Salt Pork (page 114), and Pickled Eggs (page 142).

NOTE: If you are not used to noodle-type dumplings such as these, then you can try making this dish with our dumpling recipe on page 469.

PICKLED EGGS

I fondly remember my mother making these a couple of times when I was a child. I had forgotten about the dish until I was visiting my Pennsylvania Dutch friends, the Mitmans. Mrs. Mitman served pickled eggs for lunch and I was delighted. This is a great dish for a summer-evening snack, but I'll eat them in the winter and enjoy them just as much.

This dish presents another lesson in Pennsylvania Dutch eating. There is an old custom requiring "seven sweets and seven sours." It is typical of their belief that things are to be balanced and proper. All sorts of pickles qualify for the 7-7 rule, and this egg dish is a fine "sour."

Hard-boil and peel the eggs. Put them in a covered container along with 1 sliced yellow onion and a jar of pickled beets, juice and all, and refrigerate. Let them sit for 2 days and serve.

HINT: On Making Hard-Boiled Eggs:
These are easy to prepare if you first punch a tiny hole in the large end of the egg. You can find an egg puncher for this trick in any gourmet shop. Have your eggs at room temperature. Start the eggs in cold water, uncovered, and bring to a boil. Turn to a simmer and let cook for 15 minutes. Immediately drain and run under cold water. Soak them in cold water until they cool. It is best to use a stainless-steel pan for this as aluminum will discolor.

LIVER DUMPLINGS

SERVES 6

This is just a basic food product among the hard-working Pennsylvania Dutch. It is more than a hearty soup, as the dumplings make it a whole meal. I first tasted this dish in the land of its origin, West Berlin. I will never forget it.

1½ pounds beef liver
2 eggs, beaten
2 yellow onions, peeled and chopped
3 tablespoons butter
1¼ cup bread crumbs
5 tablespoons flour
Salt and freshly ground black pepper to taste

Flour for dredging, about 1 cup
2 quarts Chicken Soup Stock (page 29) or canned chicken broth
Parsley, chopped, for garnish

Run the liver through the medium blade of your meat grinder and stir in the 2 beaten eggs.

Heat a frying pan and sauté the onions in the butter until they are clear. Stir into the onions the bread crumbs and sauté for a moment longer. Allow to cool for a moment, then stir in the liver mixture. Add the flour and salt and pepper. Roll into balls about ½ inch in diameter and dredge in flour.

Bring the stock to a boil in a 4-quart saucepan. Gently drop the dumplings into the stock and simmer, uncovered, for 20 minutes. Shake the pan to prevent the dumplings from sticking.

Serve in bowls with soup and parsley garnish.

You can use this dish as a main course if you will prepare Tomato Salad (page 125) and Sourdough Biscuits (page 460).

> HINT: **On Forming Meatballs.**
> When making meatballs of any sort, including
> liver dumplings, either oil your hands a bit now
> and then or wet them with water often. In this
> way the balls will not stick to your hands.

POTATO SOUP WITH RIVELS

SERVES 8

This is a potato-dumpling soup, and it sounds like a
double batch of starch. It is just that. The rivels, which
means "lumps," give the soup a thick richness that is
very filling. This is a very healing dish on a cold winter
day.

1 quart Chicken Soup Stock (page 29) or canned chicken broth	Salt and freshly ground black pepper to taste
4 medium potatoes, diced but not peeled	1 egg, beaten
	1 cup flour
1 tablespoon butter	2 hard-boiled eggs, peeled and chopped (page 142)
1 quart milk	
¼ cup celery leaves, chopped	Parsley, chopped, for garnish

Bring the chicken stock to a boil in a 4-quart stockpot.
Add the diced potatoes and cook until tender. Add the
butter, milk and celery leaves. Bring to a simmer and

add salt and pepper to taste. I love lots of pepper in this dish.

In a small bowl stir the beaten egg into the flour. Stir with a fork until you have a grainy mixture. Sprinkle small amounts at a time into the soup, stirring all the while with a wooden fork. Cook the rivels in the soup for 15 minutes. Be careful with these rivels, as they will lump up.

Serve with the chopped egg and parsley garnish.

SHOOFLY PIE

SERVES 8, AND HAVE LOTS OF COFFEE READY

Is this not one wonderful name? The pie is so rich with molasses that it would attract flies when the cook would leave the pie to cool on the windowsill. So, each time she passed the window, the cook would yell, "Shoo, fly!" I hope you believe that. They tell me that it is the truth.

I think you had to be raised with this one, but no real discussion on Pennsylvania Dutch cooking would be complete without it.

LIQUID LAYER
½ tablespoon baking soda
    dissolved in ¾ cup boiling water, *cooled*
½ cup molasses
1 egg yolk, beaten well

SHELL
1 unbaked 9-inch pie shell

CRUMB LAYER

¾ cup flour
½ teaspoon cinnamon
⅛ teaspoon *each* nutmeg, ginger, and cloves
½ cup brown sugar
½ teaspoon salt
2 tablespoons shortening (Crisco)

Combine the liquid ingredients. Be sure that the soda water is not hot.

Combine all the crumb ingredients except the shortening. Mix well and then stir in the shortening using a fork. Work until it is a crumb consistency.

Put one third of the crumb mixture in the bottom of the pie shell. Pour on top half of the liquid and then top with a third more crumbs. Add the rest of the liquid and top with the remaining crumbs.

Bake at 400° until the shell begins to brown, about 10 minutes. Turn oven to 325° and bake until the center is a bit firm, about 30 minutes.

RAISIN OR "FUNERAL" PIE

MAKES ONE 9-INCH PIE

Dessert among the Pennsylvania Dutch is almost always pie. This one is so named because in the old days it was often served to weary travelers who had come to the house for a funeral. It is good for the sad sick soul, and very good without the grief. But we must remember that these people see balance in all things, just as the "seven sweets and seven sours" (page 142).

Now, after that involved description, let us get on to the pie.

1½ cups seeded raisins
2 cups water
1½ cups sugar
4 tablespoons flour
3 eggs, separated
Pinch of salt
½ stick butter,
melted

Juice of 1 lemon
2 teaspoons grated
lemon rind
2 tablespoons sugar
for the meringue
1 baked 9-inch pie
shell

In a 2-quart saucepan combine the raisins, 1½ cups of
the water, and 1 cup of the sugar. Bring to a boil. In
another bowl combine the remaining ½ cup water, the
remaining ½ cup sugar plus the flour, egg yolks, and
salt. Blend well and stir into the raisin mixture. Continue stirring until thickened. Remove from the heat
and stir in the butter, lemon juice, and rind.

Allow to cool slightly.

In the meantime, prepare the meringue. Whip the
egg whites until they form stiff peaks. Whip in the sugar.
Pour the raisin mixture into the baked pie shell and
cover with the meringue.

Bake at 350° for about 10 minutes, or until golden
brown.

SHAKERS

The Shakers, or "Shaking Quakers," as they were first known, originated in France in the 1600s, part of a Protestant sect. Persecuted there, they fled to England, where they joined a radical branch of the Quakers. Their meditations, with a reliance on trances, prophecies, heavenly voices, and other signs, were marked by shouting, singing, and shaking. Thus they became known as the Shaking Quakers, and later simply Shakers.

Mother Ann Lees brought a group of eight Shakers to America in 1774. She established a wonderful and diligent community of Christians who were committed to pacifism, a communal life-style, and celibacy. Hundreds of converts joined the order and by the early 1800s the Shakers had eighteen communities and five thousand members. The simple and dedicated lives of these persons led to some interesting and highly respected art forms and food styles.

The Shaker principle at table was "Eat hearty and decent, and clean out your plate!" Their desire for simplicity and sustenance was typical of Early American cooking, and those who gathered at the table were healthy eaters and workers. The recipes that we have from these communities show a bit more color than most cooking of the time since the Shakers had developed a fine appreciation of herbs and grew them extensively.

The kitchens of the early Shakers were colorful and comfortable. Although they shunned luxury, they gathered in a communal kitchen for celebrations of good food and simple but blessed company.

Everything that the Shakers ate came from their land. They developed beautiful orchards, vegetable gardens, and made cheese and butter from the dairy herds. Honey bees were kept and large herds of cattle, hogs, sheep, chickens, ducks, geese, and turkeys were cared for.

The community offered the rest of us some interesting gifts for which they have seldom received credit. Attributing their knowledge of herb lore to Native Americans, they were highly respected herbalists and shipped herbs all over the world. They were the first to begin selling packaged seeds for home gardens and many new and creative species of fruits and vegetables were developed by Shaker horticulturists. Their most interesting gift, however, was the development of a basic compound of flour, baking soda, salt, and shortening. It was the first packaged mix and we know it now as a famous biscuit mix that will perform many tasks within the kitchen.

The Shakers were committed to establishing God's kingdom on earth. Their zeal was translated into a devotion to good design, simple processes, and methods of improving the lot of all peoples. Their furniture is still famous and much sought after. The inventions that they came up with are countless, including a buzz saw, a threshing machine, a rotary harrow, a cheese press, a water-powered butter churn, a pea sheller, a machine to pare, core, and quarter apples in a single operation, a revolving oven, and the clothespin.

With the bounty that they created through their ingenuity and diligence came a wonderful understanding of cuisine. They are credited with the creation of oyster pie and Corn Oysters (page 441). Their breads were outstanding and when the rest of the nation was cooking vegetables to death the Shakers urged us not to overcook vegetables in order to preserve the nutrients.

The following recipes will give you only a taste of a part of our culture that has all but disappeared. Their art and their recipes, however, will continue to remind us that the world may be becoming too complex for our own good.

BAKED-BEAN SOUP

SERVES 6

This is a great way to use up leftover baked beans, and the regularity with which this soup was served in Shaker communities indicates that they had a lot of leftover beans. The dish was an absolute staple, and I think it is really very good . . . and certainly hearty.

3 cups cold baked beans	1 tablespoon chili sauce
6 cups water	1 teaspoon salt
2 slices onion	½ teaspoon freshly ground black pepper
2 stalks celery with leaves	1 teaspoon sugar
1½ cups stewed canned tomatoes	2 tablespoons butter
	2 tablespoons flour

Put the beans, water, onion, and celery in a saucepan and bring to a boil for 30 minutes. They would rub this through a sieve, but I put mine through the food processor. Do the same with the tomatoes and add to the soup. Add the chili sauce and seasonings. Melt the butter and cook with the flour for 2 minutes to form a roux. Stir the roux into the soup and keep stirring over medium heat until the soup thickens a bit.

You might also try mustard or horseradish for a variation. These additions were common in the Hancock Shaker community.

SHAKER FRESH-HERB SOUP

SERVES 4–6

The Shakers were brilliant herbalists and a great deal of their income came from the many herbs that they produced. Herbs were grown for food and medicinal purposes, and the medicinal herbs were shipped all over the world. It should be of no great surprise then to see this fascinating soup. Of course, you will want to use fresh herbs in this, as I believe that dried herbs give it a very harsh flavor. If you don't have an herb garden then find a friend who does. He or she will appreciate this recipe.

1 tablespoon butter	Salt and freshly ground black pepper to taste
2 tablespoons chopped chives	½ teaspoon sugar
2 tablespoons minced chervil	6 slices toast
2 tablespoons minced sorrel	Pinch of freshly grated nutmeg
½ teaspoon finely chopped tarragon	⅓ cup freshly grated Cheddar cheese
1 cup minced celery	
1 quart Chicken Soup Stock (page 29) or canned chicken broth	

Melt the butter in an enameled, glass, or stainless-steel saucepan. Add herbs and celery and sauté for 3 minutes. Add stock, salt, pepper, and sugar. Simmer gently for

20 minutes. Place slices of toast in a tureen and pour the soup over them. Add nutmeg and sprinkle with the grated cheese. Serve very hot.

OYSTER AND HAM PIE

SERVES 6

This sounds a bit unusual but understand that pies have always been a way of stretching out meat. This is actually very delicious, as long as you use real ham and not that canned, boiled, flavorless stuff from the slicing machine at the delicatessen.

1 batch Basic Easy
    Crust (page 311),
    rolled out into
    two 9-inch circles
3 cups coarsely
    ground ham
2 tablespoons
    prepared mustard
    (I prefer Grey
    Poupon.)
2 cups shelled and
    drained oysters

2 tablespoons peeled
    and finely
    chopped yellow
    onion
½ teaspoon salt
½ teaspoon freshly
    ground black
    pepper
2 tablespoons butter
1 cup whipping cream

Line a shallow 9-inch pie plate with one of the crust circles. Mix the ham with the mustard and spread over the bottom crust. Put in a layer of oysters, and sprinkle with the chopped onion. Add salt and pepper and dot with the butter. Pour the cream over all and cover with the other crust half. Prick the top of the dough with a fork and bake in a 400° oven until flaky and brown, about 30 minutes. Serve hot or cold.

Start with the Baked-Bean Soup (page 152) and serve Stuffed Onions (page 155) along with the pie. Shaker Daily Loaf (page 155) will fill out the menu.

NOTE: Three cups of chopped hard-boiled eggs may be substituted for the ham.

STUFFED ONIONS

SERVES 6

I love onions in any form, but this recipe is particularly delicious. This is easy to make and is very basic but creative food for the Shaker table.

6 large yellow onions
1 cup cooked veal or chicken, chopped
1 cup minced celery
1 cup grated fresh corn (page 16) *or* frozen corn Niblets chopped in food processor
2 tablespoons chopped pimento (optional)
½ teaspoon paprika

2 tablespoons whipping cream
1 teaspoon salt
⅛ teaspoon freshly ground black pepper
1 cup Chicken Soup Stock (page 29) or canned chicken broth
1 tablespoon butter

Peel the onions and boil whole for 10 minutes in an enameled, glass, or stainless-steel pan. Core the center with a spoon, paring knife, or melon baller, and chop the centers finely. Make a stuffing of meat, vegetables, cream, and seasonings. Stuff the onions with this mixture. Place in a buttered 3-quart baking dish, moisten each onion with a bit of the stock, and dot each with butter. Bake in a preheated 350° oven for 20 minutes.

SHAKER DAILY LOAF

MAKES 2 LARGE LOAVES

The Shakers had communal kitchens where all the food was prepared for each and every member. Generally they had a special baking room, and this kind of bread would be coming from the oven often.

2 packages fast-acting	2 teaspoons salt
dry yeast	5 cups all-purpose flour
¼ cup warm water	Soft butter for
1¾ cup milk	greasing the bowl
3 tablespoons butter	and top of dough,
2 tablespoons sugar	about 2 tablespoons

Dissolve the yeast in warm water in large mixing bowl. Warm the milk and melt the 3 tablespoons of butter in it. Stir in the sugar and salt and allow to cool to luke-warm. Add this to the yeast bowl along with 3 cups of the flour. Beat until smooth. (I do all of this in my KitchenAid.) Add the remaining flour and knead on a floured board or marble until smooth and elastic, about 10 minutes, less time if you are using a dough hook on a good machine. Place the dough on a plastic counter and butter the top of the dough with half of the remaining butter. Cover the dough with a very large stainless-steel bowl and allow to rise until double in bulk. Punch down and shape into 2 loaves for large loaf pans. Again brush the top of the dough and allow to rise to double in bulk. Bake at 400° about 30 minutes.

CRANBERRY BREAD

MAKES 1 LOAF

This is one of the most delicious breakfast breads I know, and I like it best toasted. The simplicity of the Shaker community gathering for prayers and breakfast before a day at hard work must have been a wonderful thing. What ever happened to our morning family time together? It is gone and we may have to reschedule our lives in order to retrieve that precious time.

2 cups flour	1 egg, beaten
½ teaspoon salt	2 tablespoons melted
½ teaspoon baking	shortening or
soda	salad oil
1 cup sugar	1 cup fresh or frozen
1½ teaspoons baking	cranberries,
powder	coarsely ground
Juice and grated	½ cup walnut meats,
rind of 1 orange	coarsely chopped

Mix dry ingredients together very well in a large mixing bowl. Put the juice and grated rind in a measuring cup and add enough boiling water to make ¾ cups liquid. Add to the dry mixture. Add the egg and shortening or oil and mix just enough to moisten the flour mixture. Add cranberries and nut meats. Bake in a greased loaf pan 60 to 70 minutes at 325°. Store 24 hours before cutting.

"Land of the Pilgrims' pride..."

THE FRUGAL ONES

New England

I really did not know that New England is still so very much influenced by the kind of thinking that marked the Puritans. "Work hard and speak when spoken to." "Waste not, want not." "Eat it up, wear it out, make it do, or go without."

I traveled to New Hampshire to give a talk at the Spaulding Inn in Lancaster. The fall foliage looked like the work of a holy pyrotechnic expert. The colors of the leaves exploded and were aflame everywhere I looked. The white of the birch trees formed the canvas on which the colors were displayed, and I was calmed . . . simply calmed down by the whole of the area. I swear I could smell the history of the colonies right in the air.

I talked with two older women who had been born in the area. So had their mothers. Miss Heald and Mrs. Carr, both beyond the mark of the third quarter century, were ready for my questions, and the recipes that follow came about largely from my conversation with them. Just my talk with these two grand but frugal women helped me better understand the nature of the Yankee attitude. I think that the name "Yankee" comes from the Scotch word "yankie," meaning "a sharp or clever woman." I met two real Yankees, two women who prided themselves on knowing how to get along with very little, with knowing how to create wonderful things to eat when the cupboard held only the usual.

The talk of foods from the past in New England, foods that my two lady friends remembered from their youth, made me sorry for a time that these foods had passed from our time. But I found that many of the things that caused these two gorgeous people to talk of their childhood are *still* being served throughout New England. And I found a copy of a book that will interest you, if you wish to pursue Yankee cooking any further. It is out of print now, having been published the year I was born, 1939, but you can find one in an old bookstore, I am sure. *The New England Yankee Cookbook* was written by Imogene Wolcott.

You must remember that the word "Yankee" was used by the British soldiers as a derisive nickname for New Englanders. *Doodle,* in old English, means "a trifling, simple fellow." So they used the term "Yankee Doodle" to mean a foolish or simple New Englander. Isn't it wonderful that the people who live in the areas of those original colonies still love the term and use it as a mark of insight and respect. What did those British Redcoats know, anyhow?

> All the fine old frugal ways
> Of the early Pilgrim years
> Have the power to wake in me
> A deep sober ecstasy
> Close akin to tears.

SMOKY CHOWDER

SERVES 6

Smoked cod or haddock should be available through any good fish store. With it you can prepare this very hearty and warming chowder in just a few minutes. The recipe is an old one.

½ pound salt pork, rinsed and diced

1 large yellow onion, peeled and sliced

4 medium potatoes, peeled and cut into ¼-inch dice

Salt and pepper to taste

1 bay leaf

4 cups milk

1½ pounds smoked fillet of cod or haddock, cut into ½-inch cubes

Brown the pork in a Dutch oven. Add onion and sauté until the onion is transparent. Add the potatoes and water to cover, salt and pepper to taste, and bay leaf. Careful with the salt as the fish will add salt as well. Bring to a boil and reduce to simmer. When potatoes are almost tender, add the milk and fish and simmer for 10 minutes.

FISH CUSTARD

SERVES 4–5

This one shows true New England ingenuity. There they have a thousand ways of serving cod or haddock, and all seem to be delicious. This is a great cold evening dish.

1½ pounds haddock or cod	2 eggs, well beaten
1½ teaspoons cornstarch	Salt and pepper to taste
1½ cups milk	2 tablespoons butter, melted

In a saucepan, boil the fish just until it can be flaked or easily broken apart. Drain and flake the fish.

Dissolve the cornstarch in the milk. Add the eggs, salt and pepper to taste, and the melted butter. Place the fish in a buttered casserole and pour the milk and egg mixture over the top. Bake, uncovered, in a 350° oven for 45 minutes, or until the pudding is set.

Traditionally, this is served with Johnnycake (page 431) and mustard pickles.

CODFISH BALLS

SERVES 6

This is a classic. I am told that this has been a basic dish in New England for many generations, and I can understand why. Those folks have thought up many ways of using salt cod, cod preserved for the winter. You can find salt cod in most fish markets and in Italian markets under the name of *baccalà*.

1½ pounds dry salt cod	2 tablespoons butter
3 cups peeled and diced (½-inch pieces) potatoes	2 eggs, beaten
	Black pepper to taste

Soak the cod in water for 24 hours, changing the water 3 times. Drain and cut the cod into ½-inch pieces. Place the potatoes and fish in a saucepan and cover with fresh water. Boil until the potatoes are tender. Drain well and shake the pan over medium heat for a moment to dry the potatoes and fish a bit. Using a potato masher, mash up the fish and potatoes, being careful to avoid lumps. Add the remaining ingredients and beat with an electric mixer until the mixture is fluffy.

Deep-fry in fat that is 375°. Each ball should consist of about 1 tablespoon of the mixture. Fry only 4 or 5 at a time so that the fat maintains its temperature. Cook until light golden brown. Drain on paper towels and keep warm in oven.

NOTE: These can also be pan-fried in a bit of butter and oil. Make small cakes and fry on both sides until golden brown. Much less fat this way.

Often served with Boston Baked Beans (page 168) on Saturday night, the leftovers can be served on Sunday morning, along with a few slices of Boston Brown Bread (page 169).

CREAMED SALT COD ON BAKED POTATOES

MAKES ENOUGH SAUCE FOR AT LEAST 6 BAKED POTATOES

Another dish that is important to getting through those cold New England winters. My lady friends in New Hampshire, who gave me this recipe, claim that this dish brings back fond memories of their childhood. It is easy to make, though you have to plan ahead and soak the salt cod for at least 24 hours. New England Yankees always plan ahead. Always have!

1 pound salt cod
2 cups milk for cooking the cod
2 cups milk for sauce
3 tablespoons peeled and chopped yellow onion
1 bay leaf
Cayenne pepper to taste

½ stick (⅛ pound) butter
3 tablespoons flour
Salt to taste (careful, as the fish is salty)
2 eggs, hard-boiled and peeled
Baked potato for each person

Soak the salt cod in ample water for 24 hours, changing the water 3 times. Drain and place in a saucepan. Add the 2 cups of milk, cover, and bring to a simmer. Cook until tender, about 20 minutes.

In the meantime hard-boil the eggs and make the white sauce. Bring 2 cups of milk to a simmer and add the onion, bay leaf, and cayenne pepper. Simmer for a few minutes and then strain the milk stock. Return to the stove. In a small frying pan melt the butter and stir in the flour. Remove the milk from the burner and stir in the flour and butter. Continue to simmer, stirring constantly, until thick, about 7 minutes. Add very little salt to taste, if you must.

Separate the whites of the eggs from the yolks and grate each separately. Stir the whites into the white sauce. Drain the milk from the cooked fish and discard. Flake the fish and stir into the cream sauce.

Serve the fish sauce over opened baked potatoes with the grated egg yolk sprinkled on top.

The girls from New Hampshire told me that this was a common evening meal. I expect little else went with it, with the exception of wonderful Boston Brown Bread (page 169).

BOSTON BLACK-BEAN SOUP

SERVES 6

This soup has been popular in Boston for many generations. The colonists grew many kinds of beans for drying. This is the only way you could get through the New England winter. I think this soup could help you get through any difficulty.

2 cups dried black beans	1 cup whipping cream
2 quarts water	1 tablespoon salt
2 tablespoons flour	1 tablespoon butter
½ tablespoon peeled and minced yellow onion	6 thin slices lemon
	6 whole cloves
⅛ teaspoon black pepper	1 egg, hard-boiled and sliced for garnish
⅛ teaspoon dry mustard	½ cup dry sherry (optional)

Soak the beans overnight in ample water. Drain. Place in a 4-quart soup pot and add the 2 quarts water and salt. Cook until soft, about 2 hours, covered. Purée mixture in a food processor, using the beans and a little of the water. Return the bean purée and all of the water to the pot and simmer 15 minutes.

In a small saucepan melt the butter and stir in the flour. Cook for a moment and add the onion, pepper, and mustard. Stir in the cream and simmer, stirring constantly, until the mixture is thickened. Add this to the bean purée. Heat all just to the boiling point, being careful not to scorch the soup.

Serve in shallow bowls with a slice of lemon, a clove, and a slice of hard-boiled egg in each bowl. I also like to add a bit of dry sherry to the pot before dishing up the soup.

BOSTON BAKED BEANS

SERVES 3–4

During tough times in the very early days, the colonists in New England practically lived on salt pork and beans. The beans were brought with them from England and proved to be a wise solution to the problems offered by cold New England winters. There are many variations on this basic dish, and I suggest that you begin with some variations of your own.

2 cups navy beans	3 tablespoons dark molasses
½ teaspoon baking soda	1 tablespoon cider vinegar
1 medium yellow onion, peeled and sliced	1 teaspoon dry mustard
½ pound salt pork, cut into ¼-inch dice	¼ cup brown sugar
	1 teaspoon salt
	¼ teaspoon black pepper

Soak the beans overnight in ample water to cover. Drain the beans and cook in ample water with the baking soda. Bring to a boil and simmer for 20 minutes. Drain.

Place ⅓ of the beans in a 2-quart baking pot with a

lid. Add ⅓ of the diced salt pork and ⅓ of the onion. Add another ⅓ of the beans and repeat the layers, ending with salt pork on top. Mix the remaining ingredients with a cup of hot water and pour over the beans. Add enough additional hot water to cover the beans. Place the lidded baking pot in a 300° oven for about 4 hours, longer if the beans are not tender. Stir only once or twice during the cooking process. You will have to add additional water to the beans as they cook. Keep them just moist. Don't drown them out!

Traditionally, this dish was served on Saturday night along with brown bread and ham or frankfurters; thus the beans and wieners routine. On Sunday you could then have baked beans, brown bread, and codfish cakes . . . all for breakfast. This tradition began in very early days so that the Pilgrim housewife could bake and serve beans on Saturday and then again on Sunday morning, thus providing her with a meal and no work on the Sabbath.

BOSTON BROWN BREAD

MAKES 3 LOAVES

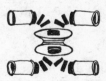

This recipe has not changed much from the days of the Pilgrims. I don't have the feeling that the Pilgrims were a fun lot to be around, what with their constant condemning of one another, but then I would not like to suffer what they went through either. Let's just enjoy the bread and forget their long and stern faces.

Once you prepare this dish you will *never* again buy brown bread in a can at the supermarket.

1 cup rye flour
1 cup cornmeal
1 cup whole-wheat
    flour
¾ teaspoon baking
    soda
1 teaspoon salt
¾ cup dark molasses
2 cups buttermilk
1 cup dark seedless
    raisins

Place all the dry ingredients in your electric mixing bowl and mix well with your machine. Add the liquid ingredients and blend well.

Grease three 1-pound coffee cans or large fruit-juice cans and place ⅓ of the batter in each. Cover each with wax paper and then aluminum foil. (How did they cook in the early days without aluminum foil?) Tie each with a bit of string so that the foil is sealed.

Place a cake rack in the bottom of a large soup pot and place the cans on the rack. Add enough boiling water to come ⅓ up the side of the cans. Cover the pot and bring it to a boil. Turn the heat down and simmer the cans for about 2½ hours. Check the water level now and then as you will need to add more water.

Remove the cans from the kettle and allow to cool just a bit. Take out the bread and serve sliced with butter. It is best hot.

YANKEE POT ROAST

SERVES 8

Just the name of this dish implies a frugal cut of meat cooked with patience until it is just right for a New England supper. My mother used to make this for me when I was little. It is still a favorite with my sons . . . though now we spike it up with a bit of wine, mushrooms, more garlic, etc. In short, it is no longer New England. New England cooking has always been rather plain and straightforward. Even my addition of garlic and thyme to this dish is going to cause some Yankee to claim that it is not "right."

⅛ pound salt pork,
   cut into ⅛-inch
   dice
4 pounds chuck roast
   Salt and pepper to
   taste
1 bay leaf
2 cloves garlic, peeled
   and sliced
2 teaspoons whole
   thyme leaves
½ cup chopped
   parsley

6 carrots, cut into
   1-inch pieces
6 medium yellow
   onions, peeled and
   cut in half
1 turnip, peeled and cut
   into ½-inch dice
6 potatoes, peeled and
   cut in half
4 tablespoons butter
4 tablespoons flour
   Kitchen Bouquet
   (optional)

Heat a large Dutch oven, about 6–7 quarts, and brown the salt pork. Remove the pork from the pan, leaving the fat in the pan. Salt and pepper the chuck roast and brown it in the fat. Brown it well on both sides, turning it with a wooden fork or spatula so you do not puncture the meat. When brown, add 2 cups of water to the pot and then the bay leaf, garlic, thyme, and parsley. Cover and simmer slowly for 2 hours, keeping about 1 cup of water in the bottom of the pot. Add the carrots, onion, and turnip; cover and cook for ½ hour. Watch that there is always a cup of water in the bottom of the pot. Add the potatoes and cook until the potatoes are tender. Watch that water!

Prepare a roux of the flour and butter by melting the butter in a small frying pan and stirring in the flour. Cook for a few moments. Remove the meat and vegetables from the pan and place on a serving platter. Thicken the gravy with the roux. Use as much or as little roux as you like. The thickness of the gravy is up to you. Correct the seasoning in the gravy and serve with the pot roast. You may wish to darken the gravy with some Kitchen Bouquet.

I cannot think of a finer menu, providing you start this meal with a dish of Smoky Chowder (page 163).

OYSTERS WITH TRIPE

SERVES 4–6

Does this not sound strange to you? In New England this is not strange at all and the dish certainly points out the fact that this nation of ours has very different tastes in very different regions. I found this to be both interesting and tasty, but then I like both tripe and oysters.

1 pound honeycomb tripe	1 pint small oysters
1 tablespoon butter	½ teaspoon salt
1 small yellow onion, peeled and chopped	¼ teaspoon black pepper
1 tablespoon flour	Toast or toasted English muffins for each person
1 cup milk	

Place the tripe in a saucepan and cover with water. Bring to a boil and cook for 5 minutes. Drain and rinse in cold water. Cover with fresh water and bring to a boil again. Simmer until the tripe is tender, about 2 hours. Drain and let cool. Cut into ¼-inch dice.

Melt the butter in the saucepan and add the chopped onion. Sauté until the onion is soft but not brown. Sprinkle in the flour and stir. Add the milk and stir with a wire whip until the milk boils and thickens. Add the tripe and oysters. Cook for about 5 minutes and then add salt and pepper to taste.

Serve at once over toast or toasted English muffins.

I like a green salad with this dish, and perhaps a bowl of Corn Chowder with Shrimp (page 437).

RED FLANNEL HASH

SERVES 4

The name for this one is amusing. Certainly it refers to the red flannel that one wore, and still wears, during the cold New England winters. The red comes from the beets. It might be fun for your children to see this dish, but I doubt that kids in our time know what red flannel is for.

This dish resembles its ancestor in England, where it was made with cabbage and called "Bubble and Squeak."

1½ cups cooked corned beef
½ cup diced (¼-inch pieces) salt pork
1½ cups coarsely chopped cooked beets (A 1-pound can of sliced beets will do nicely.)
2½ cups peeled, boiled, and diced potatoes
1 medium yellow onion, peeled and diced

1 tablespoon chopped parsley
1 teaspoon Worcestershire sauce
¼ cup half-and-half cream
Salt and black pepper to taste
¼ cup bacon drippings or oil for frying

Drain the chopped beets well.

Mix all the ingredients, except the bacon drippings or oil, together in a large bowl. Heat a 10-inch frying pan. I like to use Silverstone coated pans so that you can get this thing out of the pan. Place the bacon drippings or oil in the pan and add the hash. Press it down a bit so that it forms a nice even cake. Cook over low heat until the bottom is brown. Remove from the pan and place on a plate. Cover the cake with a second plate and turn it over. Slide it back into the pan. Brown the second side and serve hot on a large platter.

This is a full meal in itself, though I feel better with Harriet's Southern Biscuits (page 464) and a bit of green salad.

PICKLED TRIPE, PAN-FRIED

A New Hampshire lady friend told me that this was a great dish from her childhood. She also told me that I could have it at the old Parker House restaurant in Boston. (That's pronounced "Paahka House.") The dish was so pungent with vinegar that I was not terribly impressed. But they have been serving it for 132 years. So it is an old classic and this recipe is lighter tasting with vinegar. You will need to pickle your own tripe unless you live in New England.

2 pounds of honeycomb tripe, cut into 4-inch squares	1 bay leaf Salt and pepper to taste
2 carrots	1 cup white cider vinegar
1 yellow onion	

Place the tripe in a saucepan and cover with water. Bring to a boil and then drain. Rinse with cold water and cover with fresh water a second time. Add the remaining ingredients except the vinegar. Cover the pan and simmer until the tripe is tender, about 2 hours. Drain, reserving 1 cup of the broth, and add the broth and vinegar to the tripe. Place in plastic container and store in the refrigerator overnight.

Along with a bowl of Boston Black-Bean Soup (page

167) or some Boston Baked Beans (page 168), you have a complete and filling meal.

VARIATION 1 The Parker House uses a method very close to this one. Drain and rinse the pickled tripe and season each piece with salt and pepper. Sprinkle with flour and then dribble some olive oil on each piece. Sprinkle bread crumbs on each and broil slowly for a few minutes so that the crumbs are browned. You might wish to add some garlic and perhaps thyme to the bread crumbs. Serve with a mustard gravy.

MUSTARD GRAVY

1 tablespoon minced yellow onion	2 teaspoons dry mustard mixed with 1 tablespoon water
2 tablespoons butter	
2 tablespoons cider vinegar	1 cup brown gravy

Sauté the onion in the butter until brown. Add the remaining ingredients and simmer for 5 minutes. Serve with the pickled tripe.

VARIATION 2 Rinse the pickled tripe and dry with paper towels. Dip in beaten egg. Dredge in seasoned flour and pan-fry in a bit of butter until brown on both sides.

MAPLE SYRUP

There are many varieties of the gorgeous maple tree in the world. Many of these trees are said to have originated in China and Japan, where they are still very popular. There are also maple trees in Europe and about thirteen varieties that are native to North America.

However, although maple trees are found in places other than North America, maple syrup and sugar are not. Europeans have tried to get sap from their trees and have discovered that it is not necessarily the variety of tree that matters but the climate. The trees require a long cool period, during which the temperature falls below freezing in the night and rises above freezing in the day. The northeastern United States has that very climate, as do some regions in Canada.

It was the Native American who gave the Pilgrims and the colonists the gift of maple syrup and sugar. They knew how to cut the bark and drain the sap, a clear and watery liquid that must be cooked down to gain the sugar. The Indians used pots of bark, clay, or wood and condensed the liquid by placing hot rocks in the sap until it had become a syrup. The early colonists learned this process from our Native Americans, and by 1720 sugaring was a common practice among New Englanders. Indeed, the practice was so common that they produced four times what we produce today, even with the population growth since those Colonial days.

How do we account for the lack of production in our time? Expense. It is very costly to go sugaring, especially in terms of time. It takes forty gallons of sap, boiled down, to make one gallon of syrup or nine pounds of sugar. The amount of labor involved in this process is just incredible.

The colonists did make an improvement in the process of sugaring. The Native American method was to gash the trees with a hatchet. Often the trees would die during the process, so the colonists took to boring a hole in the tree and then draining the sap. When the process was completed a plug was made from wood of the same tree—it had to be the same tree—and the hole was filled. The tree thrived until the next season, when it would be bored again.

The original New Englanders preferred maple sugar to white for several reasons. One was a matter of availability. Cane sugar in early times was imported from the West Indies, making it very expensive. Maple sugar was expensive enough! Later, a second and more important reason for the Yankees to avoid white sugar came from the slave trade. The "Damn Yankees" were repulsed by slavery and white sugar began to be grown in the South, with the work done by black slaves. The Farmers Almanac from March 1803 exhorted its readers to "Prepare for making maple sugar, which is more pleasant and patriotic than that ground by the hand of slavery, and boiled down by the heat of misery."

MAPLE CANDY IN THE SNOW

This wonderful winter treat goes back to the very first days of "sugaring." The sap was cooked down to syrup stage, and then, as a special treat for the children who helped with the loading of the sap, the syrup was reduced a bit further and then poured into the snow. It would harden immediately, giving one the most delightful and chewy candy, candy with that clean and natural maple taste. I can only guess at the fun the kids used to have pouring the syrup into the snow . . . and I can only imagine what complex and bizarre patterns they thought up. This is still done in Vermont.

You can do the same thing easily. Place a pint or two of real maple syrup in a small saucepan and bring it to a light boil. Using a candy thermometer, reduce the syrup until you reach 270°. The syrup has now reached the soft ball stage and can be drizzled into the snow. If you do not have snow, use a snow-cone maker and ice cubes for the snow. If you do not have such a device, try your food processor. Simply grind up ice cubes, in small amounts, until you have enough snow for the job. If that is not possible, drizzle the syrup on a cold cookie sheet from the refrigerator. The candy will not keep more than a day or two.

MAPLE CUSTARD

SERVES 4–6—THIS IS VERY RICH!

Phil Donahue invited Willard Scott and me to do a show with him on cooking sweet things. I offered this one to Willard and he was delighted. And yes, Willard Scott is as charming a gentleman as you suspect.

This is quick and easy, and always a hit.

3 eggs, beaten	2 cups milk
½ cup maple syrup	Dash of salt

Mix all ingredients. Pour into individual molds such as small custard dishes or very small soufflé cups. Set molds in a pan of hot water and bake, uncovered, at 350° for 40 minutes or until the blade of a table knife inserted in the center comes out clean. Serve warm or chilled.

MAPLE CANDIED SWEET POTATOES

SERVES 8

It is great fun to put together two or more foods that really belong to the people called "The Americans." That's us . . . and this dish goes back to the colonies . . .

and a bit before. It is rich and different from your usual sweet-potato recipe.

5 medium sweet potatoes	1 teaspoon salt
½ cup maple syrup	¼ cup apple cider or apple juice
1 tablespoon butter	

Boil the potatoes in their jackets until nearly done. Peel, slice, and put into a baking dish. Bring the remaining ingredients to a boil and pour over the potatoes. Bake at 300°, uncovered, for 1 hour, or until the potatoes are glazed and the syrup has thickened a bit. Baste them twice or three times during the baking process.

MAPLE MASHED SWEET POTATOES

SERVES 6

The orange peel in this one may confuse you, but remember that the colonists had trade with the West Indies, and that is where they got their oranges. In the southern states this dish is still made the same way, though with molasses instead of "Yankee" maple syrup.

1 teaspoon grated orange peel, or more to taste	2 tablespoons butter, melted
4 sweet potatoes, cooked, peeled, and mashed (I like to whip mine in my electric mixer.)	3 tablespoons maple syrup

Mix the orange peel with the mashed potatoes and place the mixture in a greased baking dish. Mix the butter with the syrup and pour over the top. Bake uncovered at 350° for 25 minutes.

> HINT: **Alternatives to Maple Syrup.**
> I don't want you to avoid these recipes because
> of the high cost of maple syrup. You might try
> any of these dishes with syrup from the super-
> market or use an artificial maple extract to
> make your own. I know of one that is very
> good called Mapleine. It is produced by the
> Crescent Company in Seattle. You can find it,
> or a product like it, in many supermarkets and
> at bakery supply houses.

MAPLE CUSTARD PIE

MAKES 2 PIES

This pie is unusually good and is really very simple.
Though it goes back to early New England, if you make
this your children will think you are way ahead of the
times.

1 cup maple sugar, packed, *or* 1 cup light brown sugar plus ¼ teaspoon Mapleine (page 32)	1 tablespoon cornstarch
	½ cup cold milk
	3 eggs, slightly beaten
	½ teaspoon salt
	Two 9-inch pie crusts unbaked
2 tablespoons butter	
1½ cups milk, scalded	Nutmeg to taste

Heat the maple sugar and butter until they bubble. Add
the scalded milk and stir until the sugar is dissolved.
Mix in the cornstarch, cold milk, eggs, and salt. Pour
into the unbaked pie shells and sprinkle a bit of nutmeg
on top of each. Bake at 450° for 10 minutes, then reduce
heat to 350° and continue to bake 25 minutes longer or
until a table knife inserted in the center of the pie comes
out clean.

MAPLE CORN BREAD

MAKES 8 SQUARES

It is hard for us to accept the fact that maple syrup was a common sweetening product in Colonial times. The cost now is so high that we are surprised, and please understand that it was high even in the early days. After all, the amount of work involved in production of the syrup has always caused it to be an expensive product.

You can simply add maple syrup to your favorite corn-bread recipe or try this recipe.

1⅓ cups all-purpose flour	⅓ cup maple syrup
⅔ cup cornmeal	½ cup melted shortening or salad oil
3 teaspoons baking powder	2 eggs, slightly beaten
½ teaspoon salt	

Mix the dry ingredients together thoroughly. Add the syrup, shortening, and eggs. Stir until well mixed but do not beat. Turn into a greased 9 × 9-inch baking pan. Bake at 425° for 25 minutes.

MAPLE ICE

SERVES 5–6

This is very simple to make, providing you have an ice cream machine. The old ice crankers are great fun but you might also consider a machine like the Donvier (page 19). Sure, it takes all the fun out of the 2-hour cranking process . . . but it takes all the work out of it as well. This means that you will serve this dessert more often. It is very good.

> 2 cups maple syrup
> ½ cup water
> 1 cup whipping cream

Mix all of the above together and chill until very cold. Place in your ice cream machine and process until thick and rich.

Don't expect this to set up like regular ice cream or sherbet. It is a little too rich to be very stiff.

MAPLE-SUGAR SAUCE

MAKES 2½ CUPS

This terribly rich sauce is used on puddings, pies, ice cream, fingers, and fruit. It keeps well in the refrigerator and goes back to very early days in old Vermont.

> 2 cups maple sugar
>   *or* 2 cups light
>   brown sugar
>   and ½ teaspoon
>   Mapleine (page
>   32)
>
> 2 eggs, well beaten
> Juice of 2 fresh
>   lemons
> ½ tablespoon butter

Mix all ingredients and place in a double boiler. Cook for 20 minutes, stirring constantly until mixture thickens, and then frequently until the sauce is done.

MAPLE-SYRUP SAUCE

MAKES 1 CUP

This is particularly delicious on ice cream, though I can see it on pumpkin pie on Christmas Eve. That's how it used to be served.

1 cup maple syrup
½ cup whipping cream
1 teaspoon fresh
    lemon juice

2 egg whites, beaten
    until stiff peaks
    form

Boil the maple syrup down until it forms a thread (227° on a candy thermometer). Allow it to cool a bit. Using an electric mixer, blend the syrup, cream, and lemon juice into the egg whites. It is best to do this in the smallest bowl possible so that you can literally whip up the sauce.

APPLES IN MAPLE SYRUP

SERVES 8

Such a special treat. Apple seeds were brought from England, but the wonderful flavor of maple syrup was here waiting for those apples. This is the legitimate ancestor of the more common baked apple.

4 apples, halved and
    cored
½ cup maple syrup

1 tablespoon butter,
    melted
¾ cup water

Place the apples in a tightly fitting baking dish, cut side up. Mix the remaining ingredients and pour over the apples. Bake at 350°, uncovered, for 1½ to 2 hours, or until the apples are soft and the syrup has reduced and is fairly thick. Baste 3 or 4 times during the baking process.

PAN-FRIED APPLE SLICES WITH MAPLE SYRUP

The title of this one gives you the recipe. In early days a frontier or Colonial family did not have as many courses on the table as in later times. This dish could serve as an evening meal, or a dessert, or, for that matter, a breakfast.

Pan-fry apple slices in a little butter or bacon fat (that was common) and serve with maple syrup.

PUMPKIN

Few of us can imagine the winter holidays without pumpkin pie. It has been this way with us Americans since the Pilgrims' second Thanksgiving in 1623, but the pie was very different from the one we know now. The pumpkin was cleaned as you would for a jack-o'-lantern and filled with milk, eggs, spices, and maple syrup. When it was baked, the filling turned to a wonderful custard. The very first American cookbook, by Amelia Simmons, gives two recipes for such pies and we have evidence that the colonists also made pumpkin beer, pumpkin soup, and roasted pumpkin seeds for a snack. We have enjoyed the "American squash" in a fascinating variety of ways.

We received the gift of the yellow gourd from the Indians, of course. When European explorers hit the New World they found the Native Americans eating all kinds of squashes, but pumpkin was a favorite. The white men thought the pumpkin to be a form of giant melon. They were partly right, as the pumpkin belongs to the family Cucurbitaceae, which also includes cucumbers, gherkins, and melons. The wild ancestor of the great orange vegetable goes back to the Aztecs, Incas, and Mayan peoples, who enjoyed eating the rich seeds. The pumpkin spread north and was common by the time of European exploration, and the seekers of the New World took the squash back to Europe with them. But it remains an American vegetable, absolutely American.

The uses that we found for pumpkin in the old days were wonderfully varied and formed a basic part of our diet. The pumpkin was among the most common foods of the settlements and an old verse proves their indispensability:

For pottage, and puddings, and custards, and pies,
Our pumpkins and parsnips are common supplies.

We have pumpkins at morning and pumpkins at
  noon;
If it were not for pumpkins, we should be undoon.*

HINT: On Freezing Pumpkin.
It is easy to enjoy these pumpkin recipes year-
round, but you must do some freezing. Clean
and peel the pumpkin and cut into large pieces,
about 4 inches square. Blanch in boiling water
that contains the juice of a lemon and 2 or 3
tablespoons of olive oil, for about 4 minutes.
Drain and cool the pieces; seal in plastic bags
and freeze. Then you will be ready for some
great early American dishes all year.

If you wish to prepare mashed pumpkin for
freezing, do so without hesitation. Clean and
peel the pumpkin pieces and steam until very
tender. Run them through your food processor
and put in plastic freezing cartons. Squeeze a
little fresh lemon juice on top to prevent
browning in the freezer.

HINT: Save the Seeds for the Kids!
Wash the seeds and dry them. Place them in
a large heated frying pan along with some olive
oil, and toast until they begin to show a few
very tiny brown spots on the husk. Add a bit
of salt and cool. These are great snacks and
they are good on salads or in soups.

Newer variations on very old themes now offer us
pumpkin-filled ravioli, pumpkin—black bean soup,
pumpkin ice cream, and mini-pumpkins used to serve
bowls of hot pumpkin bisque to flashy restaurant

*Gertrude Ida Thomas, *Food of Our Forefathers* (Philadelphia: F.A.
Davis Co., 1941), pp. 169–170.

patrons all over America. I even have a couple of vegetarian friends who "stuff" a pumpkin each Thanksgiving. It is obvious we are entering a time of new appreciation for our beloved American pumpkin.

HANK'S PUMPKIN SOUP

SERVES 8–10

Hank and I met on an airplane one evening. I think you must know what it means to find a terribly interesting person sitting next to you . . . just when you are ready to die from exhaustion. Hank and his recipes proved to be so interesting that we became friends and enjoyed the flight. You will enjoy his pumpkin soup as well. It is very rich, so be prepared.

2 small pumpkins,
  about 2 pounds
  each
2 large yellow onions,
  peeled and
  chopped fine
2 cloves garlic, peeled
  and chopped fine
2 tablespoons peanut
  oil
8 cups Chicken Soup
  Stock (page 29) or
  canned chicken
  broth

1 small green hot
  pepper (optional)
2 smoked ham hocks
2 pounds chicken
  thighs or wings
Salt and pepper to
  taste

Peel the pumpkins and remove the seeds. (Hank saves them for toasting in the oven with a bit of olive oil and seasoning salt.) Dice the peeled pumpkins and set aside.

In a large pot, brown the onions and garlic in the peanut oil. Add the pumpkin, chicken stock, optional pepper, ham hocks, and chicken thighs or wings; season to taste. Cover and cook until thick and somewhat smooth, about 2 hours.

BAKED WHOLE PUMPKIN

SERVES 8

This dish was a favorite of George Washington. While it was called a pie in the old days, it's certainly not what we call a pie now. Here the custard pie is found inside the pumpkin and the whole thing is to be served up with a bit of anticipation for a very different pumpkin dessert.

1 pumpkin, 5–7 pounds	½ teaspoon freshly grated nutmeg
6 whole eggs	1 teaspoon cinnamon
2 cups whipping cream	¼ teaspoon ginger
½ cup brown sugar	2 tablespoons butter
1 tablespoon molasses	

Cut the lid off the pumpkin just as you would for a jack-o'-lantern. Remove the seeds and save for toasting later.

Mix the remaining ingredients together *with the exception of the butter*. Fill the pumpkin with this mixture and top with the butter. Cover with the pumpkin lid and place in a baking pan. Bake at 350° for 1–1½ hours, or until the mixture has set like a custard.

Serve from the pumpkin at your table, scraping some of the meat from the pumpkin with each serving.

This is an interesting substitution for the usual pumpkin pie.

BAKED PUMPKIN AND ONIONS

I can't give the amounts on this one. It's much too simple for that. It's just an old-fashioned way of serving the great American squash. Make as little or as much as you like. Your kids will love it.

Pumpkin slices, peeled,
　½ inch thick
Yellow onions, peeled
　and sliced

Salt and pepper
Melted butter or olive
　oil
Brown sugar

Clean and peel some pumpkin and cut it into thick slices. Arrange them in a buttered baking dish and add sliced onions. Add salt and pepper and a bit of melted butter or olive oil. Repeat with another layer and top with a few spoons of brown sugar.

Bake, uncovered, at 350° until tender, about 30 minutes. You may wish to cook it longer.

I generally serve this as a vegetable dish.

PUMPKIN WITH PORK

SERVES 4

I would have trouble tracing this dish to the colonists, but it's a dish that I enjoy . . . and I think they would have enjoyed it as well.

1 slice thick bacon,
　diced
2 cups fresh, peeled and
　sliced (¼-inch
　pieces) pumpkin
1 medium yellow onion,
　peeled and sliced
½ cup Chicken Soup
　Stock (page 29)
　or canned
　chicken broth

1 pound pork butt or
　shoulder, cut into
　⅛-inch strips
½ teaspoon ground
　cumin
Salt and pepper to
　taste

In a frying pan or wok, sauté the bacon until it is transparent. Add the pumpkin slices and onion. Stir around in the rendered bacon fat. Add the broth. Cover and cook over medium heat until the pumpkin is tender, about 15 minutes. Remove the vegetables from the pan.

Reheat the pan and sauté the pork until done, about 5 minutes. Add the vegetables to the pan and toss with the cumin, salt, and pepper. Cover for just a moment so that the flavors may develop.

This dish should be treated as part of a kind of Chinese menu. Plan several other vegetable dishes and add a bit of rice. Tom Jefferson would approve!

PUMPKIN WITH HAM, ONIONS, AND CORN

SERVES 6

This is the kind of dish that is fun to create with ingredients that were common and popular during Colonial times. It is terribly easy for us to cook this way. In the old days it was a pain!

- 3 cups peeled and diced (½-inch pieces) fresh pumpkin
- 1 cup Chicken Soup Stock (page 29) or canned chicken broth
- 2 tablespoons butter or olive oil
- 2 large yellow onions, peeled and sliced
- ½ pound diced (½-inch pieces) ham
- 1 box (10 ounces) frozen corn, off the cob
- Salt and pepper to taste
- Toasted pumpkin seeds, shelled, for garnish*

*Available at most gourmet shops or health food stores. If the seeds are raw, toast them in a frying pan with a tiny bit of olive oil and salt.

Place the diced pumpkin in a covered 2-quart saucepan. Add the broth and butter or olive oil; top with the onions. Cover and simmer until the pumpkin is just tender, about 15 minutes. Add the ham and corn and cook until the corn is tender, about 8 minutes. Add salt and pepper to taste. Top with toasted shelled pumpkin seeds.

This dish can become a whole meal in itself or it can be served along with a holiday meal as a vegetable dish. I am sure that is how it was used in earlier days.

PUMPKIN PIE WITH CHOCOLATE

Try this one if you want to stop traffic. Simply melt some milk chocolate bars in a double boiler and spread the melted chocolate over the top of a finished and cooled pumpkin pie. Chill a tiny bit before serving so that the chocolate will set. This is beautiful on a holiday table and everyone will be quite surprised!

PUMPKIN WAFFLES

MAKES 4–5 WAFFLES

Add a bit of canned pumpkin to your waffle batter along with some cinnamon and nutmeg—just a touch of each. Prepare your waffles in the usual way and serve with maple syrup. This great breakfast treat may stick to your waffle iron unless you use a bit of Pam spray first.

½ cup canned
   pumpkin
1 batch Mom's Basic
   Waffle Batter
   (page 293)

⅛ teaspoon cinnamon
Dash of freshly
   ground nutmeg

Stir the pumpkin into the batter, along with the spices, just prior to folding in the egg whites. Proceed as usual with the cooking. Remember that the pumpkin is going to make these waffles a bit more dense than a plain waffle. Great for dinner!

PUMPKIN MILK SHAKE

This is a fun one for the kids. It's best if you use freshly puréed pumpkin, but canned will do. For each vanilla milk shake mixture of ½ pint vanilla ice cream, ¼ cup milk, and ½ teaspoon vanilla extract, add 4 tablespoons of puréed pumpkin with rum extract to taste and a bit of nutmeg. To make it pumpkin-colored, just for fun, add 1 drop each of yellow and red food coloring.

PUMPKIN SOUFFLÉ

SERVES 6

This lovely dish can be served year-round if you have prepared some puréed pumpkin and stored it in your freezer. Otherwise, use canned. People will be impressed with this dish on a cold January evening, as it is rich and warming. *Warming* is a Colonial term for serious food!

- 2 tablespoons butter
- ¼ cup finely chopped yellow onion
- 2 teaspoons flour
- ½ cup whipping cream
- 1½ cups puréed pumpkin (canned will work)
- ½ teaspoon salt
- ¼ teaspoon freshly ground black pepper
- ¼ teaspoon freshly grated nutmeg
- Cayenne pepper to taste
- 4 egg yolks, lightly beaten
- 6 egg whites at *room temperature*
- ¼ teaspoon cream of tartar

In a frying pan, sauté the onion in the butter until transparent. Add the flour and cook until the flour and butter begin to turn a very light golden brown. Using a whisk, add the cream and cook until a thick sauce is obtained. Pour this sauce into a medium-sized mixing bowl and add the remaining ingredients, except the eggs and cream of tartar. Mix well. Then stir in the egg yolks, one at a time. A mixer is great for this.

Whip the egg whites along with the cream of tartar and gently fold into the pumpkin mixture. Do not overmix. Place in a buttered 1½-quart soufflé dish and bake in a preheated oven at 350° for about 30 minutes, or until the soufflé begins to expand and brown ever so slightly on top. Serve right away.

Serve this as a vegetable course at a light dinner. It is rich enough to stand up against anything!

CORN AND PUMPKIN STEW

SERVES 6

This simple dish is another gift from the Southwest Indians. Two early American staples are cooked together to provide variety to a rather simple diet. You will be surprised how delicious this is, though I have added an onion and black pepper for some additional flavor.

3 ears of corn *or* 1 box (10 ounces) frozen corn, off the cob	1 yellow onion, peeled and sliced
1 small pumpkin (about 3 pounds)	1 cup water Salt and pepper to taste

Shell the corn from the cob and mash to a pulp. I use my food processor for this. If using frozen corn, you need not let it defrost if you have a food processor.

Peel and seed the pumpkin and cut into small pieces. Place all ingredients in a covered saucepan and simmer until the pumpkin is soft, about 30 minutes. Serve hot.

This is a very simple but delicious vegetable dish. It should be treated as such.

PUMPKIN MUFFINS

Using my recipe for Bran Muffins the Frugal Way (page 307), prepare pumpkin and bran muffins by simply adding a bit of canned pumpkin to the dough. Two cups of freshly mixed dough will call for about ½ cup of puréed pumpkin. Add some cinnamon and nutmeg if you like. Let the batter sit in the refrigerator until the next day. The muffins will take a bit longer to cook and they will be a bit heavier due to the pumpkin. Heavy or not, the flavor of the muffins is very comforting.

PUMPKIN AND SCALLOP SOUP

SERVES 6–8

The taste of this soup is somewhere in between the colonies and American Upper Yuppie. You decide. I like it!

- 4 tablespoons olive oil
- 1 clove garlic, peeled and crushed
- 1 stalk celery, minced
- 1 medium yellow onion, peeled and coarsely chopped
- ⅓ cup flour
- 1 quart Fish Stock (page 31), Chicken Soup Stock (page 29), canned fish broth, or canned chicken broth

- ¼ teaspoon allspice
- ⅛ teaspoon mace
- 1 tablespoon Worcestershire sauce
  Dash Tabasco
- 1 cup frozen squash
- 1 cup canned pumpkin
- 1 cup whipping cream
  Salt and freshly ground black pepper to taste
- 1 pound fresh bay scallops

Heat a 4-quart pot and add the oil. Sauté the garlic, celery, and onion until the onion is clear. Add the flour, cooking and stirring over medium heat for a few minutes to form a roux. Add the stock and stir with a wire whip until the mixture begins to thicken. Add the remaining ingredients *except* the cream, salt, pepper, and scallops. Simmer, covered, for ½ hour, stirring often. Add the cream and season to taste with salt and pepper. Add the scallops and heat just a few minutes. Do not overcook the scallops. Serve immediately.

NOTE: A very small amount of freshly grated ginger will bring some additional Yuppie flavor to this dish.

CRANBERRY

Cranberries are a native North American fruit with relatives growing wild in the bogs and marshes of Northern Europe. Ours is the largest variety, however, and the only one that is seriously cultivated. And do we cultivate it! I cannot imagine the winter holidays without cranberry sauce.

When the Pilgrims arrived in America, they were instructed in extensive use of the cranberry by the Native Americans. The Indians ate cranberries raw and cooked, and pounded them into pemmican with meat and fat for use during the winter. The mashed fruit was used on wounds to draw out poisons and infection, and the berries were used for dye in making rugs and blankets. We assume that the North American Indians brought cranberries to the first Thanksgiving dinner, since the fruit would have been plentiful at that time. Among the Delaware tribe in New Jersey, the berries were known as the symbol of peace, and Chief Pakimintzen, who distributed cranberries often at tribal peace feasts, came to be known as "Cranberry Eater."

The fruit is also known as the "bounce berry" because of its bouncy quality. There is a story of an old fellow who had a bad leg and could not carry the berries down from his storage racks. So, he simply allowed them to tumble down the stairs to the ground level. He discovered that the firm, ripe berries bounced to the bottom, while the bruised fruit remained on the steps. They tell me that this is still the principle behind commercial cranberry separators in our time. No, no, not an enormous staircase, a machine. A machine does it!

In the old days one could harvest cranberries by hand. In our time, of course, the fruit harvesting is done by machine. However, I like to think of the early folk who used this very American fruit for jams, jellies, sauces, cakes, muffins, pies, relishes, and, of course, wine.

You will be surprised at the versatility of the cranberry after you read some of the following recipes.

> HINT: **Don't Use Aluminum.**
> When cooking cranberries be sure to use stainless steel, glass, or porcelain-covered cookware. Aluminum will discolor, due to the acid in the berries.

FREEZING CRANBERRIES

This dish is so simple that I should not even tell you about it. If you have trouble finding frozen cranberries year round, then buy bags of them during the cranberry season and stock your freezer. That is all there is to it. Frozen berries will work in all the recipes in this section.

CRANBERRY FOOL

SERVES 8

The name is more fun than the dish itself. This dish was brought with the colonists from England, where a fool was made of many different kinds of fruit. The meaning of the name? It comes from the French term "fouler," which means to crush.

1 can (16 ounces) sweetened cranberries	1 tablespoon grated orange peel
½ teaspoon almond extract	1 pint whipping cream

Pour the cranberries into a medium-sized food processor and grind them up. Mix with the almond extract and the orange peel. Whip the cream and gently fold it into the cranberry mixture. Serve in very small dishes or wineglasses.

CRANBERRY CHEDDAR SANDWICH

This pleasant snack sounds very unusual, but it simply makes good use of Early American food products. You and I can use a toaster/oven/broiler. In the old days you would have to make this dish in a broiler in front of the fire.

Toast some good French bread slices. Butter the slices and then spread a layer of canned whole cranberry sauce on each. Top with thinly sliced sharp Cheddar cheese. Broil until the cheese is bubbly and hot.

PLYMOUTH CRANBERRY PIE

SERVES 8

Have you ever tried a cranberry pie? I hadn't, and it's not likely that you have either. In Colonial times this was a popular treat, using the native American berries.

4 cups cranberries
1½ cups sugar
3 tablespoons cornstarch
1 egg, lightly beaten
½ teaspoon almond extract
Pastry for a 2-crust 9-inch pie

Preheat the oven to 400°. Wash and pick over cranberries; drain thoroughly. Chop cranberries and mix with sugar and cornstarch. Mix egg and almond extract and combine with cranberries. Line a 9-inch pie plate with half the pastry. Add cranberry mixture. Cover with strips of pastry arranged in a lattice, and seal edges. Bake 10 minutes. Reduce heat to 350° and continue baking about 35 minutes, or until cranberries are soft and pastry is browned.

CRANBERRY ORANGE RELISH

Some years ago my mother stopped serving normal cranberry relish at holiday meals. By "normal" I mean that jellied stuff you buy in a can. Instead, she began serving this relish. It is terribly simple to make, and now I much prefer it to the sweeter jellied type.

> 1 pound (4 cups) fresh cranberries
> 2 oranges
> 2 cups sugar

Wash the cranberries and chop them up in your food processor or hand grinder. Peel the oranges, remove the seeds, and put the rind and the orange pulp through the chopper or food processor, too. Mix together with sugar and let stand a few hours before serving.

CRANBERRY SALAD MOLD

SERVES 10

I swore I would never put a gelatin salad mold in a cookbook. The memories of pear slices in green gelatin, or canned fruit cocktail and red gelatin . . . well, these memories do nothing for my appetite. But here it is, the first wiggly salad I have ever proposed. Thank goodness it is my mother's recipe and not mine. It is unusually good.

½ pound fresh cranberries (2 cups)	1 cup chopped walnuts
	1 package (3 ounces) raspberry Jell-O
⅓ cup orange rind	1 package (3 ounces) lemon Jell-O
1 cup orange juice	
1 cup celery, chopped fine	3 cups water

Grind up the cranberries and orange rind. I use my medium-sized food processor, or you can use a hand grinder.

Heat the water and prepare the gelatin as per the instructions on the package. Add all other ingredients and chill in a 2-quart mold.

SPICED CRANBERRIES

SERVES 6–8 AS A CONDIMENT

You cannot have too many good cranberry relish recipes. This one comes from the turn of the century, and it is just great with any kind of poultry. I especially enjoy it with roast duck.

1 quart fresh cranberries	2 sticks cinnamon, broken
½ cup water	⅛ teaspoon ground mace
12 whole cloves	
12 whole allspice	1 cup brown sugar

Place the berries in a covered pot. Add the water. Tie the whole spices in a little cheesecloth bag and add to the pot, along with the mace. Cover and simmer until the fruit is soft and broken, about 25 minutes. Remove the spice bag and discard. Run the berries through the food processor or press through a colander and return to the pan. Stir in the sugar over heat until dissolved. Cool in refrigerator before serving.

CRANBERRY ICE

SERVES 6–8 AS A MIDMEAL SHERBET COURSE

This is colorful, refreshing, and easy, though the work that went into something like this in Colonial days was considerable. Ice had to be stored from the wintertime and then used in hand-cranked ice cream makers. One had to stir for a long time to get a nice smooth texture. You and I can do it in a matter of minutes.

3 cups fresh cranberries	1½ cups sugar
3 cups water	1 teaspoon fresh lemon juice

Simmer the cranberries and water in a covered stainless-steel pot until they are very tender, about 10 minutes. Strain the berries, reserving the juice, and purée in a food processor with some of the juice. Add the remaining juice, sugar, and lemon juice. Refrigerate until chilled and freeze in a Donvier ice cream maker (page 19). Or you can freeze mixture in a small pan in the freezer, stirring every 15 minutes or so until a nice texture is achieved.

CRANBERRY MUFFINS

MAKES 12 MUFFINS

These are great for any meal, including breakfast. Using a medium-sized food processor or hand grinder, coarsely grind 1 cup of fresh cranberries. Add this to 4 cups of your favorite muffin batter and proceed with the baking.

CRANBERRY DUMPLINGS

For a very different-flavored dumpling, one that will go particularly well with chicken stew, add ½ cup ground-up fresh cranberries, along with 2 tablespoons sugar, to the Dumplings recipe (page 469) and proceed with the cooking.

Careful, these may become addictive in your household, in which case you can use frozen cranberries off-season.

SKILLET CRANBERRIES FOR A SLACK OVEN

SERVES 6–8 AS A RELISH

In 1767, John Adams wrote the following in his journal: "Arrived at Dr. Tuft's where I found a fine Wild Goose on the Spit, and Cranberries in the Skillet for Dinner." This is what he tasted.

> **1 pound fresh cranberries**
> **2 cups brown or white sugar**
> **¼ cup brandy**

Spread the cranberries in an iron skillet that has a cover. Sprinkle the sugar over the berries, cover the skillet, and place in a "slack" oven (250°) for 1 hour. Remove the lid and pour the brandy into the skillet. They are now ready to serve.

CHICKEN WITH CRANBERRIES

SERVES 3–4

I like dishes that can be prepared ahead of time and then placed in the oven until dinnertime. It gives me a chance to relax and get myself together before the family gathers. This is such a dish.

1 chicken, 3 to 3½ pounds
1 cup flour
Salt and pepper to taste
Cayenne pepper to taste
1 cup peanut oil for frying
1 can (16 ounces) whole sweetened cranberries
¼ cup peeled and chopped yellow onion
¾ cup orange juice
¼ teaspoon *each* ground cinnamon and ginger

Cut up the chicken and pat dry with paper towels. Mix the flour with the salt and both peppers, and dredge each piece of chicken. Pan-fry in the peanut oil just until brown, turning once.

In the meantime, mix all remaining ingredients in a stainless-steel saucepan and bring to a boil. Pour this over the chicken and cover. Cook slowly for 35 to 40 minutes or until the chicken is very tender.

A Sweet Potato Soufflé (page 213) goes well with this dish.

CRANBERRY ROAST PORK

SERVES 4–5

Pigs were a common meat source in Colonial times, and while I cannot confirm my suspicion, I suspect that someone used to roast pork with a glaze much like this one. If not, you and I can enjoy it anyhow. The kids will love this dish.

4 pounds pork roast,
  boneless and tied
  with string
Salt and freshly
  ground black
  pepper to taste
1 can (16 ounces) whole
  sweetened
  cranberries

¼ cup peeled and
  chopped yellow
  onion
¾ cup orange juice
¼ teaspoon *each*
  ground cinnamon
  and ginger

Rub the roast with salt and pepper, and place on a rack in a baking pan. Roast at 325° for 2½ to 3 hours, or until an inserted meat thermometer registers 175°.

In the meantime, combine all the remaining ingredients in a stainless-steel saucepan and bring to a boil. Remove from the heat.

Halfway through the roasting process, begin basting the roast every 15 minutes with the cranberry mixture. The remaining sauce can be served on the side with the thinly sliced pork.

Serve along with Wild Rice with Mushrooms and Onions (page 451) for a smashing meal.

SWEET POTATOES WITH CRANBERRIES

This is an interesting twist on what I assume is an old combination. Old or not, the ingredients are totally American and just delicious.

Grind up 2 cups of fresh cranberries and add them to the Sweet Potato Soufflé (page 213). You will enjoy this.

"O beautiful for spacious skies..."

DOWN SOUTH

SOUTHERN COOKIN'

There really is such a thing as southern hospitality, and it is not hard to define. It consists of the sure and recognizable fact that people are glad you are there, and they treat you accordingly. In the South the comfort that is offered to prove your welcome is warm, and sometimes quiet and a bit slow. I mean that respectfully, of course.

I have had meals in Atlanta, and Covington, Georgia, in Richmond, Virginia, Mount Vernon and Colonial Williamsburg. I have judged cooking contests in Mobile, Alabama, and had barbecue in North Carolina. I have had peach pies, corn soufflés, mint juleps, black-eyed peas, fried okra, crowder peas, and catfish with hushpuppies. I have eaten pecan pie, pickled peaches, homemade biscuits, and Southern-fried chicken. I have tasted squash cooked until it turned to candy, and turnip greens so fresh that I wanted nothing more. Why am I telling you about all of this food when I am trying to discuss the meaning of southern hospitality! You know the answer, of course. Southern hospitality is good food, generally simply prepared, and *always* graciously served.

I love southern cooking. I love the idea of a screened-in porch on a warm day with friends about. I love the clinking of ice cubes in iced tea or lemonade. I love the Sunday afternoon supper with friends after church, and fried chicken, of course.

There is a certain attitude in the South, an attitude that says, "Calm down and enjoy yourself." It is a wonderful bit of healing and I really should go there more often. So that you do not become confused by what I am trying to do in this section I should explain that by Southern Cookin', I mean dishes that are found in Georgia, Mississippi, Alabama, Virginia, and North and South Carolina. Many of the other states will be discussed in another section.

SWEET POTATO SOUFFLÉ

SERVES 8

This is simply a fancy way of serving sweet potatoes. In the North we eat sweet potatoes only during the winter holidays, but in the South this dish is on the table at every Sunday supper. We would be wise in the North to put a wider variety of vegetables on the table regularly, and the South can teach us how to do it. This one can be served very often.

6 sweet potatoes, medium (I like the darker potatoes, usually misnamed "yams" in our supermarkets.)
½ teaspoon salt
2 tablespoons butter
1 egg, beaten
½ cup raisins
3 tablespoons grated orange rind
¼ cup whipping cream or half-and-half
Pinch of freshly grated nutmeg
1 cup miniature marshmallows

Boil the potatoes with the skins on until tender. Peel, and run the vegetables through a potato ricer into an electric mixing bowl. Add the remaining ingredients, except the optional marshmallows, and whip until light. I use my KitchenAid for this and the potatoes are absolutely fluffy! Place in a baking dish and top with the marshmallows. Bake at 375° for 10 minutes or until the marshmallows brown and the dish is hot.

SCALLOPED OYSTERS

SERVES 4–6

In the Pacific Northwest, my home, it is rare that you see cooked oysters since we eat them raw just as soon as they come from the water. I was suspicious of this dish when a southern lady friend told me about it . . . but my suspicions were wrong. This is delicious and terribly easy.

6 tablespoons butter, melted	**1 egg, beaten**
½ cup bread crumbs	**½ cup milk**
1 quart oysters, shucked	**Pinch of mace**
2 cups oyster crackers	**Salt and pepper to taste**

Stir 3 tablespoons of the butter into the bread crumbs.

Drain the oysters in a colander, reserving the juice for some other use. Grind the crackers a bit in a medium-sized food processor or with a rolling pin. Don't make them too fine. Place ⅓ of the oysters in a buttered 2-quart baking dish and sprinkle ½ the cracker crumbs on top. Repeat a layer of oysters and one of cracker crumbs and then top with the remaining oysters.

Mix the remaining ingredients (including the remaining butter, but not the bread crumbs) and pour over the dish. Top with the remaining bread crumbs and bake at 350° for 30 minutes. Serve immediately.

I like this dish with a Corn Relish (page 441) and a Cranberry Salad Mold (page 203).

SOUTHERN HAM

The hams that drip at you in the meat-market case in our time are not at all like the hams of old days. The old-style hams are still available, but they come from the South, to be more specific, Virginia. Western and eastern hams, for the most part, are injected with water, salt, and chemicals until they blow up like a balloon . . . and shrink like a popped balloon when you bake them. In Virginia the old way is still used. The ham is cured with salt and pepper, smoked, and hung to dry, and I mean dry. The weight loss is terrific since there is little water left in the meat. In the food business, water is where the weight is and therefore the money is in the water. You can understand why a Virginia ham will cost you around fifty dollars. The most common name from the state is that of Smithfield.

Since the ham has been cured for so long, it must be highly salted. Before cooking, place the ham in a sink full of hot water, and scrub hard with a good bristle brush. I soak mine for 2 days in fresh water, changing the water twice. The ham is then ready for use.

Fried Virginia ham is a wonder, but it is very salty. The ham is sliced and then pan-fried. When the ham is put on the plate and water is then added to the pan to dissolve the wonderful reddish-brown remains that stick to the bottom . . . you have red-eye gravy.

To bake a ham you need to boil it first. The instructions will be on the package. In order to reduce the salt I put the ham in a big pot, cover with water, and bring to a simmer. I then discard the water and follow the directions on the ham package. I like to let mine cool in the water a bit rather than take it out right away. It will remain moist if you do that. The ham is then baked and glazed. Recipes for a fine glaze come on the package, too. Remember that though these hams appear expensive, they are so rich that one will feed half the neighborhood.

Try the Oyster Sauce (page 114) on the ham, along with Cream of Peanut Soup (page 111) and Ragoo of Onions (page 113).

FRIED CHICKEN IN BACON FAT

SERVES 3–4

In the South the practice of using bacon fat goes way back to your great-great-great-grandma. Lard did not have the same flavor and little else was available. Bacon fat, or "drippin' " was used both for flavoring and for fat in cooking. While I will admit that this is not for those of us who are cholesterol conscious it is absolutely delicious . . . now and then.

1 chicken, about 3½ pounds, cut up	1 teaspoon black pepper
2 cups flour	1 tablespoon poultry seasoning
1 tablespoon salt	
2 teaspoons paprika	1 cup bacon drippings

Mix the flour with the seasonings and dredge the chicken in the coating. Pan-fry in the preheated bacon fat using medium heat. Turn the chicken until golden brown and done to your taste. This should take about 30 minutes. Drain well on paper towels before serving.

TO MAKE CREAM OR COUNTRY GRAVY

Pour off the grease, leaving 2 to 3 tablespoons in the pan. Add 2 tablespoons butter, 4 tablespoons flour, and stir and cook until golden brown. Using a wire whip, add 2 cups of milk to the pan, stirring constantly until the mixture thickens. Add salt and pepper to taste. The gravy is served over hot biscuits or rice. I am told that in Georgia one *never* pours the gravy over the chicken.

Serve with a Sweet Potato Soufflé (page 213), Baked Creamed Corn (page 434), and Harriet's Southern Biscuits (page 464).

CHICKEN SALAD WITH COOKED DRESSING

I am told that this is the solution to supper on a hot southern summer day. This is great as a main supper or luncheon dish. It is terrific in a sandwich and it is perfect for a snack in the middle of the night. Don't overcook the chicken, please.

COOKED DRESSING

¼ cup cream
¼ cup Chicken Soup Stock (page 29) or canned chicken broth
½ cup cider vinegar

2 egg yolks
1 tablespoon flour
2 tablespoons sugar
1 tablespoon dry mustard
Salt and white pepper to taste

Place all the ingredients in a double boiler and mix with electric mixer or wire whip. Place double boiler on the heat and cook, stirring constantly, until the mixture thickens. Cool before using.

THE CHICKEN SALAD

Cold cooked chicken, diced
Celery, chopped
Yellow onion, peeled and chopped fine (optional) (You may want to try this with green onions for a change.)

½ portion good mayonnaise mixed with ½ portion cooked dressing (above)
Salt and pepper to taste

Mix all to taste and serve chilled.

CHICKEN BRUNSWICK STEW

SERVES 8

This is another southern basic. It is really more than an ordinary stew and can be served at a fancy dinner or an informal supper. I must have run across fifteen variations on this dish and I know I have not even begun to hear about the rest of the possibilities.

3 tablespoons bacon drippings
1 chicken, about 3 pounds, cut up
2 cups water
2½ cups canned tomatoes, or fresh, chopped
2 yellow onions, peeled and sliced
½ teaspoon sugar
½ cup dry white wine
1 package (10 ounces) frozen lima beans
1 package (10 ounces) frozen corn Niblets

1 package (10 ounces) frozen okra, sliced
1 cup toasted bread crumbs (Toast in oven on a cookie sheet.)
2 teaspoons salt, or to taste
½ teaspoon freshly ground black pepper, or to taste
3 tablespoons Worcestershire sauce
½ teaspoon Tabasco, or to taste

Heat a large Dutch oven and add the bacon fat. Fry the chicken until lightly brown and add the water, tomatoes, onions, sugar, and wine. Cover and bring to a simmer. Cook for 1¼ hours. Remove chicken from the pot and allow to cool enough to handle. Debone chicken and discard skin and bones. Tear meat into small pieces and set aside. Add remaining ingredients to the pot and bring to a boil. Reduce heat and simmer for 30 minutes, uncovered. Add the chicken and cook for another 10 minutes. Correct the seasoning.

This goes well with Spiced Cranberries (page 204) and a big green salad.

HOPPIN' JOHN

SERVES 4–6

This dish looks like a normal starch dish, but the name is intriguing. In the South it is served as often as you wish, but always on New Year's Day, in which case it is to bring you good luck. I am told that the children were so fond of this dish in the old days that they would hop about the kitchen waiting for it to cook, thus giving it the name.

It can be made with black-eyed peas, red lentils, or dried field peas, but the remaining ingredients are always constant.

1 cup dried fried peas (cowpeas)	1 cup raw long-grain rice
4 cups water	1 teaspoon salt
1 medium onion, sliced	Black pepper, freshly ground, to taste
½ pound bacon, thick-sliced, cut in ½-inch pieces	

Put the peas and water in a 2-quart covered saucepan and bring to a boil. Reduce to a simmer and cook the peas, covered, until just barely tender, about 1 hour 45 minutes. You will have to add additional water during the cooking process. Watch that the peas do not dry out. Drain the peas, reserving the water, and return them to the kettle.

Sauté the onion along with the bacon until the onion is clear. Add to the pot along with the rice and 2½ cups of the reserved liquid. Add the seasonings. Cover and bring to a boil. Reduce heat and simmer for 15 minutes, covered. Allow the dish to rest off the heat for 10 minutes before you lift the lid.

1,2,3,4 CAKE

When a southern lady, and she *is* a lady, told me about this cake I responded with utter ignorance. She could not believe that I had never heard of such a thing. The recipe resembles a fine pound cake in terms of both flavor and texture. Sliced thin, with a cup of black coffee, it makes a wonderful southern afternoon snack.

2 sticks, ½ pound, butter	1 cup, minus 1 tablespoon, milk
2 cups sugar	
4 eggs, separated	½ teaspoon lemon extract
3 cups flour	
2 teaspoons baking powder	½ teaspoon vanilla

Using an electric mixer, cream the butter, sugar, and egg yolks. Mix the flour and baking powder together and sift into the creamed mixture, adding alternately with the milk. Add the flavorings. Whip the egg whites to form stiff peaks and gently fold into the batter. Bake in a loaf pan in a preheated oven at 300° for 1¼ hours, or until a toothpick stuck into the center of the cake comes out clean.

LANE CAKE

The real joy here is not the cake itself but the filling. This is just a stupendous flavor for the center of a dessert. I can see the family just waiting for dinner to finish so that they can tear into this one!

3 round vanilla layer cakes
(Use your favorite recipe or a mix.)

FILLING

8 egg yolks	1 cup pecans
1 cup sugar	¾ cup dry white wine
½ cup butter, room temperature	1 teaspoon vanilla
1 cup raisins	

Beat the yolks until well blended and add other ingredients. Mix well and place in a double boiler. Cook, stirring often, until thick. Spread the filling between the cake layers.

Traditionally, the cake was covered with a white vanilla butter icing and that is what I prefer. Place this on a footed cake plate and watch the excitement!

PECAN PIE

There are certain dishes that bring back memories, sometimes of a person. I had a dear friend in graduate school in theology by the name of Ora Lee. She was raised in Virginia and she gave me this recipe. I make one now and start to laugh over the good times that we shared and then I become terribly sad that I have lost track of her. Perhaps this recipe will cause her to get in touch with me and we can eat this terrific pie together . . . again.

½ stick, ¼ cup, butter	1 tablespoon flour
1 cup light-brown sugar	1 teaspoon vanilla
1 cup white corn syrup	½ teaspoon cinnamon
3 eggs	1 unbaked 9-inch pie shell
⅛ teaspoon salt	1 cup pecans

Using your electric mixture, cream the butter and sugar together. Add the syrup and whip until light. In a separate bowl, whip the eggs and salt together until light and fluffy. Combine the eggs with the sugar mixture along with the flour, vanilla, and cinnamon. Mix well and pour into pie crust. Sprinkle pecans on top and bake in a 350° oven for 50 minutes.

HUGUENOT TORTE

SERVES 16

This is another wonderful dish that I had never heard of. My southern friends all seem to know about it but the North has been deprived!

This is very rich stuff resembling an apple crisp. I can understand its popularity in the South. I found the recipe in a wonderful book called *Charleston Receipts* collected by the Junior League of Charleston and published in 1950.

4 eggs
3 cups sugar
8 tablespoons flour
5 teaspoons baking powder
½ teaspoon salt
2 cups cored and chopped tart cooking apples

2 cups chopped pecans or walnuts
2 teaspoons vanilla
Whipped cream, flavored and sweetened for topping

Beat the eggs in electric mixer until very frothy and lemon-colored. Add other ingredients, except the whipped cream, in above order. Pour into two well-buttered baking dishes about 8 × 12 inches. Bake in 325° oven about 45 minutes or until crusty and brown. To serve, scoop up with pancake turner (keeping crusty part on top), pile on a large plate, and cover with whipped cream and a sprinkling of the chopped nuts, or make individual servings.

PICKLED PEACHES

MAKES 4 QUARTS

This dish is so much a part of Sunday dinner that I cannot imagine the table without it. Several pickles are served at a formal southern meal, and Sunday is always formal. It is a day for the family to gather about the table and enjoy some fine food. There were no excuses accepted for your absence at Sunday dinner... but I suppose that custom in the South has gone with the wind as it has in most of the rest of the country. Shame on us!

2 pounds, about 7 cups, sugar
2 cups white vinegar
2 sticks cinnamon
2 tablespoons whole cloves
4 quarts ripe peaches

Boil the sugar, vinegar, and spices for 20 minutes. Drop the peeled fruit in, a few at a time, and cook until tender. Pack in hot sterilized jars, adding syrup to ½ inch of the top. Seal.

> HINT: **On Peeling Fresh Peaches.**
> Blanch the peaches in boiling water for about 2 minutes and then plunge them into cold water. The peel will come off very easily.

NEW ORLEANS

If you have never been to New Orleans for a meal, stop reading right now and call the airlines. You must go. I am still convinced that New Orleans is the best restaurant city in America, and I will stand by that conviction. The others? New York, San Francisco, Chicago, Seattle, and Boston. Yes, I am aware of the fact that you might not agree with my list. No, please don't write and tell me how wrong I am. I love eating in these cities and I get to New Orleans whenever I can.

The history of the city is the history of the most interesting food and cultural conglomeration in America. The French settled the area with the explorer La Salle in 1682. By 1722 New Orleans was the capital of the region and other people began to arrive. One interesting group consisted of fifty girls sent from "houses of correction" in Paris, and these were the only girls in town. By 1762 Louis XV had decided that the colony named after him was more trouble than it was worth and gave the Louisiana territory to Spain, which meant another wave of varied immigration. Along with the Spanish came a group of Acadians from France. They were joined by another group of Acadians, all of whom had been displaced from French Nova Scotia by conquering British. By the mid-eighteenth century they all had settled together in the swamplands and waterways of New Orleans. Their name became corrupted into "Cajuns," a name that they still bear, and bear proudly.

At about the same time a title was given to the residents of New Orleans. The name "Criollo" was given to all residents of European descent and their heirs. This soon became "Creole."

The Spanish had a very open immigration policy and the city began to take on fascinating ethnic colors. The culture was further broadened in the 1790s, when French refugees fled the slave uprisings in Santo Domingo (now Haiti). These Santo Domingoans brought with them any blacks and mulattoes they could, who, incidentally, brought voodoo with them.

When Napoleon came to power in France he decided that Spain should return Louisiana to France. He then quickly sold the area to the United States. In 1803 the famous Louisiana Purchase brought the colorful area into American ownership for $11.25 million and the cancellation of a $3.75 million debt. In 1812 Louisiana became the eighteenth state.

The blending of many wonderful ethnic backgrounds has now given us the famous Cajun and Creole food. Both of these styles have French roots but with incredible influences from all of the other cultures in the area. I suspect that the major difference between Creole and Cajun is like that which you find between French city cooking and country-peasant cooking. The Cajuns moved to the country and brought their country cuisine with them while the Creole kitchen of the rich planters is much closer to a grand cuisine. The whole of the city has been influenced by the Spanish sense for high seasoning, African cooks, and allspice from the West Indies. Haitian, Native American Indian, and German cooks each contributed to the collage that we call New Orleans.

I should mention some friends in New Orleans. Howard Mitcham's insights have been valuable to me. Ella and Dick Brennan, at Commander's Palace, run one of the finest restaurants in the city. You must also eat at the Bon Ton, a Cajun place that is just south of heaven. Chez Helene's is a wonderful black eating house with food you will not forget. Galatoires is good on a good day, but very inconsistent. Try an oyster loaf at the Felix Oyster Bar and outside courtyard dining at Naw'lins Cookery. Forget about places like Christian's and Pascal Manale's. They have certainly fallen from grace. You will probably have a very difficult time finding a bad meal in the French Quarter of the city.

JAMBALAYA

SERVES 8

Originally this dish, like so many dishes that have become classics, was designed to use up leftovers. The dish stands in that great tradition of frugal cooks who could not afford to throw anything away, or, in the more profound tradition, that good community of cooks who *refused* to throw out any edible leftovers. This bit of Cajun ingenuity is now common all over New Orleans, and there are as many variations on this dish as any one I know. I think I love them all!

2 pounds pork spareribs, cut into single-bone pieces

3 tablespoons peanut oil

1 large yellow onion, peeled and chopped

2 green peppers, cored and chopped

3 cloves garlic, peeled and chopped fine

4 ribs celery, chopped

6 green onions, chopped

1 can (28 ounces) whole tomatoes, crushed with your hands

3½ cups Chicken Soup Stock (page 29) or canned chicken broth

½ pound smoked hot-link sausage, sliced in ¼-inch pieces

1 cup diced ham

3 tablespoons chopped parsley

2 teaspoons Tabasco

¼ cup Worcestershire sauce

3 teaspoons whole thyme leaves

Salt and freshly ground black pepper to taste

2 cups uncooked converted rice

Place the spareribs on a broiling rack and bake them in a 400° oven until brown, about 15 to 20 minutes. Set aside.

In the meantime heat a large frying pan and add the oil. Sauté the yellow onion, green peppers, garlic, celery, and green onion until all is tender. Place the vegetables and the ribs in a 12-quart stockpot, along with the tomatoes and chicken stock. Cover and simmer for 1 hour.

Pan-fry the sliced sausage until it just begins to brown. Deglaze (page 23) the pan with a bit of the broth and add the pan drippings to the stockpot. Set the sausage aside.

Add the remaining ingredients, except the sausage and rice, and simmer, covered, for another 20 minutes. Add the sausage and rice and simmer for 25 minutes. Correct the seasoning.

EGGPLANT CASSEROLE

SERVES 8

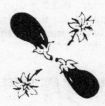

I really cannot understand why the "Northerners" don't eat more eggplant. To me it is the most delicious vegetable imaginable. I once did a whole show on nothing but eggplant. I want you to give this dish a serious chance. It will pay off, I promise!

½ cup peanut oil
2 large yellow onions, peeled and chopped
6 cloves garlic, peeled and chopped fine
4 medium-size, unpeeled eggplants, cut in ½-inch dice
3 ribs celery, chopped
1 green sweet bell pepper, cored and chopped
½ teaspoon whole thyme leaves
½ cup chopped parsley
3 tablespoons tomato paste
2 pounds lean ground pork
1 teaspoon Tabasco
2 teaspoons Worcestershire sauce
Salt and freshly ground black pepper to taste
1 egg, beaten
½ cup bread crumbs

Heat a large Dutch oven and add the oil. Lightly brown the yellow onions and garlic and then add the eggplant, celery, green pepper, thyme, parsley, and tomato paste. Sauté, covered, stirring often, until the vegetables are very tender, about 20 minutes.

In the meantime pan-brown the pork. Drain the fat and discard.

When the vegetables are tender stir in the pork, Tabasco, Worcestershire sauce, salt and pepper, and the egg. Place in a 2-quart baking dish and sprinkle the bread crumbs on top. Bake uncovered in a 350° oven until the top is lightly browned and the dish is very hot, about 35 to 40 minutes.

SHRIMP ETOUFFÉE

SERVES 5–6

The idea of cooking a sauce for hours does not appeal to most American home cooks . . . but this is the only way that a proper etouffée can be made. The name refers to "smothering" the seafood with a heavy sauce, and it is certainly heavy. This method of cooking has its roots in Creole cuisine, and if you take the time to prepare this dish properly you will be very proud of your Creole skills.

3 tablespoons peanut oil
3 tablespoons flour
1 yellow onion, peeled and chopped
½ green sweet bell pepper, seeded and chopped
3 ribs celery, chopped
3 cloves garlic, peeled and crushed
3 tablespoons tomato paste
1¼ cups Basic Brown Soup Stock (page 28) or canned beef broth
1 cup dry white wine
2 bay leaves
1 teaspoon whole basil leaves

1 teaspoon whole thyme leaves
1 tablespoon plus ½ teaspoon Tabasco
¼ teaspoon freshly ground black pepper
1 teaspoon salt
4 green onions, chopped
1½ pounds shrimp, peeled (These need to be uncooked, and about 35 to 40 per pound.)
¼ cup chopped parsley
Cooked rice

Heat a large Dutch oven and add the oil and flour. Toast this to a peanut-butter-colored roux. This should take about 15 minutes over medium heat. Be careful not to burn this. Stir often.

Add the yellow onion, bell pepper, celery, and garlic. Sauté for about 10 minutes or until the vegetables are tender. Stir in the tomato paste, followed by the beef stock and wine. Stir constantly until this mixture thickens. Add the remaining ingredients, except the shrimp, parsley, and rice. Simmer, covered, for about 45 minutes.

Add the shrimp and parsley and simmer for 20 minutes, uncovered.

Serve over cooked rice.

This is great with Corn Pudding (page 433) and perhaps Eggplant Casserole (page 229).

PICKLED PORK

I am always happily confused over the wonderful variations that one finds in New Orleans cooking. The reasons are obvious enough. So many different cuisines cooked together in the same neighborhood, a neighborhood that is supplied with some of the best basic food products in the nation.

During my last trip to New Orleans I was told by an elderly black woman that I did not understand what red beans and rice really were since I did not use pickled pork in my two previous cookbooks. Well, this one is to set me straight. Obviously this method of curing pork started simply as a method of preservation, and it became a necessary part of the complex flavors of the French Quarter. The meat can be purchased in New Orleans in any market, but those of us in the North are bound to make our own. This recipe is from a wonderful resource book by John Mariani called *The Dictionary of American Food and Drink*.

½ cup mustard seed
1 tablespoon celery seed
2 tablespoons Tabasco
1 quart distilled white vinegar
1 bay leaf
1 tablespoon kosher salt

12 peppercorns
6 cloves garlic, peeled and cracked, not smashed
2 pounds boneless pork butt, cut into 2-inch cubes

Combine everything except the pork in a stainless-steel pan and boil for 3 minutes. Cool and place in a refrigerator container (plastic, glass, or stainless steel) and add the pork. Stir to remove bubbles. Cover and refrigerate for 3 days.

RED BEANS AND RICE

SERVES 6–8

A woman who was born and raised in Louisiana recently sent me this recipe and told me it was authentic. Furthermore, she told me that the person who sent me my previous authentic recipe was way off base. Everybody's recipe is authentic in some way, I am sure, so here we go on our third variation of a New Orleans classic.

Actually this is authentic if you are one who believes that the dish must contain pickled pork. In any case it is delicious.

1 pound red beans, soaked overnight	1 tablespoon Worcestershire sauce
1 medium yellow onion, peeled and chopped	2 teaspoons Tabasco
	2 whole bay leaves
1 bunch green onions, chopped	1 teaspoon whole thyme leaves
7 cloves garlic, peeled and chopped fine	Salt and freshly ground black pepper to taste
½ cup chopped parsley	1 pound smoked sausage, cut in 1-inch pieces
1 rib celery, chopped	1 pound Pickled Pork (page 232), cut into 1-inch cubes and *rinsed*
½ cup catsup	
1 green sweet bell pepper, seeded and chopped	Cooked rice

Drain the beans. Put them in a 6-quart heavy pot and add 3 quarts of fresh water. Cover and simmer for 1 hour, or until the beans are tender. Watch that the water does not boil down too far. The beans must be covered with water at all times. Add the rest of the ingredients, except the cooked rice, to the pot and more water to cover, if needed. Simmer, partially covered, for 1 to 1½ hours or until the liquid has thickened. Serve over the cooked rice.

PASTA WITH OYSTERS AND SHRIMP

SERVES 4–5 AS MAIN DISH

I cannot even remember where in New Orleans I first tasted this dish . . . but I certainly remember the dish itself. The important thing here is the cooking of the roux. It is this dark flour-oil mixture that gives the dish both its color and depth. You must try this soon.

- 2 tablespoons peanut oil
- 1 medium yellow onion, chopped
- 2 tablespoons flour
- 1 teaspoon anchovy paste
- 1 pint small oysters
- 1 pound shrimp, raw and peeled (32 to 40 per pound)
- Salt and freshly ground black pepper to taste
- 1½ pints half-and-half
- 2 shots Tabasco
- 1 teaspoon Worcestershire sauce
- ½ teaspoon whole thyme leaves
- ½ pound cooked pasta
- 4 green onions, chopped, for garnish

Heat a large frying pan and add the oil. Stir in the flour and cook this mixture until it is the color of light peanut butter, being careful not to burn it. Add the onions and sauté until limp. Stir in the anchovy paste and the half-and-half, stirring carefully with a plastic whip to avoid lumps. Turn to a light simmer and add the Tabasco, Worcestershire sauce, and thyme and simmer for 10 minutes. Add the oysters and shrimp and heat for a few minutes. Do not overcook the seafood. Add salt and pepper to taste and serve over the hot pasta. Garnish with chopped green onion.

   All you need to complete a menu with this rich dish is a big green salad and a dry white wine.

SHRIMP REMOULADE

SERVES 4

This is another one of those classic New Orleans dishes that appears on every menu in town. However, the variations are endless and exciting. Traditionally this great dressing is served over cold shrimp, but I find that it goes well with many cold seafoods and seafood salads.

½ cup finely chopped celery

½ cup finely chopped green onions

½ cup finely chopped parsley

¼ cup finely chopped dill pickle

1½ tablespoons peeled and very finely chopped garlic

¾ cup Creole mustard *or* stone-ground mustard or grained mustard

2 tablespoons horseradish

¾ cup salad oil

⅛ cup red wine vinegar

¾ teaspoon salt or to taste

1 tablespoon Worcestershire sauce

1 pound boiled shrimp, peeled and deveined

4 leaves of crisp romaine or green-leaf lettuce

Combine all ingredients except the shrimp and lettuce. Whisk thoroughly until well blended. Chill before serving over the shrimp on lettuce beds.

OYSTERS ALVIN

SERVES 3–4 AS A FIRST COURSE, OR 2 FOR DINNER

The Bon Ton restaurant in New Orleans is one of my favorite places for really fine food. The bills are not high, the staff is terrific, and the food is generally outstanding. Oh, they have some off nights like all restaurants seem to have, but I have a better time more often at the Bon Ton than just about any place I can name in New Orleans. The food is Cajun and the whole operation is a delight. During one of my recent pilgrimages Wayne Pierce, the proprietor, brought me a new dish and asked me what I thought. He had developed it in terms of Cajun flavors and named it after the original owner of this old New Orleans restaurant. He gave me the recipe and the results will convince you that you should take the next flight to New Orleans, or learn to do more Cajun cooking at home. Actually, this dish is not at all complex.

1 dozen small oysters, shucked	Juice of ½ lemon
2 cups flour	Salt and freshly ground black pepper to taste (about ¼ teaspoon each)
2 cups peanut oil for frying	
¼ stick margarine	
4 large fresh mushrooms, sliced	¼ teaspoon paprika
¼ cup Basic Brown Soup Stock (page 28) or canned beef broth	1 teaspoon chopped parsley

Dredge the oysters in the flour. Deep-fry in hot oil (350°) until golden brown. Set aside.

Melt the margarine in a large skillet and sauté the mushrooms until just barely soft. Add the beef stock along with the lemon juice. Simmer 2 minutes. Place the oysters in the skillet. Sprinkle with the salt, pepper, and paprika. Place under a broiler until the oysters are crisp. Do not stir. Serve crisp side up in sauce. Sprinkle parsley over the top.

You may wish to correct the seasoning in the sauce or you may wish to remove the crisp oysters to a platter and reduce (page 25) the sauce.

This can be served as an appetizer or main course. If serving as a main course, start with Backwoods Gumbo (page 237) and then serve Dirty Rice (page 238) with the oysters.

BACKWOODS GUMBO

SERVES 8–10

A fellow from the bayous of Louisiana came running
up to me in an airport and shouted out a set of ingredients. He then explained it was a backwoods gumbo,
the kind his grandma made for him when he was a boy.
This is not as complex as a normal gumbo and therefore
is easy to make. It is a good and frugal meal.

2 pounds chicken
    gizzards, cut into
    ½-inch dice
2 pounds turkey necks
    or chicken necks
4 tablespoons peanut oil
    (Grandma used
    lard.)
4 tablespoons flour
4 ribs celery, chopped
1 large yellow onion,
    peeled and chopped
1 green sweet bell
    pepper, seeded and
    chopped
3 cloves garlic, peeled
    and chopped fine
1 can (14½ ounces)
    whole tomatoes,
    crushed with your
    hands

1 teaspoon whole
    thyme leaves
1 teaspoon whole
    basil leaves
3 whole bay leaves
2 tablespoons filé
    powder
2 tablespoons
    Worcestershire
    sauce
1 teaspoon Tabasco
1 teaspoon salt
¼ teaspoon freshly
    ground black
    pepper, or to
    taste
1 pound smoked
    hot sausage,
    cut into 1-inch
    pieces
3–4 cups cooked long-
    grain rice

Place the gizzards and necks in a 12-quart stockpot and add 3 to 4 quarts of water. Cover and simmer until tender, about 2 hours. Set aside to cool.

Heat a large black frying pan and add the oil and flour. Stir over medium heat until the mixture becomes a peanut-butter-colored roux, about 10 to 15 minutes. Add the celery, onion, green pepper, garlic, and tomatoes and cook, stirring all the time, until almost tender. Stir in the remaining ingredients except the sausage and the rice and simmer a few minutes until thickened.

Strain the necks and gizzards from the kettle, reserving the broth. Place the poultry pieces and the vegetable mixture in the kettle, along with 2 quarts of the reserved broth. Stir over medium heat until the mixture thickens. Simmer for 30 minutes. Add the sausage and cook for an additional 15 minutes.

Serve over ¼ cup of cooked rice in each bowl.

DIRTY RICE

SERVES 8–10

Just calm down! The name comes not from the ingredients or even the process, but from the appearance of the rice. The chicken livers and gizzards give this wonderfully flavored old down-home dish a rather "dirty" look. I really do love this stuff and your kids will enjoy it as well as the funny name. The dish is Creole.

6 cups Chicken Soup Stock (page 29) or canned chicken broth	2 cloves garlic, peeled and crushed
1 pound chicken gizzards	1 large green sweet bell pepper, seeded and chopped
1 pound chicken livers	4 ribs celery, coarsely chopped

1 teaspoon salt
1 tablespoon
    Worcestershire
    sauce
½ teaspoon cayenne,
    or more to taste
3 tablespoons olive oil
    or bacon
    drippings
2 medium yellow
    onions, peeled
    and chopped

1 pound lean ground
    pork
1 pound bulk Italian
    sausage, hot or
    mild
2 cups uncooked long-
    grain rice
Freshly ground
    black pepper to
    taste
4 green onions,
    chopped
¼ cup chopped
    parsley

Heat the chicken stock in a 12-quart pot and add the gizzards and livers, along with the salt, Worcestershire sauce, and cayenne. Cover and lightly boil for 30 minutes.

In the meantime chop all of the vegetables. Heat a large frying pan and add the oil or bacon drippings and sauté the yellow onion, garlic, green pepper, and celery until tender. Remove from the pan.

Add the ground pork and sausage to the frying pan and sauté until lightly browned. Drain the meat in a colander and discard the fat.

Remove the livers and gizzards from the chicken stock, reserving the stock. Cool them for a moment and coarsely grind in your meat grinder. Add the gizzards and livers, along with the browned meats, to the vegetables. Place all in the stockpot and add ½ cup of the chicken stock. Cover and simmer for 20 minutes.

Meanwhile, using 4 cups of the reserved chicken stock, cook the rice (page 447). Add the cooked rice to the completed vegetables and meat and gently stir in the green onions and parsley. Taste for salt and pepper and serve.

SOUL!

Soul food was born in the rural South, and it was born out of destitution and sheer necessity. The slaves who were forced to come to this country had to develop a style of cooking based on the barest of necessities, and the ingenuity that gave birth to this cuisine has to be highly respected and admired. That style, now referred to as "soul," brings back memories of your childhood in Virginia or in Chicago where you were raised by parents or grandparents who came North. To say someone understands soul is to say they understand the feelings of warmth, creativity, and downright hard times that marked the life of the early American black, and in many cases still does.

Remember that there were black citizens in this country long before the slave trade began. It was the African black who brought with him a style of cooking from Africa and adapted it to genuinely American foodstuffs. The American sweet potato thus was treated like the African yam, and grits reminded early blacks of an African grain called *foo-foo*. Okra was called *gomos* in Africa and Africans were already familiar with black-eyed peas. The peanut, which originated in South America, had been taken to Africa by traders. The blacks who came to this country brought the peanut with them and taught America how to use it and enjoy it.

There were many new foods in America, of course. Corn, squashes, lima beans, tomatoes were all new to the African and most slaves were allowed to grow these vegetables on their tiny private family plots. The plantation generally issued a limited supply of flour, salt pork, and corn. Cornmeal was a basic part of the diet and everything else had to be raised.

On occasion the slaves were given the parts of the pig rejected by the slave masters and plantation owners. These included the entrails or chitterlings, the feet and snout, the stomach linings or hog maws, and the neck bones. These lowly parts of the hog gave rise to a comment that referred to eating the better cuts or upper cuts on the animal. "Well, aren't you eating high on the hog!" These lowly leftovers were turned into delicacies that are still appreciated in the black community.

The contribution that soul cooking has made to American culture is hard to overestimate. Remember that both George Washington and Thomas Jefferson had kitchens run by black cooks. Black cooks almost single-handedly ran the dining cars during the great days of the American railroad industry, and black cooks were behind almost every major hotel restaurant from New York to Chicago, from Seattle to Miami, from Los Angeles to Buffalo.

The point behind this book is borne out by the meaning of soul cooking. It is obvious that we eat certain foods to recall special warm and wonderful memories, though those foods were eaten in earlier times because we had nothing else. Now we eat them because we don't have to . . . we choose to, and remember. As I understand it that is what soul is all about.

Other dishes that would be typical:

Grits (page 302)
Pickled pigs' feet
Boiled pigs' feet
Fried Catfish (page 263)
Corn Fritters (page 432)
Barbecued Spareribs (page 379)
Sweet Potato Pie (page 347)
Sweet Potatoes, Soul-Style (page 347)

CHITTERLINGS

SERVES 4–5

There is probably no other dish that brings out the word "soul" more strongly than this one. These are the intestines of the pig, washed and soaked, cleaned and pulled, then cooked for hours until they are tender. I admit they take a bit of getting used to, but like all foods of your childhood, once you learn to enjoy them you long for them for the rest of your life.

The name of this dish is generally pronounced "chit-lins." It comes from the Middle English name for body organs, "chitirling."

Yes, I have come to enjoy them now and then.

5 pounds of chitterlings, cleaned
2 yellow onions, peeled and diced
3 dried whole red peppers
1 cup chopped celery
1 tablespoon Seasoning Salt (page 247)
Salt to taste (very little)
1 cup Chicken Soup Stock (page 29) or canned chicken broth
1 green sweet bell pepper, cored and chopped

The chitterlings can be purchased in central-area meat markets, frozen and ready to go. The only problem is the cleaning. You must open each piece and scrap the fat. The fat is discarded as it has a very strong flavor.

Cut into 6-inch lengths and rinse in fresh water several times. Soak overnight in the refrigerator in salt water.

Rinse the chitterlings and place in a heavy kettle with a tight-fitting lid. Add all other ingredients *except* the green bell pepper. Simmer for 2–3 hours until tender. Add the chopped bell pepper and cook for an additional 15 minutes.

FRIED CHITTERLINGS

Prepare chitterlings as above. Cut into 3-inch pieces and dip in egg wash (2 eggs whipped with 4 tablespoons water) and then into cracker crumbs. Deep-fry or pan-fry until golden brown.

PORK NECK BONES AND SAUERKRAUT

Pork neck bones are one of the most flavorful parts of the pig. There is not much meat on the bones, of course, so they are not expensive. They can be used as a flavoring for greens and for making soups. Or they can be placed in a covered pot with sauerkraut and simmered until they are deliciously tender. I put a pinch of sugar and some fried onions in my sauerkraut and then load the pot with the neck bones.

COLLARD GREENS

SERVES 4

In earlier times in our culture, slaves were allowed to grow a few crops for themselves, but they obviously were not crops that the "house" would want to claim. Collard greens are a mite bitter if you don't know what to do with them, so collard greens became a part of the soul diet in the South.

This recipe is simple and just delicious. Don't talk to me about cooking greens too long. In this case it is part of the tradition.

4 bunches collard
   greens
2 cups Chicken Soup
   Stock (page 29) or
   canned chicken
   broth

Salt and pepper to
   taste
Dash of Tabasco
2 tablespoons bacon
   drippings

Wash the greens very well. Shake dry and place in a kettle. Add the chicken broth and bring to a full boil. Lower the heat and keep the pot at a heavy simmer until the greens are tender and to your liking. Add the seasonings and bacon fat.

CHICKEN AND DUMPLINGS

This is another method of using one chicken to feed several people. The dumplings are a wonderfully frugal way to enjoy a full meal.

Prepare the chicken according to Nettie Smith's Chicken and Noodles recipe (page 465), omitting the noodles. Instead, cut down on the liquid in the final pot and drop dumplings (page 469) on top. Cook according to the dumpling recipe.

I love a dish of Collard Greens (page 245) on the side and some of Harriet's Southern Biscuits (page 464).

CHICKEN-FRIED PORK CHOPS

SERVES 4

I will admit that you are adding more fat to this dish by deep-frying a pork chop. However, if you pan-fry the chop you can eliminate a lot of the fat and still have a very tasty meal. This would be part of a traditional breakfast in an old southern home.

4 good-sized pork chops, trimmed of fat	¾ cup cornmeal Seasoning Salt to taste*
2 eggs, beaten	Black pepper, freshly ground, to taste
3 tablespoons water	Peanut oil for pan-frying
¼ cup flour	

Whip the eggs with 3 tablespoons water in order to make an egg wash. Mix the remaining ingredients, except the oil, together and place on a plate. Dip the chops into the egg wash and then into the coating mix. Pan-fry in a bit of oil over medium heat until golden brown and done to your taste.

Serve Sweet Potatoes, Soul-Style (page 347), along with some Fried Okra (below).

*Seasoning Salt
Makes ⅓ Cup

While I do not use much of this in my regular cooking it is common in soul cooking. Rather than purchase the stuff, you can make your own Seasoning Salt. You can also avoid the MSG that is found in most commercial seasoning salts. And this will cost you about ⅓ of the price of the big labels!

3 tablespoons salt	1 teaspoon sugar
1 tablespoon paprika	1 teaspoon onion
1 tablespoon celery salt	powder
2 teaspoons garlic	½ teaspoon cayenne
powder	½ teaspoon turmeric

Mix together and keep in a sealed jar.

FRIED OKRA

SERVES 4–6

Some good things take time. (Oh, I sound like a cheap wine commercial.) In the case of okra I know of no way to get to this delicious vegetable except through slow and proper cooking. Every black cook agrees with me,

I am sure. So, calm down and be prepared for okra that is wonderful and tasty. And no, it will not be "slippery."

1½ pounds fresh okra	Oil for pan-frying
1 egg, beaten	(Bacon grease is
2 tablespoons water	traditional but
1 cup cornmeal	peanut oil works
Salt and pepper to taste	fine. Olive oil is delicious with this!)

Cut the tops off the okra and cut into ½-inch slices. Mix the egg with 2 tablespoons water and toss with the okra. Add the cornmeal and salt and pepper. Mix well so that all pieces are coated. Pan-fry in a bit of oil over medium heat. Shake so that the pieces separate and brown evenly on both sides. You may have to do this in 2 batches.

This dish must be cooked slowly and carefully so that the okra dries out a bit in the cooking.

BLACK-EYED PEAS AND HAM HOCKS

SERVES 6

Most Yankees have never seen a black-eyed pea. Actually, it is a bean, and it has a marvelous sort of smoky flavor that cooks up beautifully in the midst of a wonderful soul menu.

This is not an expensive dish. Most soul dishes are not expensive . . . which is one of the points behind "soul." This is, however, terribly nutritious and enjoyable.

2 pounds smoked
   ham hocks, cut
   into 2-inch slices
½ pound black-eyed
   peas, soaked for
   4 hours and
   drained
2 stalks celery,
   chopped
1 yellow onion, peeled
   and chopped

1 green sweet bell
   pepper, seeded
   and chopped
½ teaspoon crushed
   red pepper flakes,
   or to taste
Salt and pepper to
   taste (Careful
   with the salt. The
   hocks are already
   salty.)

Place the ham hocks in a covered kettle and add just enough water to barely cover. Cover with the lid and bring to a boil. Simmer for 2 hours, or until tender. Add the peas, drained, along with the remaining ingredients. Careful with the salt! Cook, covered, until the peas are tender, about 45 minutes.

You may wish to remove the lid and reduce some of the juices before serving.

This dish offers soup, meat, and sustenance. Add a salad and some rolls and enjoy.

PEANUTS

This legume—yes, the peanut is not a nut at all—is so much a part of American life that one cannot estimate the mental damage and frustration that would occur among our youth if we were to run out of peanut butter. I cannot imagine the pain and ruin!

Actually, the peanut is a native South American legume. It is not a nut, of course, because it does not grow on trees above the ground. It grows in a pod beneath the ground. In any case the early Spanish and Portuguese explorers found the native South Americans cultivating the peanut and the Europeans took the treat home with them. We assume that Portuguese slave traders then took the peanut into Africa, where it became very popular. Later, peanuts were put on slave ships to provide food and assurance for the long voyage. The slaves brought peanuts into the New World, where they also taught the early Americans how to eat them. Tom Jefferson tried growing peanuts at Monticello in about 1791.

Now the story gets to be more interesting. The whites in the colonies were not very taken by the peanut, but they would allow the slaves to grow them. So nice! The colonists thought peanuts fit only as food for swine. Little happened with the peanut crop in this country, outside of the blacks' interest in keeping the peanut for home use, until the Civil War. Wartime oil shortages promoted the use of peanut oil as never before, both industrially and for consumption. Tasted and appreciated by Union soldiers, the peanut emerged from the conflict with a reputation for good taste and a bad background.

It was not until the famous black scientist, Dr. George Washington Carver, began to teach us about the uses for the peanut that the American form of the "goober" became really popular. The brilliant doctor came up with 300 uses for peanuts. Then it happened. A St. Louis doctor invented peanut butter and promoted it

as a health food at the 1904 St. Louis World's Fair.
Today half of the peanuts used in the United States go
into peanut butter. Now, peanut butter is American!

PEANUTS ROASTED IN THE SHELL

It is not difficult to find raw peanuts in the shell. Roasting them at home is really great fun, especially if you
have your children do this at a party. Get ready for a
real mess because most American kids have never
tasted freshly roasted peanuts. You will have shells all
over the house.

Roast the peanuts, in the shell, on a cookie sheet at
about 315° for about 15 minutes.

If you insist on salting them, first simply soak them
in a very strong salt brine and then drain them very
well. This will be hard to do at home since the things
will float and not absorb much saline solution. At the
factory they put them in a vacuum chamber and draw
out the air, which is, of course, replaced by the solution.
Drain them well and remember that they will take
longer to roast since they need to dry out in your oven
first.

Serve the peanuts in little paper bags, the kind that
we used to get at the circus. What fun!

THE PEANUT-BUTTER SANDWICH

I cannot imagine what would happen to the American
culture if we did not have the peanut-butter sandwich.
We all used to eat them and sometimes we enjoyed
clever combinations. I assume you have tried all of the

following, but in case you have not, here are some of the more bizarre combinations that I have come across.

Peanut Butter and Mayonnaise on Toast
It must be toast! I ate these often as a child.

Peanut Butter and Sardine Sandwich
No, I am not trying to make you sorry that you bought this book. Bosco, my dear friend and cameraman in Chicago, claims this is great. No, I have not tried it. Yes, I think you are going to try it!

Peanut Butter and Relish
Not bad for a man who lives on hamburgers and french fries. Fonzie, another cameraman in Chicago, claims this is to die for. I expect you would!

PEANUT SOUP

SERVES 4

This recipe is to be found in cookbooks from all over the country... and since about 1850. When you tell your kids that you are making peanut-butter soup, get ready for some wisecracks... and make plenty since they will love it.

3 cups Chicken Soup
Stock (page 29) or
canned chicken
broth
1 yellow onion, peeled
and chopped
2 carrots, unpeeled
and sliced

¼ cup uncooked rice
½ teaspoon salt
⅛ teaspoon cayenne
pepper or more
to taste
½ cup peanut butter

In a 2-quart covered saucepan simmer the chicken
stock, onion, and carrots, covered, for 30 minutes.
Purée all in a food blender or food processor and return
to the pan. Add the rice, salt, and cayenne pepper;
cover and simmer for an additional 20 minutes, or until
the rice is tender. Stir in the peanut butter and serve.

PEA CHOP
Peanut and Chicken Stew
(Africa)

SERVES 5–6

This dish actually came from Africa, but then that's
how we got our own peanuts returned to us in the first
place. John Clark, a dear man in Batavia, Illinois,
wanted to cook this for me and I was smart enough to
take him up on his offer. At the time he gave me this
recipe he was dying of cancer . . . and he cooked for me.
Just a few days before his death I finished the Peanut
Show and sent him a copy of the tape. He was not
communicating much but he woke up when he heard
that the tape had arrived. He watched the whole show
and then said, "That silly Jeff. He forgot to put some
more crushed peanuts on top." He died shortly there-
after.

You see, I have a very wonderful job, and I meet
wonderful people. And John, dear heart, I shall never
forget to put some crushed peanuts on top, I promise!

This dish is extraordinarily good. Though it sounds

strange, I cannot imagine anyone not liking this combination of chicken and peanut sauce.

2 chickens, about 3 pounds each, cut up
4 ounces unsweetened shredded coconut
½ cup peeled and sliced yellow onions
½ tablespoon dill weed
2 whole bay leaves
½ cup peanut butter
Cornstarch to thicken
Salt and freshly ground black pepper to taste

5 bananas (not too ripe), peeled and halved lengthwise
Butter for frying the bananas
Cooked long-grain rice, enough for your table (page 447)
1 can unsweetened pineapple chunks, chilled
½ cup dry-roasted peanuts, chopped fairly fine

Pan-brown the chicken, skin on. While the chicken is browning, toast the coconut on a cookie sheet in a 375° oven. Watch it carefully. You want it just barely light golden brown, and it will take little time.

Place the browned chicken in a 4- to 6-quart pot and add the onions, dill and bay leaves. Add enough water to not quite cover. Bring to a boil and then turn down to a simmer and cover and cook for 45 minutes. Remove the chicken from the pot and set aside. You may wish to remove the skin and discard.

Add ½ cup of the stock to the peanut butter and mix well. Pour this peanut sauce into the stock and thicken the stock with cornstarch dissolved in water. Start with about 3 tablespoons cornstarch dissolved in ½ cup water. Stir into the stock in a quick fashion and stir over heat until thick. If this is not thick enough for you, add more cornstarch and water. Then, add salt and pepper to taste. Return the chicken to the pot.

Fry the bananas in a bit of butter just until they are browned. This will take little time.

This dish is traditionally served buffet style. The guests put rice on their plates, then chicken and gravy on top. The fried bananas and pineapple are next, with the coconut and chopped peanuts providing the topping.

John claimed that it was traditional to fill your plate 3 times. By this time I expect that he has the Holy Spirit enjoying this dish!

John served nothing more with this meal. It stands complete.

BEEF ON A STICK WITH PEANUT SAUCE
Saté
(Indonesia)

SERVES 5–6

What is a recipe from Indonesia doing in an American cookbook? Because peanuts came from the Americas to Indonesia, that's why. And besides, I love this recipe. Great for the barbecue!

1 **round steak (2 pounds), trimmed of fat**

THE MARINADE

2 **cloves garlic, crushed**

1 **teaspoon ground coriander**

3 **tablespoons finely diced yellow onion**

1 **tablespoon brown sugar**

1 **teaspoon fresh lemon juice**

2 **tablespoons light soy sauce**

3 **tablespoons dry sherry**

THE SAUCE

1 cup dry-roasted unsalted peanuts	1 tablespoon fresh lemon juice
½ cup light soy sauce Dash of Tabasco, or to taste	½ yellow onion, peeled, diced, and pan-fried until brown
2 tablespoons light brown sugar	

Cut the meat into thin strips, being careful to remove the fat. Mix the marinade and soak the meat strips for at least ½ hour. Put the meat on bamboo skewers in an S pattern.

Prepare the sauce by grinding the peanuts in a food blender or medium-sized food processor. Place in a bowl and add all other ingredients for the sauce.

Broil the sticks of meat over charcoal or under the broiler. Cook just until barely browned, about 4 minutes on each side. You want the meat to be fairly rare and tender.

Spoon the sauce over the meat when you serve.

I like a sliced cucumber salad with a Vinaigrette Dressing (page 384). You need add only plain Steamed Rice (page 447) and the menu is complete.

NOTE: This sauce is great on other meat dishes as well. And I love it on fish.

HINT: Rules for a Good Soufflé

1. Have the eggs at room temperature.

2. Be sure the sauce is not too hot when you blend in the flavoring ingredients.

3. *Fold* in the egg whites; don't stir them in. Folding means that you use a rubber spatula to gently roll the batter over the egg whites in a circular or folding motion. You don't want the egg whites to collapse.

4. Be prepared to serve it the *minute* it comes from the oven. Soufflés fall like two-year-old children . . . all the time.

PEANUT BUTTER AND CHEESE SOUFFLÉ

SERVES 4–6 AS A SIDE DISH

Please stop laughing. You paid plenty for this book and I didn't write it for laughs! This dish is really very good and the flavor of cheese and peanuts is not new in American cuisine. Thomas Jefferson was very fond of this sort of thing, I'm sure.

3½ tablespoons butter
4½ tablespoons flour
1½ cups hot milk
½ teaspoon salt
Pinch cayenne
Pinch freshly
    ground nutmeg

6 tablespoons
    creamy peanut
    butter
6 egg yolks
1 cup coarsely
    grated Jack
    cheese
8 egg whites
½ teaspoon cream of
    tartar

Read the hints first. Soufflés are actually very easy.

In a saucepan melt the butter and stir in the flour. Cook for just a few minutes. Remove from heat. Stir in the hot milk, using a wire whisk, and return the pan to the heat. Stir until thickened. Add the salt, cayenne, nutmeg, and peanut butter. Stir until all ingredients are well incorporated. Remove from heat.

Stir in the egg yolks using the whisk. Stir in the cheese with a rubber spatula and set aside to cool for a few minutes.

Beat the egg whites, along with the cream of tartar, until they are stiff and form nice peaks. Very gently, very gently (No, this is not a typo) very gently, fold the cheese sauce into the egg whites. Place in a 1½- to 2-quart soufflé dish and bake for 25–30 minutes at 375°. Serve a minute ago!

Serve as a luncheon dish or as a first course.

PEANUT-BUTTER MILK SHAKE

Stir 2 or 3 tablespoons of hot tap water into the same amount of creamy peanut butter. Add to your favorite vanilla milk-shake recipe (see Pumpkin Milk Shake, page 195) and enjoy!

PEANUT-BUTTER CORN MUFFINS

All right, so you could have thought this one up yourself. Well, I have already got it in a book, so there! Corn and peanuts belong together, and this recipe will prove my point.

Mix a batch of corn-bread batter (page 430). Grease your muffin pans or spray them with Pam. Put 2 tablespoons of batter in the bottom of each cup and then add 1 tablespoon of crunchy-style peanut butter. Add the remaining bit of batter and bake as usual.

When you serve these, ask the younger children how they think you got the peanut butter into the middle of the muffin. I'll bet you get some wonderful answers.

PEANUT-BUTTER WAFFLES OR PANCAKES

These are just wonderful with the flavor of maple syrup. Simply blend 3 or 4 tablespoons of peanut butter with an equal amount of hot tap water. Stir with a table fork in a cup. When smooth, add it to your favorite waffle or pancake batter recipe.

CATFISH

The first time I was ever in the South, I was invited to visit with one of my classmates in theology. We traveled to his home base in Covington, Georgia, where I met his gracious parents. When they asked me what I wanted for dinner, I replied, "Something really Georgia!" We got into the car and drove to a roadside restaurant for catfish and hushpuppies. I felt as if I were in a foreign land. I had never seen such a dish, though I had heard of it, of course. Catfish was not to be found up North, at least not in 1962. Since that time all has changed in the catfish market.

Today fresh catfish can be purchased in most larger American cities, and it is the darling of the trend-setting crowd. It is low in fat and calories, lower even than chicken, and it is very versatile. A plain catfish fry is fun, but you will also enjoy it creamed or grilled. I expect that you can purchase your catfish already skinned. If not, simply hook the head of the dead fish on a nail that you have driven through a board. Holding on to the tail of the fish, pull the skin off using a pair of pliers. This method works for me, but remember, "There is more than one way to skin a cat!" (That's what that old phrase means.)

There are approximately twenty-eight different species of catfish in North America, and they range in size from the inch-long madtom to the giant blue catfish, which can weigh 120 pounds. While the fish does exist in many other parts of the world, it seems to be more popular here than anywhere else. People in the old South, black and white alike, used to pull catfish from the bayous and canals. While in the old days the fish was free it now has become so popular that the demand can be met only through the use of highly technical catfish farms. The Mississippi Catfish Institute (you didn't know that there was such a thing, did you?) claims that they have raised about 212 million pounds of the cats during 1986 alone. Since the production is increasing at a tremendous rate, we can be sure that we will see more fresh catfish on the market in the future.

These recipes are simple and absolutely delicious.

FRIED CATFISH

SERVES 4–5

This is the quickest way I know to enjoy the flavor of catfish. Soaking in milk makes the fish mild in taste and tender in texture. You don't necessarily have to deep-fry this one, though that is the most common method used in the South. I like it pan-fried just as well. It is a completely different dish.

4 pounds catfish
   fillets
1 cup milk for
   soaking
½ cup flour
1½ cups cornmeal
   Salt and pepper to
   taste

2 teaspoons Crab and
   Shrimp Seasoning
   (page 408) *or*
   Bookbinder's crab
   and shrimp
   seasoning
Oil or butter for
   deep-frying or
   pan-frying

Cut the fillets into serving pieces of about 4 ounces each. Soak all the fish in the milk for 1 hour. Mix the flour, cornmeal, salt and pepper, and the crab and shrimp seasoning together. Drain the fish and dredge in the cornmeal mixture.

Deep-fry in 375° oil, a few pieces at a time, until

golden brown. Keep pieces warm in a 200° oven until all is complete, *or* pan-fry on both sides in a bit of oil or butter until the fish is lightly browned and done to your liking. Do not overcook catfish.

Traditionally, deep-fried catfish was served with hushpuppies. I am convinced that you also need a great deal of very cold beer with this catfish fry.

HUSHPUPPIES

SERVES 4–5

Howard Mitcham, a New Orleans authority on just about everything, is a wonderful and charming man. He explains that hushpuppies got their name in ante-bellum days ("before the war"). In the summertime the slaves cooked their meals over an outdoor fire. Over-come by ravenous hunger and by the delicious smells rising from the skillet, the family dog would walk around crying and whining. The cook would toss him one of these deep-fried tidbits and say, "Now. Hush, puppy!" Hushpuppies may be spoon-dropped, patted into small cakes, or rolled into balls. The spoon-dropped type are the easiest and seem to be the most crispy and tasty. You can fry them in the same fat in which you have cooked the catfish.

This is Mitcham's recipe:

1 cup cornmeal	2 teaspoons baking
1 cup flour	powder
1 medium yellow	1 teaspoon salt
onion, peeled and	½ teaspoon freshly
finely chopped	ground black
6 green onions, finely	pepper
chopped (Use only	1 egg, beaten
2 inches of the	¾ cup buttermilk
green part.)	

Mix the dry ingredients and the onions together. Blend
the egg with the buttermilk and stir into the dry ingredients. You will have a very thick batter.

Allow the batter to sit for ½ hour and then drop by
the tablespoonful into deep fat at 375°. Deep-fry until
golden brown. Drain on paper towels and keep warm
in a 200° oven until serving.

GRILLED CATFISH

Now that catfish has become an "in" food, you will find
it in the most elegant grill houses. This recipe contains
nothing fancy, but putting the fish on a charcoal grill is
just wonderful. Easy and quick, and very flavorful.

> Catfish fillets
> Olive oil
> Freshly squeezed lemon
>   juice
> Salt and freshly ground
>   black pepper to taste

Mix a bit of olive oil, lemon juice, salt and pepper
together and whip to the consistency of a salad dressing.
Marinate the fish in this mixture for ½ hour before
grilling. Grill over charcoal for about 5 minutes on a
side, or until the fish is lightly browned and begins to
flake a bit. Do not overcook.

BLACKENED CATFISH

SERVES 6

Okay, so I admit that I too am tired of everyone blackening everything. This method, however, is very easy and the results unusually good. I prefer this to blackened redfish (which is nearing the endangered-species list), blackened chicken, and, Lord save us all, blackened oysters. Why would you do such a thing to a perfectly innocent oyster?

This is the only time that you have ever seen me use garlic and onion powders . . . but this is the only way you can do this dish.

SPICE MIX

2 tablespoons sweet paprika	1½ teaspoons cayenne pepper
2½ tablespoons salt	2 teaspoons lemon pepper*
1 teaspoon onion powder	1 teaspoon whole thyme leaves
1½ teaspoons garlic powder	1½ teaspoons whole basil leaves

Mix together and store in a lidded jar. You will probably not need all of this mix for this particular recipe. Use it on other meats as well.

*Lemon pepper is a blend that can be found in the spice section of the local supermarket.

    4 **catfish fillets (total weight**
      about 3 pounds)
  ½ **stick butter**
  ¼ **cup olive oil**

Heat a black iron frying pan for at least 10 minutes over very high heat.

Cut each of the fillets in half. Melt the butter and mix with the olive oil. Place the spice mix on a plate. Dip the fish into the butter and oil and then dredge on both sides in the spice mix. Fry in a very hot pan just a few minutes on each side. This must be done in a room with a very good kitchen fan or out in the backyard over a very hot charcoal barbecue fire.

Serve this with a great deal of beer, an enormous green salad, and Macaroni Pie (page 130).

POACHED CATFISH

SERVES 6

This recipe is just what it claims to be, a simple poaching job on a low-class fish. However, this process raises the fish to glory! Remember that we are dealing with very few calories here, and the flavor and texture taste like something very expensive!

    4 **catfish fillets (about**
      3 pounds)
    4 **cups Chicken Soup**
      Stock (page 29)
      or canned
      chicken broth
  ½ **cup dry white wine**
  2 **tablespoons white**
      vinegar
  3 **tablespoons very**
      coarsely chopped
      fresh parsley

  2 **sprigs fresh dill** *or* ½
      teaspoon dried dill
  3 **slices fresh lemon**
  1 **teaspoon salt**
      Butter, melted for
      topping
      Salt and freshly
      ground black
      pepper to taste

In a 6-quart soup pot bring the above ingredients, except the butter and the fish, to a boil. Place the fish in the poaching liquid and simmer, covered, for 8–10 minutes. The fish is done when it barely begins to flake.

Do not overcook the fish. Serve with melted butter and salt and freshly ground black pepper.

I like this along with Pasta with Fresh Asparagus and Scallops (page 495).

CATFISH WITH SHRIMP SAUCE
(New Orleans)

SERVES 6

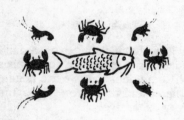

This is from a most interesting collection of recipes from New Orleans. The cook is a fellow called Jesse. The cookbook, long out of print, is called *Jesse's Creole and Deep South Recipes.* He has a wonderful sensitivity, as this recipe shows. It will take some time to prepare but it is well worth it.

4 catfish fillets
  (about 3 pounds
  total)
Salt and pepper to
  taste
½ cup butter, melted
2½ tablespoons peanut
  or olive oil
½ small yellow onion,
  peeled and finely
  chopped
2 tablespoons finely
  chopped celery
2 tablespoons butter
½ pound fresh
  mushrooms,
  sliced
1 heaping tablespoon
  flour

¼ cup Fish Stock
  (page 31) or
  clam juice
Dash Tabasco
Juice of ½ lemon
2 tablespoons
  Worcestershire
  sauce
⅓ cup dry sherry
1 tablespoon finely
  chopped parsley
¼ pound shrimp,
  cooked and
  cleaned (cocktail
  or salad shrimp
  are fine for this)

Salt and pepper the fillets. Mix the melted butter and
oil in an oven-proof baking dish. (Pyrex would be fine.)
Dredge the fillets in the mixture and broil, basting often
with the butter and oil mixture. Do not overcook. The
fish will barely begin to brown and will just begin to
flake.

Meanwhile, prepare the sauce by sautéing the onion
and celery in the 2 tablespoons butter. When clear add
the mushrooms and sauté for 3 minutes. Stir in the flour.
Work out all lumps. Add the fish stock or clam juice,
Tabasco, lemon juice, Worcestershire sauce, dry
sherry, and parsley. Simmer for a moment until thick
and then add the shrimp. Cook for just a minute and
top the fish with the sauce.

I serve this over pasta along with Peas and Salt Pork
(page 122).

CREAMED CATFISH

SERVES 4–5

Sound like a bit much? This marks a change in the eating habits of whites in the South. When they began eating catfish it had to be dressed up a bit, since educated whites were not to be seen eating lower-class food. Well, this is educated catfish and anyone could be seen eating this. It is popular in New Orleans . . . with all kinds of people.

4 catfish fillets (about 3 pounds, total weight)	¼ cup peeled and chopped shallots
Salt and pepper to taste	¼ cup tomato sauce
Dash of cayenne	1½ cups whipping cream
3 tablespoons butter, melted (Use microwave.)	Juice of ½ lemon
	2 cups dry white wine
	⅓ cup finely chopped parsley

Salt and pepper the fillets along with a dash of cayenne. Place in a covered stove-top dish or sauté pan. Mix together the butter, shallots, tomato sauce, 1 cup of the cream, lemon juice, and the white wine. Pour over the fish and simmer, covered, for 20 minutes or until the fish barely flakes. Gently remove the fish to a warm platter. Add the remaining cream and the parsley to the sauce and bring it to a boil. Reduce the sauce until it thickens and pour it over the fish.

Try this over a nice dish, such as Rice with Burned Almonds (page 394).

CRAWFISH

The lowly crawfish, also called a crawdad, crayfish, or mudbug, lives in many American lakes, ponds, rivers, flooded swampy areas, and even roadside ditches. He is not uncommon in the rest of the world, as he can be found in fresh water on every continent except Africa. He is particularly prized in Scandinavia, where great summer-evening crawfish feasts are held.

If he is to be found in other countries, why do I include this tiny lobsterlike crustacean in a strictly American cookbook? Because ours are the biggest and the best, and we seem to have done more with them than anybody else. They are terribly popular in New Orleans, where they can be found in the bayous. They also grow profusely in my part of the country, the Pacific Northwest. From here we ship vast amounts of the critters to Norway, France, and Sweden! A restaurant in Portland, Oregon, Jake's Crawfish House, has been serving the crawfish since 1892. It is a marvelous place.

This tasty creature is celebrating a new popularity in America. Most of the attention he is getting comes from the current craze for New Orleans cuisine. A good portion of this country, until recently, saw the mudbug as a food for poor people, a food that could be gathered free in the waterways . . . and nice middle-class folk weren't to be seen down there grubbing in the mud for crawdaddies. But things have changed!

The season is from early spring through the summer, though you can now buy frozen crawfish meat. It is not bad, not bad at all. And we now have commercial crawfish farms that are producing fine-quality creatures in abundance. This has improved the availability of this freshwater delicacy and it has also taught us a lesson about creative farming. Most of the crawfish farmers are actually rice farmers, and the food producers have realized that they can produce two crops from the same area at the same time. Now that is a lesson in frugal food management.

Crawfish taste like a freshwater lobster or crab, and they are very sweet and versatile. But, like most really fine old American dishes, crawfish put you through a considerable amount of work to get to the meal. The cleaning and cooking process is explained below, but we should talk first about eating them from the shell. Once they are boiled (page 275), you break off the head and suck out the wonderful juices. Don't pay attention if people are watching—they are just jealous. Then, crack the tail from the belly side and peel it off. Devein the meat, if you are one of those, and enjoy. Use your thumb to remove the yellow liver and fat from the head. Crack the claws with your teeth and draw out the meat. This is just great eating!

NOTE: All recipes in this section, except the recipe for Boiled Crawfish, assume that you are using cooked crawfish. If you do not want to go to the trouble of boiling them according to the recipe, you can use the meat in the other recipes if you clean the crawfish and then plunge them into boiling water. Allow to sit for 5 minutes and then drain. They are ready to be shelled and cooked any way you wish.

HINT: **On Cleaning Crawfish.**
Since these creatures live in the mud, it is important to clean them properly or you will have mud in your food.
1. Wash well with fresh water.

2. Soak them in a saltwater bath for about 8 minutes to purge them of mud.

3. Rinse well in a colander and you are ready to cook them.

CRAWFISH BOURBON ORLEANS

SERVES 4–6

I tasted this dish in a hotel in New Orleans that is now under new management. The chef gave out the recipe and I was very taken by it. You have got to love this one!

1 cup Fish Stock (page 31) or canned fish broth, *reduced* to 1 tablespoon *or* 1 tablespoon commercial shrimp base with 1 tablespoon hot water

1 tablespoon minced shallots

1 tablespoon minced garlic

2 tablespoons butter

1 pound crawfish tail meat, cooked and peeled

2 tablespoons white wine

4 tablespoons bourbon whiskey

2 cups heavy cream or half-and-half

1 tablespoon butter

Salt and pepper to taste (careful on the salt)

Reduce the stock.

In large frying pan, sauté the shallots and garlic in 2 tablespoons of butter until clear. Add the crawfish, reduced stock, wine, bourbon, and salt and pepper. Flame, or light with a match, being very careful that there are no children around . . . or nice guests for that matter. Add the cream and reduce the sauce for 3 to 4 minutes. Finish the sauce by swirling in the final tablespoon of butter.

We are talking rich here!

Serve over cooked pasta or rice, along with a green salad and Peas with Salt Pork (page 122).

BOILED CRAWFISH

SERVES 3–4 AS A MAIN COURSE

This is a compilation of several recipes, and I think it comes off better than any of the individual versions. I have eaten these mudbugs from New Orleans to Portland. This is great stuff, hot or cold.

4 quarts water
¾ cup salt
1½ fresh lemons, sliced
5 stalks celery, chopped
4 tablespoons Worcestershire sauce
4 cloves garlic, chopped

1½ large yellow onions, peeled and sliced
1 small package commercial shrimp boil spices
Tabasco to taste
6 pounds live crawfish, washed and soaked in salt water (see cleaning on page 273)

Place all but the crawfish in a large kettle and bring to a boil, covered. Simmer for 15 minutes so that you create a good rich stock and then add the crawfish. Cover and bring back to a boil. Boil for 7 minutes, *no more,* and then turn off the heat, leaving the lid on the kettle. The crawfish may be served after a few minutes or chilled in the refrigerator.

One needs only beer and good bread with these critters.

CRAWFISH NEWBURG

SERVES 3–4

This is a very high-class use of the formerly low-class mudbug. It is wonderful, isn't it, how peasant dishes become expensive classics once the rest of the culture catches on to the glories of inventing dishes out of sheer necessity? We have certainly gone beyond necessity in this one, since it is a blend of the freshwater crawfish and a very fancy and rich sauce. I love this one, too.

3 tablespoons butter
1 small yellow onion, peeled and chopped
3 tablespoons flour
2 cups Fish Stock (page 31), canned fish broth, or clam juice
1 cup whipping cream
1 egg
2 tablespoons dry sherry

½ teaspoon paprika
Salt and freshly ground pepper to taste
1 pound crawfish tails, cooked and cleaned (page 273)
2 cups cooked rice
Parsley, chopped, for garnish

Heat a 2-quart soup pot, add the butter and the onion, and sauté until the onion is clear. Stir in the flour and cook for a few minutes to form a roux. Do not let it darken. Add the fish stock, stirring carefully, and bring the whole to a boil. Reduce the heat and simmer 15 minutes, stirring until it thickens. Combine the cream, egg, and ½ cup of the hot stock and whip together. Stir this mixture back into the pot. Turn the heat to low and add the remaining ingredients, except the crawfish, rice, and parsley. Keep warm until you are about to serve. Then stir in the crawfish, heat for a moment, and serve over the rice with a parsley garnish.

I enjoy a glass of cold dry white wine and a green salad with my Newburg. Anything else would be too rich.

CRAWFISH OMELET

Use some of the leftover Crawfish Etouffée (below) for omelet filling. Delicious!

CRAWFISH ETOUFFÉE

SERVES 4–6

The term *etouffée* means "smothered." Most of us in the North assume that it is so called because the sauce is so thick that it smothers the crawfish. After one taste of this dish you will understand that the crawfish is also smothered with flavor.

This is one of my favorite crawfish dishes . . . ever!

2 cups fresh crawfish tails, cooked, peeled, and cleaned

4 tablespoons *each* flour and butter, cooked together to form a brown roux

1 cup finely chopped yellow onions

1 cup finely chopped green onions

½ cup finely chopped celery

1 teaspoon finely chopped garlic

2 green sweet bell peppers, seeded and chopped

1 cup chopped parsley

1 can (16 ounces) tomatoes, drained and chopped

1 cup white wine

1 cup Fish Stock (page 31) or canned fish broth

1 tablespoon whole thyme leaves

1 tablespoon Worcestershire sauce

¼ teaspoon cayenne pepper

1 teaspoon freshly ground black pepper

1 teaspoon ground cumin

1 teaspoon salt Tabasco to taste

4–6 cups cooked white rice

Boil the crawfish (page 275), drain, and cool. Save as much of the "butter" or the fat that is found in the head as you wish. You will need 1 pound of meat, about 2 cups.

In a heavy 5- to 6-quart metal casserole, prepare the roux and toast it gently until light brown. Add the yellow onions, green onions, celery, garlic, green bell peppers, and parsley, and cook over medium heat until the vegetables are soft.

Add the tomatoes to the pot, stirring carefully so that the mixture begins to thicken. Add the white wine, fish stock, and all seasonings. Simmer for 30 minutes and then stir in the crawfish meat and fat, if any.

Serve over the hot rice along with Fried Okra (page 247) and perhaps some Eggplant Casserole (page 229).

"I love thy rocks and rills..."

EDIBLE COMFORTS

TURKEY

While the turkey may be one of the dumbest animals in God's creation, she is nevertheless precious to us Americans. The old bird is American, and has been since before the Europeans discovered the New World.

The bird originated in North and Central America. Indians domesticated turkeys in Mexico, the southwestern United States, North Carolina, and Virginia, some as early as A.D. 400. However, since the wild bird was so abundant and easy to hunt, most of the Native Americans found it unnecessary to raise turkeys. At a refuse pile, near an Indian camp in Kentucky, turkey bones were exceeded in number only by those of deer. This site was dated by radiocarbon as existing before 3000 B.C.

Cortez and his armies found the Aztecs with domesticated turkeys when they entered the Valley of Mexico in 1519. Like so many other American products, the bird was taken by the explorers back to Europe, and by the early 1600s turkey was popular all over the Continent. Now, here is the interesting part. The bird that was found in the New England colonies by our European foremothers and forefathers is not the bird that we know today. The colonists became fond of American turkeys, all right, but it was the domesticated bird that they preferred, and they brought it back to this country from Europe! What a long trip for the poor bird to take, only to wind up on the dinner table anyhow. So, the turkey that you and I eat now is not the eastern wild variety but rather a subspecies from the descendants of the Mexican bird.

In the early days, the wild bird that was served in the colonies was enormous, up to forty pounds each. The bird was so very American that Ben Franklin claimed that we should never have chosen the eagle as our national symbol. The eagle is a bit shifty and dishonest, said Ben, and therefore we should have chosen the true American bird, the turkey. I wonder if Mr. Franklin, sometime fellow of Philadelphia, realized that turkeys are literally too dumb to come in out of the rain.

In our time the turkey is generally served on holidays, and I think this practice is very shortsighted. The meat is lean, low in fat, high in protein, delicious in flavor, and terribly versatile. We now have fresh, uncooked, sliced turkey breast in all supermarkets and I can do anything with turkey slices that I can do with chicken or veal slices. Enough of this wintertime confining of our bird. Up with summer and spring dishes of turkey!

ROAST TURKEY WITH SHERRY BUTTER

The turkeys that the Pilgrims ate must have been terribly stringy and tough old birds. In our time we have developed a lovely bird and there is simply no excuse for dry turkey meat. You can use either a frozen or a fresh turkey in this recipe, and the injection of butter and sherry will promise you a moist and lovely feast.

9–12 pound turkey
Salt and pepper to
taste

1 stick butter *or* ½
cup olive or salad
oil
½ cup dry cocktail
sherry

Clean the bird and remove the giblets. Save the giblets and neck for soup stock. Remove the wing tips, or first section of the wing, and add to the soup stock. Salt and pepper the bird inside and out, and stuff, if you wish.

After stuffing, secure the opening with string or thread, or simply close the opening by folding the skin over it and securing the legs. Instructions are generally included with the bird. Tie the wings to the body, and the legs together. Melt the butter and allow to cool for a few minutes (or use oil). Stir in the dry sherry. Using an injecting needle or plastic flavor injector (available in most gourmet shops—see page 14), inject the butter and sherry mixture into each of the legs, the thighs, and finally the breast. Just put a bit in 2 or 3 places in each of the mentioned parts. Rub the bird with a bit more butter or oil and roast in your usual manner.

I bake the bird at 325°, uncovered, about 15 minutes a pound. If you are stuffing the bird, add 1 hour for the dressing. A 9- to 12-pound stuffed bird will take between 3½ and 4 hours. A meat thermometer placed in the thigh should register 180°. Baste the bird with its own juices 2 or 3 times during the roasting.

OYSTER AND CORN BREAD STUFFING

STUFFS A 9- TO 12- POUND BIRD

This dish goes back 300 years. The colonists lived on corn, clams, and oysters . . . and now and then a turkey. The recipe is easy and unusually good. I urge you to try it soon.

4 stalks celery,
  chopped
1 yellow onion, peeled
  and chopped
½ stick butter
  Giblets
5 cups Corn Bread
  crumbs (page
  430)
¼ cup chopped
  parsley
1 teaspoon basil

1 teaspoon salt
½ teaspoon paprika
⅛ teaspoon freshly
  grated nutmeg
2 teaspoons whole
  sage leaves,
  rubbed
2 eggs, beaten
½ pint small oysters,
  juice and all
  Salt and pepper to
  taste

In a medium-sized frying pan, sauté the celery and onion in the butter until transparent. Set aside. Cook the giblets (the heart, liver, gizzard, neck, and tips of the wings) in about 1 quart of water. Cover and simmer until the gizzard is tender, about 1½ hours. Allow the meat to cool in the broth and in the meantime make the corn bread crumbs. I simply break up the corn bread and place it on a cookie sheet in a very low oven until the bread is dry enough to crumble up into very small pieces. Place the crumbs in a large mixing bowl.

Remove the meat from the bones and coarsely grind the meat, reserving the broth. Place the meat and sautéed vegetables in the bread-crumb bowl along with the remaining ingredients. Add about 3 cups of the giblet broth and season with salt and pepper to taste. The amount of broth that you add will depend upon how moist a dressing you like.

PLAIN OLD TURKEY GRAVY

People are always telling me that they cannot make good gravy. The secret to simplicity is in the roux and dry sherry. It's easy!

2–3 cups of broth (I make the broth from the bones of my last turkey and freeze the broth for the next turkey.)

Pan drippings from the turkey, fat removed (I use a plastic gravy skimmer.)

Roux—4 tablespoons butter in which you have cooked 4 tablespoons flour (Simply cook in another frying pan until the roux turns a very light brown.)

¼ cup dry sherry

Kitchen Bouquet to desired color

Salt and pepper to taste

Add the broth to the skimmed drippings and reduce by one third (page 25). Remove from the heat and stir in the roux, using a wire whip. Return to the heat and cook, stirring, until the mixture thickens. Add the sherry and Kitchen Bouquet, just to the desired color. Salt and pepper to taste. If too thick, add a bit more broth and cook for a few moments.

Sautéed mushrooms make a nice addition to this gravy. If you are still unhappy with your efforts, try adding some Maggi seasoning liquid (page 32), a fine product from Switzerland. It is most helpful.

TURKEY WITH BLEU CHEESE SAUCE

My editor, Maria, is so clever. Whenever we eat together in New York, I learn something new about food. She just threw this recipe off one evening while we were on a New York walk. I love it!

Simply slice cooked turkey, either roasted or poached, and serve it with a bit of turkey gravy in which you have dissolved some bleu cheese to taste. Delicious.

Add a grand Tomato Salad, Jefferson-style (page 125), and perhaps some Fried Corn with Green Chile (page 443).

TURKEY WITH LEMON AND CAPERS

SERVES 8

This is very much like my recipe in an earlier book for Chicken Piccata, but in this case I use sliced turkey breast. It is now readily available in most supermarkets, and since it is low in fat and there is no waste, I recommend it for regular eating. Don't overcook this and you will be very pleased with the results.

8 slices boneless turkey breast (1½ pounds total weight)	6–8 tablespoons peanut or olive oil
Salt and pepper to taste	½ cup dry white wine
½ cup flour	3 tablespoons drained capers, chopped if large
Egg wash—2 eggs whipped with 4 tablespoons water	Juice of 1 lemon
4 cups fresh bread crumbs	2 tablespoons chopped parsley
	1 lemon, sliced thin for garnish

Using a wooden or metal meat pounder, pound the meat a bit between a heavy plastic sheet (see page 18) until the slices are about double their former size. Salt and pepper each, and dust with a bit of the flour. Dip into the egg wash and then into the crumbs, which have been placed on a plate.

Fry two pieces at a time in a bit of the oil. Cook only 2 or 3 minutes on each side, as you want them lightly browned, not dry. Remove and keep warm on a platter.

Deglaze the pan (page 23) with the wine. Add the capers and lemon juice, and reduce (page 25) for a minute. Pour over the turkey and garnish with the parsley and lemon slices.

For a special addition, try adding some crushed garlic to the pan just before you deglaze it. Delicious!

Since this is a quick one, I would serve it with a nice green salad, rolls, and a dry white wine. That's enough!

POACHED TURKEY BREAST OR HIND PORTION

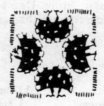

These cuts of turkey are now available frozen year-round. We are silly not to make better use of this wonderful meat.

Place the melted hindquarter or breast in enough Chicken Soup Stock (page 29, or use canned chicken broth) to cover and simmer, lid on, for about 40 minutes. Allow the meat to cool a bit in the broth and it's ready to serve. Store the meat with the broth in the refrigerator.

TURKEY IN GREEN CHILE

SERVES 4

I assume that a Southwest Indian cook would prepare a meal in this manner. It is a new way to understand turkey, and it is about time we understood the "old bird."

1 turkey hindquarter, about 2–2½ pounds	1 recipe Blended Red Chile Pods (page 61) using green chiles in place of red chiles
2 tablespoons olive oil	

In a covered Dutch oven, brown the defrosted hindquarter in the oil. Add the sauce and simmer, covered, until the meat is tender, about 1 hour.

Serve this along with Baked Pumpkin and Onions (page 192) and you will have a very nice Santa Fe meal.

TURKEY IN RED CHILE

SERVES 4

This one sounds hot, and it is . . . but not in terms of spice power. The dish is amazingly mild and very flavorful. This would be great in any season of the year.

1 turkey hindquarter, about 2–2½ pounds	2 cups Blended Red Chile Pods (page 61)
2 tablespoons olive oil	

Brown the defrosted hindquarter in the oil, in a Dutch oven. Add the sauce and simmer, covered, until tender, about 1 hour.

I like Rice with Cheese and Onions (page 448) with this dish. A light salad and very heavy, dry red wine would complete a nice menu.

TURKEY WITH MUSHROOMS AND MARSALA

You are probably just as good as I am at thinking up ways to use leftovers, but I really do like this simple but flavorful solution to using turkey "again."

Mushrooms, sliced	Gravy
Butter or olive oil for	Marsala wine to taste
sautéing	Cooked turkey

Sauté the mushrooms in butter or olive oil. Cook them just until they begin to brown. You need a hot pan for this.

Add a bit of gravy and the Marsala to taste. You can use either sweet or dry wine, according to your family's preference. Add the leftover turkey and heat. This is good over toast, rice, noodles, fingers, and so on.

TURKEY WITH RED PASTA SAUCE

Try this: Chop up some Poached Turkey (page 288) and simmer for a few minutes in your favorite red pasta sauce. Serve over pasta for an unusual treat.

A green salad and very crunchy Italian rolls will complete a nice menu.

WAFFLES

Now, be patient with me and I will get around to the reason for my including waffles in an all-American cookbook.

It is hard to tell where waffles actually began. France has been making them for a long time, and so have Holland and Germany. Waffles are mentioned in twelfth-century French ballads (the French will sing about anything!) and the original word for waffle iron, *fer à gaufres,* appeared in print in 1433. But, while the history goes back a long way, these *gaufres,* as they were called, were probably much closer to the thin waffled cookie that we know today than to the thick and yummy waffle that we celebrate here in America.

One theory about their background, and I do love this one, concerns a Crusader who returned from the Holy Wars and entered his house, still wearing his cross-meshed foil and armor. He greeted his wife and sat down, terribly tired, but he sat on a freshly made pancake. The waffled pattern given the pancake thus . . . oh, never mind. You know the rest of the story. Boy, the research that I go through when I do a recipe for you!

Now the American part. Waffles were known in England and therefore to the American Pilgrims. But it is Thomas Jefferson who is given the credit for bringing a waffle iron back from Europe and he was the first one to serve waffles at a formal waffle party. (No, it was not an electric waffle iron.) "Waffle parties" became popular in the latter part of the 1700s due, I am sure, to Tom's enthusiasm. By the 1800s vendors on city streets were selling waffles that were covered with butter and molasses or maple syrup.

The old waffle irons had to be heated on the top of the wood stove. When the electric waffle iron was invented, early in the 1900s, waffles became very popular not only as a breakfast food but as a Sunday night supper dish. My mother used to tickle us with waffles with fresh strawberries on Sunday evenings when I was

292

a child. Now catch this one. In Baltimore kidney stew served on waffles is a traditional Sunday evening specialty. I want to try that one too.

MOM'S BASIC WAFFLE BATTER

MAKES 4–5 WAFFLES

We would often have waffles for dinner when I was a child. I suppose you have the same story. They were crispy and delicious. Once in a while we would have fresh strawberries on top, or perhaps freshly picked wild mountain blackberries. I have the recipe that Mom used to use but mine were never quite so crisp and wonderful. I finally figured out what was wrong. Mom always used an old-fashioned electric waffle iron, the kind to which the first waffle *always* stuck. It never failed. Now we have a Teflon-coated waffle iron and nothing sticks . . . and the waffles are always soggy. If you can, find an old waffle iron at a garage sale and clean it up. Spray it with Pam and you will have no problem . . . and the waffles will crunch. My mother bought a new waffle iron a few years ago and she has been most unhappy with it. I found her an old one the other day at a junk shop in Chicago. I hauled it home on the plane and presented it to her. She feels better and the waffles are crunchy again.

1¾ cups all-purpose flour	4 tablespoons melted butter or oil
2 teaspoons baking powder	1½ cups milk
½ teaspoon salt	3 egg whites, beaten until stiff
1 tablespoon sugar	
3 egg yolks, beaten	

Mix the dry ingredients together. I use my electric mixer for this. Mix the egg yolks, melted butter or oil, and milk together and blend into the dry mixture. Do not overmix. Fold in, most gently, the beaten egg whites.

NOTE: My frugal mother would often use sour milk in this recipe. In that case she would add a bit of baking soda, perhaps 1 teaspoon.

CHOCOLATE WAFFLES

Blend a bit of chocolate syrup into the basic batter and enjoy a nice change. You must use Pam spray for this one as the batter will be very rich and a bit sticky.

PEANUT-BUTTER WAFFLES

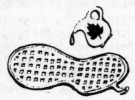

Using a fork, stir 4 tablespoons of hot tap water into a glass that contains 4 tablespoons of creamy peanut butter. Stir into the basic batter and call the kids!

BANANA WAFFLES

Mom used to buy old brown and overripe bananas at the market and smash them up for banana waffles. I just realized that I have not tasted those for years . . . and I think I'm going to go heat up the waffle iron.

CORNMEAL WAFFLES

This one is a bit crunchy and very American. Add ½ cup cornmeal to the batter and go to it with the waffle iron. These have always been popular in New England.

BACON WAFFLES

I am sure that you have tried these before, but just in case I shall suggest a favorite of my sons, Channing and Jason.

Fry the bacon first and then place a slice or two on top of the batter when you put it in the iron. The boys think I thought that up . . . and I have never had the nerve to tell them the truth.

CLAM WAFFLES

This is another from my childhood. During World War II my mother was very clever at stretching the food dollar. In this case one 6½-ounce can of minced clams was drained and added to the basic batter. That is the flavor of the Pacific Northwest.

BELGIAN WAFFLES

MAKES 4 WAFFLES

These became popular during the World's Fair in Seattle in 1962 and again in New York in 1964.

For this old classic you need a special waffle iron, the Belgian Waffle Maker. The Nordic Ware people have good ones on the market, either stovetop or electric. This recipe is from their collection.

4 eggs, separated	1 cup flour
½ teaspoon vanilla	½ teaspoon salt
3 tablespoons butter, melted	1 cup milk

Beat egg yolks until very light. Add vanilla and butter. Combine flour and salt and add with milk to egg mixture. Beat well. Beat egg whites until stiff and very gently fold into batter.

Bake in a Belgian waffle iron. I use Pam spray to prevent sticking.

These are often served with strawberries and powdered sugar. An unusual and very rich treat.

GAUFRETTE

MAKES ABOUT 24 *GAUFRETTES*

This is probably the oldest form of the waffle that we can find today. It is actually a thin wafer affair, covered with a light waffle pattern. The original irons came from France. Nordic Ware used to make such an iron, and I have one. They are great fun to use but the market will be the market. Nordic stopped making them due to lack of demand. I hope that this effort will get them back in action. The recipe is from Nordic as well.

2 egg whites
¾ cup confectioners' sugar
¼ teaspoon vanilla
⅛ teaspoon salt
½ cup flour
4 tablespoons butter, melted and cooled

Beat the egg whites until stiff. Sift in the confectioners' sugar, folding in very gently. Add the vanilla and salt, and then sift in the flour, again folding in gently. Finally, fold in the melted and cooled butter.

Place the iron on top of a gas flame at medium heat. Put one teaspoon of batter on the heated iron and turn the iron two or three times on top of the burner until the wafer is golden brown. It takes a little practice to get these going but they are delicious and it is worth the effort.

KRUM KAKER

MAKES 3 DOZEN *KRUM KAKER*

This is a Norwegian waffle cookie and I have watched my mother make these each Christmas for as long as I can remember. The irons, which sit on the top of the burner, can be found in any Scandinavian gift shop. Be sure to buy the wooden cone for rolling them too.

3 eggs	¾ cup flour plus 2
¾ cup sugar	tablespoons
½ cup butter, melted	¼ cup potato flour*
and cooled	1 teaspoon ground
1 tablespoon brandy	cardamom seed

Beat the eggs and stir in the sugar. Add the remaining ingredients and beat until smooth.

Chill for ½ hour before using.

Place the iron on top of a gas flame at medium heat. Put a tablespoon or so of batter on the hot iron and turn two or three times over the stove until the *krum kaker* is golden brown. It is then removed from the iron and rolled on a wooden cone. When cool you will understand why it is called "crumb cookie" in Norwegian.

The cones are filled with whipped cream just before serving.

*Available in most gourmet shops and Scandinavian food stores

PIZZELLE

MAKES 36 *PIZZELLE*

This is the Italian version of the waffle, and the Italian immigrants brought their irons with them from the old country. They are rolled much like the Krum Kaker and filled with flavored whipped cream or sweet Ricotta-cheese (sweeten 1 cup Ricotta with ¼ cup powdered sugar) fillings. You can buy an electric iron from the Vitantonio Company. This is their delicious recipe as well.

6 eggs	2 tablespoons vanilla
1½ cups sugar	or anise extract
1 cup margarine,	3½ cups flour
melted (Do not	4 teaspoons baking
use more than 1	powder
cup.)	

Beat the eggs and sugar together until light and smooth. Add the margarine and vanilla. Sift in the flour and baking powder and mix until smooth.

These are cooked on top of the stove in the same way as the Krum Kaker or Gaufrette. They are usually served flat with powdered sugar on top.

GINNY'S ORANGE WAFFLES

My friend Ginny Miller in Tacoma has become a sort of cooking chum through the years. I first met her because she is married to my doctor. She has given me several recipes and I usually have the nerve to print them for you.

While on tour with my last cookbook, the one on cooking with wine, I told a reporter, "I put wine in everything but waffles." Ginny heard about this remark and called me. "You clown, why don't you put wine in waffles?" said she with her usual tact and charm. She offered me the following recipe. It is delicious.

Add a few tablespoons of Cointreau or orange liqueur to the basic waffle batter. Serve the waffles with whipped cream into which you have grated orange peel. Such a breakfast. And this is my doctor's wife!

AMERICAN BREAKFASTS

I am told, by people who claim to know, that breakfast is the most important meal of the day. They talk about energy, sustenance, that sort of thing. But most of us eat the same thing every morning . . . and that is not very good for us. Fried eggs and bacon get to be a bit too much if you have them regularly. There are so many other possibilities for that first meal of the day. There is no reason to repeat yourself in the kitchen each morning, and it is such an important meal that I think we should have fun with it.

In addition to the early American dishes in this section, I think you should also consider the following:

Whole-grain breads
Fried Cornmeal Mush (page 429)
Hominy and Eggs (page 439)
Creamed Hominy on Toast (page 439)
Rice with milk and cinnamon (page 450)
Mimosa cocktail of orange juice and champagne
Scrapple (page 100)
Corn Bread (page 430) crumbled with hot milk
Corn Fritters, Pan-Fried (page 432)
Sourdough Pancakes (page 461)
Steamed Rice (page 447) with milk, sugar, and
    cinnamon
Peanut-Butter Waffles or Pancakes (page 260)
Clam Pancakes (page 421)
Waffles (page 291)
Pan-Fried Apple Slices with Maple Syrup (page 185)
Raisin Scones (page 468)
Monticello Muffins (page 123)
Stewed Pretzels (page 99)
Cranberry Cheddar Sandwich (page 202)
Fried Creamed Salt Pork (page 477)
Hot Chocolate Drink to Die For (page 340)
Shaker Daily Loaf (page 155)

There now. That should get you started. We have very little time left in this world for boredom, very little time left, indeed.

BISCUITS AND GRAVY

SERVES 4

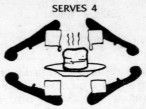

To many people in this country this old southern breakfast favorite sounds like something cheap or inferior to a real breakfast of bacon and eggs. It actually has roots in England and was a common meal from very early times in America.

I have tasted biscuits and gravy all over the country, and the meals have ranged from simply inedible to wonderful. St. Louis makes great biscuits and gravy. Atlanta can do it too. Florida? Forget about it.

The secret to good gravy is the sausage. Use a quality pork sausage that is low in fat and not filled with heavy seasoning and salt. The dish takes very few minutes to make and it just makes the day.

½ pound pork
    breakfast sausage
    (bulk)
2 tablespoons
    chopped yellow
    onions
3 tablespoons flour

2 cups hot milk
Salt and pepper to
    taste
1 batch of Harriet's
    Southern Biscuits
    (page 464)

This dish is made in a frying pan. Heat the pan and fry the sausage and onion until the sausage is brown and the onion clear. Drain off all grease except for 2 tablespoons. Stir in the flour and cook for just a minute. Add the hot milk. I heat mine in the microwave. Stir constantly until the mixture thickens and then season with salt and pepper. I doubt that you will need much salt, but pepper will be a must.

Serve over warm opened biscuits.

GRITS

We are not talking about a food product here so much as we are talking about a memory, a life-style, a childhood, a commitment, a dish that was popular during the worst times in the history of the South. When there was little else to eat one could always have grits. Following the War Between the States everyone ate grits— poor white trash, landowners, black farmhands. Now it is eaten not because one has to but because one can choose to eat this old recipe left over from difficult times.

I can just hear you grits lovers yelling that I am being unfair. No, the truth of the matter is that I love grits. When I was in graduate school studying theology, the inevitable would happen each evening. Several of us could take only so many hours of studying, so we would run out to eat an extra meal about ten or eleven in the evening. We found a place in Chatham, New Jersey, called Mother's, though Mother was a Greek fellow who bore no resemblance to my mother. None at all. He would cook us fried eggs and potatoes for very little money, and we went often. One night Carrol, a big lad from the South, yelled, "I can't stand it any longer. These eggs are perfect but there are no grits." I did not know what grits were, so he wrote to his mother and she shipped us a box. Since we had no kitchen we took them to our Greek "Mother" and Carrol taught him how they were to be prepared. At last we sat down to grits and eggs. Carrol smiled and said, "That's better!" I then realized that he was not hungry for grits as much as he was lonely for home. That's what grits are for.

Buy a box in the supermarket and cook according to the instructions on the box. You cook them just like cream of wheat. A puddle of grits is placed on the plate and topped with butter and black pepper. Fried eggs and toast go on the side. The egg yolk must run into the grits. . . . Oh, I think I'll go call Carrol.

GRITS WITH CHEESE

SERVES 4

This is another treat from my Texas cook, Harriet Fields. You will know that it is Harriet's recipe because she puts Tabasco in it . . . for breakfast! Harriet puts Tabasco and hot green peppers in everything, so this dish should not strike us as strange. It is unusually good and she serves it as a side dish at dinner as well as at breakfast.

1 cup grits	Salt and freshly
½ cup milk	ground black pepper
1 egg, beaten	to taste
½ pound Cheddar cheese, coarsely grated	Tabasco to taste

Cook the grits according to the directions on the package. Blend the milk and egg together and stir into the grits. Add remaining ingredients. Be careful with the salt as the cheese makes it a bit salty to start with.

Pour into a greased 8 × 8-inch glass baking dish and bake at 375° for 45 minutes, stirring once after the first 30 minutes.

CREAMED CHIPPED BEEF ON TOAST

SERVES 4 FOR BREAKFAST

This is actually a very popular dish made so by the Pennsylvania Dutch. It was immortalized by the U.S. Army, the troops having thought up an unprintable name that is now abbreviated and actually used on every truck-stop breakfast-joint menu in the country. I love it, if prepared properly. It makes for a great change at breakfast time, regardless of your memories of bad versions of this dish while in the army. I happen to know that there are a lot of closet S.O.S. eaters out there!

3 tablespoons butter	¼ teaspoon paprika
3 tablespoons peeled and chopped yellow onion	Black pepper, freshly ground, to taste
3 tablespoons flour	Tabasco (optional)
2 cups hot milk	1 tablespoon dry sherry
½ pound dried chipped beef	

In a heavy saucepan melt the butter and sauté the yellow onion until clear. Stir in the flour with a whisk and then the hot milk, stirring all the time until the mixture thickens. I heat my milk in a microwave. When the mixture is thick, add the remaining ingredients and heat for a moment. Serve over toast. Calm down, it is very good!

HINT: **On Premade Cream Sauce.**
Make a batch of this cream sauce, omitting the chipped beef, and keep it in your refrigerator. It will heat up beautifully in the microwave in no time. Morning is tough enough as it is.

EGGS IN FRIED BREAD

SERVES 1

One of the worst breakfasts I have ever eaten in my life was at the Salvation Army Hostel in Dublin, Ireland. I was a student and we traveled on very little money. The hostel offered "Rasher and Fried Bread." (Rasher is bacon.) It sounded good and it was cheap. Lord, it should have been. The bread was fried in old bacon fat that was so rancid we almost died.

Fried bread makes a delicious breakfast. When the boys were little I would serve them the following dish and we could create quite a game at the breakfast table. Channing called the dish "Eggs Looking at You." I hope your father made it for you when you were little.

> **2 slices whole-wheat toast**
> **Butter**
> **2 eggs**

Cut a hole about 2 inches in diameter in the center of each slice of bread. Butter the bread on both sides and pan-fry gently until brown on both sides. Crack an egg into each hole and cover the pan until the eggs are set.

ENGLISH MUFFINS WITH CHEESE SAUCE

SERVES 2

This is a favorite breakfast at our house. It does not take long to prepare and it is delicious as well as filling. Its background is the old Welsh rarebit, of course.

1 cup milk	Worcestershire sauce to taste
½ cup sharp Cheddar cheese, coarsely grated	Salt to taste
1½ tablespoons *each* butter and flour cooked together to form a roux (page 25)	Black pepper, freshly ground, to taste
	2 teaspoons dry sherry
	Tabasco to taste
	2 English muffins, split and toasted

Heat the milk in a small saucepan. Stir in the cheese and thicken with the roux. The roux can be made in the microwave. Stir the milk and cheese mixture over medium heat until it is thick. Add remaining seasonings to taste.

Serve on the toasted English muffins.

BACON ON TOAST WITH CREAM SAUCE

This one is from New Hampshire. My lady friends there told me that they had this for breakfast often as little girls. While I don't want you eating bacon every morning, there is something to be said for a few slices of old-fashioned cured New England bacon. A lot can be said!

Pan-fried or microwaved bacon	Cream sauce (use the recipe for Creamed Chipped Beef [page 303], omitting the chipped beef)
Toast	

The cream sauce can be made a day or two ahead and then warmed in the microwave in no time.

Place the bacon on the toast and top with cream sauce. Then pour black coffee and open the windows so that you can smell the fresh New Hampshire air. (This works best if you are in New Hampshire!)

BRAN MUFFINS THE FRUGAL WAY

MAKES 6 DOZEN MUFFINS

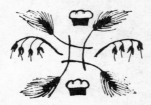

This is a great recipe because it is delicious, healthy, and there is no waste. None. You can keep it covered in the refrigerator for up to 6 weeks! That means you can get up in the morning and while you are getting cleaned up you can be baking a batch of muffins for breakfast. Takes no time at all! This recipe makes 6 dozen muffins, so you will be set for a while.

5 teaspoons baking soda	4 cups All-Bran
1 cup butter	2 cups 40 percent bran flakes
2 cups sugar	5 cups all-purpose flour
4 eggs	1 quart buttermilk

Dissolve the baking soda in 2 cups boiling water (microwave). Set aside to cool.

With your electric mixer cream the butter and the sugar and beat in the eggs. Remove bowl from machine and stir in, by hand, the remaining ingredients. Finally, stir in the soda water.

Keep the batter covered in the refrigerator for weeks. Bake in muffin pans in a 375° oven for 30 minutes.

You will love these!

Pot Pies

I was discussing this section of recipes with Karen Arena, a dear friend who has traveled with me a great deal. She told me that Mario, her husband, just loves pot pies. When I asked her what kind she makes for him, she replied, "What do you mean, 'make'? I defrost pies for him!" These recipes are for poor Mario.

The background of this wonderful American dish is English, of course. The English have been making pastries and pies for hundreds of years, and the "four and twenty blackbirds, baked in a pie" of nursery-rhyme fame actually did exist. The top piecrust was baked and then placed on top of a large casserole containing live birds. There was a spring mechanism in the top crust that could be released as the pie was "set before the King. When the pie was opened the birds began to sing." It must have been a mess!

The English practice of making meat pies, called "savory" rather than sweet, was brought to the colonies. The Americans, however, used a much deeper dish and called the creation a "Pot Pie." It was generally filled with leftover chicken gizzards, hearts, etc., and then highly seasoned and covered with a pastry top. The term "pot pie" first appeared in print in this country in 1792, and the dish held us together through difficult financial times. Then it happened. In 1951 the Swanson company offered the first frozen fully prepared entrée . . . the chicken pot pie. No pot, just an aluminum-foil pie plate, and the frozen-food business was under way. It is a shame to admit that most Americans stopped making homey pot pies when the frozen ones became available.

The following recipes will help you get started with dishes that I know your family will appreciate. Remember, almost anything can go into a pot pie so it is a very frugal way to cook.

BASIC EASY CRUST

MAKES ENOUGH FOR 4–5 INDIVIDUAL POT PIES

This is a very easy yet flaky piecrust. I use a pastry blender (page 17), for me an absolute must. Some people get away with blending with a fork, but I rarely have any luck doing this. In the old days lard was used instead of the lighter shortenings that we have now. Lard does make a delicious crust, but it is really hard on the old heart. I suggest the following:

3 cups all-purpose flour	1 egg
1 teaspoon salt	1 tablespoon white vinegar
½ cup margarine	3–4 tablespoons ice water
½ cup Crisco	

In a medium-size bowl stir the flour and salt together. Cut in the shortenings using a pastry blender. Keep working the flour and shortening until the mixture is rather grainy, like coarse cornmeal. Mix the egg and vinegar together and, using a wooden fork, stir the mixture into the flour. Add enough ice water so that the dough barely holds together. Place on a marble pastry board or a plastic countertop and knead for just a few turns, enough so that the dough holds together and becomes rollable.

I roll my dough out on a piece of waxed paper. It is easy to handle that way. If you have a marble rolling pin this will be easy. If you use a wooden one be sure to dust a teaspoon of flour on it a couple of times when you are rolling the dough.

NOTE: If you wish to use this recipe for a fruit or sweet pie simply stir in 1 tablespoon of sugar along with the flour and salt. This recipe will make enough dough for one 9-inch pie with two crusts, top and bottom.

PORK, HAM, AND SAUSAGE PIE

SERVES 4

Why, this sounds just like an effort to use up leftover meats! Exactly. That is the point of the pot-pie concept, and it always has been. In the old days you would have these meats sort of sitting around, but in our time we will probably have to start from scratch. If you have a leftover pork roast go ahead and use it and avoid cooking fresh pork.

1½ pounds boneless pork roast
2 whole bay leaves
½ teaspoon whole sage leaves, rubbed
Salt and black pepper to taste
½ pound ham (Buy real ham from the butcher, not canned or boiled ham. You will need one good slice. Remove the round bone.)
½ pound bulk breakfast sausage

1 yellow onion, peeled and sliced
3 tablespoons chopped fresh parsley
¼ teaspoon whole sage leaves, rubbed
¼ teaspoon savory
Salt and pepper to taste
3 tablespoons *each* butter and flour cooked together to form a roux (page 25)
1 batch Basic Easy Crust (page 311)

Place the pork in a small saucepan just big enough to hold it and add enough water to come halfway up the side of the roast. Add the bay leaves, sage, and salt and pepper. Cover and simmer for 1 hour. Remove the pork from the broth, reserving the broth, and allow the meat to cool. Cut it into ½-inch cubes.

Cut the ham into ½-inch cubes. Roll the sausage into small balls ½ inch in diameter. Brown the sausage balls in a frying pan and set aside. In the same frying pan sauté the yellow onion until lightly browned.

Put 1½ cups of the pork broth into a saucepan and bring to a simmer. Add the remaining seasonings and thicken with the roux. Mix the gravy with the meats and fill the pies. Make 1 large pie or 4 smaller individual pies. Cover with the easy crust and bake at 375° for 45 minutes, or until the crust is golden brown.

Start your meal with a hearty soup, such as Corn Chowder with Shrimp (page 437), and then move on to this unusual American pie.

STEAK AND KIDNEY PIE

SERVES 4

This is an old English classic that remained popular with the colonists. Before you reject this recipe because it contains kidney, I hope you will calm down and at least taste a good steak and kidney pie. I love this dish and our family is fond of it as well. I have never served it to anyone who was not surprised at how good it is. Even my television crew in Chicago was taken by this one. That should prove it!

3 slices bacon, cut into large dice

1½ pounds chuck steak, well trimmed, cut into ½-inch dice

About 1½ cups Basic Brown Soup Stock (page 28) or canned beef broth

½ cup Madeira wine

2 cloves garlic, crushed

2 veal or lamb kidneys, cleaned of inner fat and cut into ½-inch cubes

2 tablespoons chopped yellow onions

3 tablespoons chopped parsley

1 teaspoon whole thyme leaves, or to taste

¼ – ½ teaspoon whole sage leaves, rubbed, or to taste

Salt and black pepper to taste (I like lots of black pepper in this dish.)

3 tablespoons *each* butter and flour cooked together to form a roux (page 25)

1 batch Basic Easy Crust (page 311)

Heat a heavy black-iron kettle or Dutch oven and lightly brown the bacon. Turn up the heat and brown the beef cubes well. Add enough beef stock to barely cover and put a lid on the pot. Simmer the meat until tender, about ½ hour.

Add the remaining ingredients except the roux. Continue cooking for another 15 minutes. Thicken the sauce with the roux.

Roll out the crust and make one large pot pie or 4 small individual pot pies.

Bake 45 minutes at 375° or until the crust is brown and flaky.

A good dry wine and a big salad is about all you need to complete this fine English meal.

STEAK AND MUSHROOM PIE

SERVES 4

This one is for the less adventuresome, but it is delicious even without the kidney.

Substitute sautéed mushrooms for the kidneys in the previous recipe for Steak and Kidney Pie. Use about 1 pound of fresh mushrooms and sauté them in a hot pan with a little butter. Omit the kidneys from the recipe and proceed as above. Add the mushrooms just after you thicken the sauce with the roux.

COLD PORK PIE

SERVES 4–5

I am going to tell you a story about this one. Something new, eh? In 1960, when I was a sophomore in college, a dear friend and I traveled for several months in Europe. We ate very well on the Continent, even on student budgets, but when we arrived in Great Britain things changed. The food was not very good at the time and we found ourselves living on cold pork pies purchased in English delicatessens. We had eaten them for a solid week when we arrived in Wales. A charming Welshwoman invited us home for a "typical Welsh meal." We were so excited at the prospect of something new and home-cooked. Need I go on with this story? You guessed it. A cold pork pie.

I have added a bit of flavor to this dish that was *not* to be found in the Welsh version, nor is this cooked in the traditional Welsh manner. It is much more typical of early-American cooking.

1½ pounds fresh
   coarsely ground
   lean pork (best to
   grind your own)
1 yellow onion, peeled
   and chopped
2 eggs, beaten
¼ teaspoon cayenne
   pepper
¼ teaspoon sage
2 tablespoons
   Worcestershire
   sauce
Salt and black
   pepper to taste
1 batch Basic Easy
   Crust (page 311)

Mix all of the above together, except the crust, and place in an 8-inch deep-dish pie plate. Bake, covered, at 375° for ½ hour. Remove from oven and pour off the accumulated fat. Cover with the crust topping and return to the oven for 45 minutes, or until the crust is golden brown and flaky.

Allow to cool completely before serving.

This is great for a first course, a midnight snack, or a luncheon dish.

CHICKEN POT PIE WITH ONIONS AND SALT PORK

SERVES 4–5

The addition of salt pork to this dish certainly marks it as an old meal from the colonies. The combination sounds a bit strange to us, but salt pork was a common flavoring in the old days. People literally lived on salt pork and beans, thus the origin of the line about "scraping the bottom of the barrel." It was the salt-pork barrel, and when you touched bottom you were in serious trouble.

This is a very enjoyable dish and I have blanched the salt pork so that some of the saltiness and fattiness have been removed.

1 **chicken, cooked and deboned**

1 **cup baby onions**

2 **cups Chicken Soup Stock (page 29) or canned chicken broth *or* make broth from the bones**

2 **tablespoons *each* butter and flour cooked together to form a roux (page 25)**

½ **teaspoon paprika**

2 **tablespoons chopped fresh parsley**

1 **batch Basic Easy Crust (page 311)**

½ **pound salt pork Salt and pepper to taste (Careful with the salt! The salt pork should do it.)**

Cook and debone the chicken as in the previous recipe. Make stock if you wish just as above.

Parboil the onions for 5 minutes and then cool in cold water. Peel the onions and set aside.

Thicken the stock with the roux, as above. Add the paprika and parsley, along with the salt and pepper.

Cut the salt pork into ¼-inch dice. Quickly blanch in boiling water and then drain and sauté in a small frying pan until the pork begins to brown. Drain the fat from the pan.

Mix the boneless chicken, onions, and sauce together. Place in a 2½-quart casserole or soufflé dish and top with the diced salt pork. Roll out the crust and place on top.

Bake in a 375° oven for 45 minutes.

Add a good corn dish, such as Fried Corn with Green Chile (page 443), along with a green salad, and you will have full menu.

CHICKEN PIE WITH BISCUIT TOPPING

SERVES 5–6

This is an oldie and a goodie. The biscuit topping puffs up and provides you with a whole meal in a wonderful form. Yes, if you don't want to make your own biscuit dough you can use good old Bisquick.

1 whole chicken, 3–3½ pounds
1 bay leaf
¼ teaspoon thyme
Butter or olive oil for pan-frying
½ yellow onion, peeled and chopped
3 stalks celery, chopped
2 carrots, sliced
2 tablespoons chopped parsley
2 cups Chicken Soup Stock (page 29) or canned chicken broth or make broth from the bones as directed below

4 tablespoons *each* butter and flour cooked together to form a roux (page 25)
½ pound mushrooms, sliced and lightly sautéed in butter or olive oil
Salt and pepper to taste
2 hard-boiled eggs, sliced
1 batch Harriet's Southern Biscuit dough (page 464)

Place the chicken in a 2-quart saucepan and add enough water to barely cover. Bring to a boil and then turn down the heat to a simmer. Cover and simmer for ½ hour. Allow the chicken to cool in the liquid. Take the chicken from the pot, reserving the liquid, and remove the skin and bones. Cut the meat into ½-inch cubes, cover, and set aside. You can do this the day before if you wish.

Place the bones in the cooking liquid and add the dry herbs. Cover and simmer for 1 hour. This will provide you with the cooking broth.

Heat a frying pan and add a bit of butter or oil. Sauté the onion, celery, and carrots until they just begin to brown.

Place the vegetables in a saucepan, along with the parsley, and add 2 cups of chicken stock. Prepare the roux and bring the vegetables and stock to a simmer. Thicken with the roux. Blend the sauce with the chicken meat and sautéed mushrooms. Season with salt and pepper and place in a deep baking dish. A 2-quart soufflé dish should do nicely. Top the mixture with the hard-boiled egg slices.

Roll out enough biscuit dough to make a lid for the pie that is ¼-inch thick, unbaked.

Bake at 425° for 20 minutes, or until the top is high and lightly browned.

CLAM AND CHICKEN PIE

SERVES 4

Old cookbooks offer strange combinations. At least they seem strange in terms of today's eating habits. This dish was not considered particularly off the normal track in earlier days. I have tried it and find it to be delicious. There is nothing wrong with mixing seafood with chicken. And besides, I need no excuse for putting clams in anything.

1 whole chicken, 3–3½ pounds
½ cup Chicken Soup Stock (page 29) or canned chicken broth
½ cup cream, half-and-half, or milk
2 tablespoons *each* butter and flour cooked together to form a roux (page 25)

1 teaspoon salt
Dash of cayenne pepper
1 cup chopped celery
2 cans (6½ ounces each) Gorton's diced clams, drained
2 hard-boiled eggs, sliced
1 batch Basic Easy Crust (page 311)

Cook the chicken according to the recipe for Chicken Pie with Biscuit Topping on page 318. Remove skin and debone the chicken. Make your own broth if you wish.

Heat the cream or milk along with the chicken stock. Thicken with the roux as in the Chicken and Biscuit Topping recipe. Add the salt, cayenne, and celery, and bring to a simmer. Add the chicken and drained clams. Place in a baking dish just large enough to hold everything and top with the sliced eggs. Roll out the crust and cover the pie. Bake at 375° for 45 minutes, or until the crust is golden brown and flaky.

Serve along with Cabbage and Salt Pork (page 114), and you will have a typical Colonial meal.

ADDITIONAL POT PIE POSSIBILITIES After reading through these recipes you can easily design the following possible pot pies for yourself.

Chicken, Sausage, and Mushroom Pie
Rabbit Pie
Pigeon Pie
Squirrel Pie (still popular in the South)
Quail Pie
Chicken Curry Pie
Beef Curry Pie
Ham, Mushrooms, Tomatoes, and Pepperoni in
  Light Cream Sauce Pie
Vegetable Pie
Sausage, Onion, and Mushroom Pie
Lamb and Artichoke Stew Pie

APPLES

No, apples are not strictly American, but the phrase "as American as apple pie" is. The question is, why?

Apples go back thousands of years, with varieties coming from all over Asia and the Middle East. The Romans took apples with them when on conquests, so the seeds were spread throughout Western Europe, and by the time Columbus sailed for the New World, apples were the most important cultivated crop in most of Europe.

American apple history begins with the Pilgrims bringing seeds with them from England in 1620. (You wondered how I was going to "Americanize" the apple, didn't you?) The Jamestown settlers also listed apple seeds among the provisions that they brought to the colony. By 1741, New England was exporting apples to the West Indies. The American apple industry was under way.

As people began moving west in America, so did the apple. The seeds were carefully planted along the trails so that those who came behind might find refreshment. Yes, Virginia, there really was a Johnny Appleseed. He was one of those persons moving west, and he was a preacher, a follower of Swedenborg. Johnny's mission was to see that the Middle West had apple trees. He gathered seeds at the cider presses in western Pennsylvania and then took off by canoe to plant his trees. He began his journey in 1800, barefoot and actually wearing a saucepan for a hat, armed with apple seeds and the message of the good Swedenborg people. He started nurseries on more than ten thousand square miles of the American frontier. He made it out to Fort Wayne, Indiana, and had to stop his wonderful work. He died in 1845 at the age of seventy-one. Now, next time you make an apple pie for your children, be sure that they thank both God and Johnny Appleseed!

Apples came to my state, Washington, in the spring of 1827. The seeds were planted at Fort Vancouver and now Washington is responsible for 50 percent of all apples sold fresh in America. We are the leading apple-producing state, with New York and New Jersey running next.

The number of varieties of apples that we now have in this country is amazing. Many came about by selective cutting, some by crossbreeding, but most by grafting. The five varieties that you will see throughout American supermarkets are the McIntosh, Red Delicious, Golden Delicious, Jonathan, and Rome Beauty. For cooking I love the Granny Smith.

You will note that I do not have a recipe for apple pie in this section. I really want you to think of other things to do with this fruit that has been with us since the moment the first European explorers hit the New World.

HINT: **To Peel and Core Apples in a Hurry.**
There is a wonderful machine on the market that will actually peel an apple in nothing flat. It will also slice and core it. It is distributed by Norpro and is explained on page 16.

FRIED APPLES WITH CURRY

SERVES 5–6 AS A RELISH

This is a great side dish or relish for any kind of meat course. The flavor is mild but sweet, and the curry sets the natural sugar of the apples.

4 apples (Granny Smith are best, but any can do.)	3 tablespoons butter
	1 tablespoon curry powder
1 medium yellow onion, peeled and sliced thin	Salt and pepper to taste

Core and wedge the apples with an apple/pear corer-cutter (page 16), or do the same by hand. Heat a frying pan and sauté the onions with the butter until they are clear. Add the apples and sauté until the apples are not quite tender. Add the seasonings and toss.

APPLE BUTTER STEAK

SERVES 7

I know that this sounds like I'm pushing it, but one of my former cooks, Scott, came running over with this recipe and told me I had to try it. I think he developed it when he came home one night and found little in the pantry except apple butter. What do you think could have caused him to come up with such a recipe? Interesting that he always has soy, sherry, and fresh ginger on hand. It is really quite good.

1 flank steak, about 1½ pounds	2 tablespoons dry sherry
4 tablespoons apple butter	¼ teaspoon freshly grated ginger
2 tablespoons light soy sauce	4 green onions, chopped

Place the steak on a plate. Mix the remaining ingredients together and rub 2 tablespoons onto the steak, both sides. Allow to marinate for ½ hour and then broil on an oven rack to your liking. I enjoy mine a bit rare. Turn once. Slice the steak across the grain of the meat and place the pieces in an oven-proof dish. Pour the remaining sauce on top of the meat and place under the broiler for just a few moments, thus allowing it to glaze a bit.

This is delicious served with Rice with Cheese and Onions (page 448).

HINT: **On Keeping Cut Apples From Turning Brown**

Prevent this problem by cutting the apples and immediately placing them in salt water or water in which you have placed a bit of lemon juice. The problem of browning is gone. This also works for pears.

APPLE AND CABBAGE

SERVES 6–8 AS A VEGETABLE DISH

This is more typical of Pennsylvania Dutch cooking than anything else. The apples add a sweetness to the harsh taste of that old lifesaver, cabbage. This dish works well as an accompaniment to most meals.

3 slices bacon, diced
1 large yellow onion, peeled and sliced
2 heads cabbage, cored and sliced as for sauerkraut
3 Granny Smith or other cooking apples, cored and sliced

½ teaspoon whole caraway seeds
½ cup dry white wine
Salt and freshly ground black pepper to taste

Heat a large Dutch oven and sauté the bacon until clear. Add the onions and sauté until they barely begin to brown. Add the remaining ingredients and cook, covered, stirring often, until all is tender.

APPLE BEEF BRISKET

SERVES 8–10

Viewers send me recipes all the time. Most of the time I am very anxious to try such offerings. On occasion, though this is rare, someone will send me a list of prepared mixes that he or she blends together to get a . . . a dish of some sort. Not so with this offering. It takes a while to cook, but you can do much of the work ahead of time. It is very good.

1 beef brisket, 4–5 pounds, trimmed of fat
1 large yellow onion, peeled and quartered
2 large cloves garlic, peeled and chopped
10 cloves garlic, whole
1 jar (10 ounces) apple jelly
⅓ cup dry white wine

3 tablespoons Dijon mustard (Grey Poupon is fine.)
2 green onions, chopped
½ teaspoon salt
¾ teaspoon freshly ground black pepper
¾ teaspoon curry powder
1 cup apple juice
¼ cup chopped parsley, for garnish

Place the brisket, onion, chopped garlic, and garlic cloves in a large Dutch oven. Add water to cover and bring to a boil. Reduce heat, cover, and simmer 2½ hours, or until the brisket is tender. Drain brisket. (If you wish you can keep the brisket covered with the water and refrigerate it overnight. This will help prepare for the next day.)

In a small saucepan mix together the apple jelly, wine, mustard, green onions, salt, pepper, and curry powder. Heat until the jelly melts. (This can be done in your microwave in just minutes.)

Place brisket in a shallow roasting pan and brush

some of the jelly mixture over the top. Bake at 325°
for 45 minutes, basting 3 or 4 times with the remaining
jelly mixture.

Remove the meat to a platter to keep warm. Place
the pan on a hot burner and deglaze (page 23) with the
apple juice. Reduce (page 25) the juice for a moment
and place in a gravy boat. Serve alongside the meat.

Slice brisket and serve with parsley garnish.

Since this is a rich dish, I suggest you serve it with
Frittorta (page 391) and some Spiced Cranberries (page
204).

QUICK APPLE TART

SERVES 6

I rarely eat dessert, but I do live in one of the most
important apple-producing regions in the world. Now
and then I have to enjoy an apple dessert and this one
is easy and very tasty. It comes from our Washington
State Apple Commission.

⅓ cup butter	2 (about ¾ pound) Granny Smith apples, pared and sliced thin
¼ cup powdered sugar	
1 egg	
⅛ teaspoon salt	¼ cup sugar
1⅓ cups flour	¼ teaspoon cinnamon
2 tablespoons butter for sautéing apples	2 tablespoons orange or ginger marmalade, melted

Beat butter and sugar together until light and fluffy.
Beat in the egg and salt. Gradually stir in the flour until
a soft dough is formed. Cover tightly and refrigerate
for 30 minutes. Then roll dough on a lightly floured
surface to a 10-inch circle. Place in a 9-inch glass quiche
pan or round tart pan.

Heat a medium frying pan and add the 2 tablespoons

butter. Sauté the apples in the butter for about 5 minutes. Add the ¼ cup sugar and the cinnamon. Toss.

Arrange the apple slices in the pastry shell and bake at 375° for 15 to 20 minutes, or until the pastry is golden. Brush the apples with the marmalade and return to the oven for about 2 minutes. Remove and cool a bit before serving.

APPLE STIR-FRIED PORK

SERVES 6

Have you thought about garlic with apples? Well, the two belong together, absolutely belong together. This is a quick dish that is not terribly sweet, as you would expect, but very flavorful.

- 2 pounds pork steak, deboned and cut into ⅛-inch strips
- 2 tablespoons light soy sauce
- 2 tablespoons dry sherry
- ¼ teaspoon freshly grated ginger
- 3 tablespoons peanut oil
- 4 cloves garlic, peeled and sliced paper thin

- 1 large yellow onion, peeled and sliced
- 3 Golden Delicious apples, cored and sliced
- 1 tablespoon sesame oil
- ¼ teaspoon freshly ground black pepper
- 4 green onions, chopped, for garnish

Cut the pork steak as instructed and marinate for 15 minutes in the soy, sherry, and ginger. Heat a wok or large frying pan and add the oil and garlic. Drain the marinade from the meat and sauté the meat over very high heat until done to your liking, about 6 minutes. Remove the meat from the pan and add the onion slices. Sauté until tender and then add the apple slices. Sauté just until they begin to brown. Return the meat to the pan, add the sesame oil and pepper, and toss. Top with the green onions as a garnish. Serve immediately.

This is a whole meal if you simply add Macaroni Pie (page 130) and a green salad.

APPLE COBBLER

SERVES 6–8

We know that the apple seeds brought from England were intended for this very dish. Apple cobbler goes back to the time of the Pilgrims, and since it is so easy to make you should offer this bit of edible history to your family very soon.

3 tablespoons butter for sautéing the apples	¼ pound butter, melted (Use microwave.)
2 pounds cooking apples, cored, peeled, and sliced	1 cup flour
	2 teaspoons baking powder
	1 teaspoon salt
½ cup raisins	½ cup milk
1¼ cups sugar	Vanilla ice cream or whipped cream for topping
¼ teaspoon cinnamon	
⅛ teaspoon nutmeg	

Heat a frying pan and add the 3 tablespoons butter. Put the apples and raisins in the pan and sauté for a few minutes over medium heat until they are tender. Add ¼ cup of the sugar, and the spices. Stir and set aside.

Pour the melted butter into a 7 × 11 × 2-inch baking dish. Mix the remaining cup of sugar with the flour, baking powder, and salt. Mix well and then stir in the milk. Spread this batter on top of the butter.

Pour the apple mixture over the batter and bake in a 350° oven for about 50 minutes, or until the crust is golden brown.

Serve this warm, topped with vanilla ice cream or whipped cream.

CHOCOLATE

Americans seem to think that the sweet breakfast drink that they celebrate only in the winter is a drink from some other culture, Europe perhaps. Or those wonderful chocolates with the creamy center. Maybe France? Not so! It all began in Central America and it belongs to us. Cocoa and chocolate are American!

Cocoa and chocolate's recorded history began with Cortez and the Spanish conquistadores in 1519. They found the Aztec emperor Montezuma drinking a liquor prepared from the cacao (or cocoa) tree . . . and they called it an aphrodisiac! We think that the cacao tree actually originated in the river valleys of South America and was carried north into Mexico by the Mayans during the seventh century.

The importance that the cacao bean had for these early cultures stems from the fact that it is rich in fat and is therefore a great food source. However, the place that the bean had in legend and folklore indicates that the bean was considered a gift from the gods and was to be seen as an integral part of the culture. When the Spaniards arrived in Mexico they found that cacao was in such abundance that it was used as currency in Yucatán. During this time a rabbit cost ten beans, a pumpkin four, a live slave one hundred, and the services of a girlfriend for the night, ten.

The drink that was made from the bean in the old days is nothing like the sweet drink we know now. The original was made with a great deal of red pepper and no sugar at all. I have developed a recipe for you that might give you a hint of the original flavor. It is not the sort of thing that you are going to serve your children just before you send them off to school.

The Spanish became very fond of chocolate drink after sugar was added. They took the bean back to Spain and it was used primarily as a drink until 1828, when a Dutchman, Conrad van Houten, came up with a method of pressing the oil, or cocoa butter, from the bean, thus creating a new product. This was cocoa powder, and eventually led to a chocolate that could absorb large amounts of sugar.

In 1847 the English firm of Fry and Sons began producing "eating chocolate" and the treat soon hit the Continent. We have never recovered from those wonderful first experiments. And then in Switzerland, milk chocolate was developed by Daniel Peter and Henri Nestlé. Rodolphe Lindt brought the product to fulfillment when he produced a chocolate that would "melt in your mouth." To this day the Swiss eat more chocolates than anyone in the world, consuming about twenty-two pounds per person per year. Americans eat fourteen pounds per person.

The following set of recipes does not include instructions for chocolate cake or chocolate-chip cookies. You have enough of those. What I have done is attempt to show you other possibilities for using this wonderful flavor.

CHOCOLATL DRINK

SERVES 2

This is the correct spelling, and if the descriptions of the Cortez party are correct, then this is the drink. When the Aztecs were drinking a beverage made from the cacao tree it tasted nothing like what we know in our time. The drink that Montezuma loved, and supposedly drank by the potful, had hot pepper in it and no sugar at all. After reading some of the responses of the Europeans to the beverage, I have developed the following easy recipe. I doubt that you will be drinking this every morning but it is fun to try now and then.

2 cups Chicken Soup
    Stock (page 29)
    or canned
    chicken broth

½ teaspoon plain
    cocoa powder
    Tabasco to taste
½ teaspoon vanilla
½ teaspoon cinnamon

That's it. Heat the chicken stock and season it with the cocoa, Tabasco, vanilla, and cinnamon.

MEXICAN CHOCOLATE DRINK

For this one you must find a Mexican or Latin American grocery. Look for chocolate beverage blocks made by Ibarra. The round molded confection is made up of cocoa, sugar, ground almonds, and cinnamon. Two wedges are broken off and they are melted with milk. You then use a wooden chocolate whipper called a *molinillo* to mix the drink and put a bit of froth on the top. The mixer, the *molinillo,* goes back hundreds of years . . . but I use my food blender. Heat two wedges of chocolate for each cup of milk. When it is hot pour into the blender and whip for just a moment. My sons, Channing and Jason, are much more likely to come to the breakfast table on a cold winter morning if I threaten them with Mexican chocolate drink.

GREEN CHILE BROWNIES

Now this one is a kick! It is a cross between the pepper flavor of the cocoa drink of the Aztecs and the sweetness of chocolate that is so enjoyed in our country. It is so simple that you will laugh at me, and it is so delicious that your guests will laugh at you!

Mix two or three 4-ounce cans of Ortega-brand diced green chiles into your next batch of brownies. When I tested this (oh boy, I am going to be in trouble with you now) I used a box brownie mix. The results were just smashing. Start with 2 cans of chiles for a batch and then move it up to 3 if you wish.

COCOA BLACK-BEAN SOUP

SERVES 8–10

I want you to understand that cocoa was used in cooking long before it was loaded with vanilla and sugar. This recipe will surprise you, as the cocoa adds an interesting bit of depth to a good black-bean soup.

Chocolate freaks will not recognize this flavor, but they will love it!

1 pound dried black beans
10 cups water
1 teaspoon salt
1 large green sweet bell pepper, cored and halved
⅔ cup peanut oil or salad oil
1 large yellow onion, peeled and sliced
4 cloves garlic, peeled and minced
1 small green hot pepper, halved and seeded

3 teaspoons salt, or to taste
½ teaspoon freshly ground black pepper
1½ tablespoons plain cocoa powder
1 bay leaf
¼ teaspoon whole cumin seed
1 teaspoon sugar
2½ tablespoons red wine vinegar
2½ tablespoons olive oil

Rinse the black beans and soak overnight in the 10 cups of water, along with 1 teaspoon salt and the green bell pepper.

In a large, heavy-bottomed 6-quart soup pot, bring the beans, soaking water, and pepper to a boil. Simmer until tender, about 45 minutes. Remove the green-pepper pieces and discard.

Heat the peanut oil in a deep frying pan or heavy saucepan. Sauté the onion, garlic, and green hot pepper until soft. Remove 2½ cups of the bean broth from the pot and add it to the frying pan. Simmer this mixture for 10 minutes. Strain the onions, garlic, and hot pepper from the broth and discard them. Add the seasoned broth to the soup pot. Add salt, pepper, cocoa, bay leaf, cumin, and sugar. Bring to a boil and simmer, covered, for about 1½ hours, or until the soup thickens. You may have to add more water if too much of the liquid cooks away.

Before serving, add the vinegar and olive oil. Mix well.

COCOA RYE BREAD

MAKES 3 LOAVES

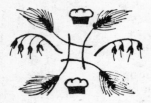

The flavor of cocoa in rye bread is so natural to me that I cannot understand why I did not try this before. I am wondering now how good a stiff shot of cocoa would be in pumpernickel. This recipe is easy and tasty and it will help change your mind about chocolate having to be sweet.

As always, you will need a good kitchen scale in order to make good bread.

2 packages quick-rising dry yeast
2½ cups tepid water (95°)
3 cups rye flour *plus* enough white flour to make up 2 pounds total

3 tablespoons plain cocoa powder
1 teaspoon salt, dissolved in 1 teaspoon water
3 tablespoons cornmeal for the baking sheets

I do all of this in my KitchenAid so there is no work to making bread, no work at all.

In your electric mixer bowl dissolve the yeast in the water. Let sit for 5 minutes.

Measure out the flour on a scale. I use a lunch sack for this. Mix the flour up a bit and add 4 cups of the mixed flour to the water mix. Beat with your mixer; I use my batter blade for this, for about 10 minutes. Add the cocoa powder and the salt water. Mix well and then work in the rest of the flour, using the dough hook. If you do not have a powerful mixing machine it is best to stir the remaining flour in by hand.

Knead on a floured board or on a piece of marble until the dough is very smooth, about 15 minutes. If you use a machine for this it will take half that time.

Place the dough on a plastic countertop and cover with a very large stainless-steel bowl. Allow to rise once until double in bulk and punch down. Allow to rise a second time and punch down again. Shape into 3 loaves and place on cookie sheets sprinkled with cornmeal. Allow the loaves to rise until double in bulk.

Bake in the upper third of a 450° oven for about 25 minutes, or until the loaves are light brown and hollow-sounding when you tap them on the bottom.

CHOCOLATE POULTRY SAUCE

MAKES 3½ CUPS

This is actually a *mole* sauce, short-cut style. The chocolate gives the sauce a wonderful lift and it can be used to enlighten otherwise dry cooked poultry.

2 tablespoons peanut oil

1 medium yellow onion, peeled and chopped

2 cloves garlic, peeled and minced

1 green sweet bell pepper, cored and chopped

¼ cup raisins

½ cup whole canned tomatoes

¾ teaspoon ground cinnamon

½ teaspoon ground cloves

¼ teaspoon ground cumin

¼ cup sesame seeds

½ cup cocktail sauce

½ teaspoon Tabasco, or more to taste

2 cups Chicken Soup Stock (page 29) or canned chicken broth

2 squares (1 ounce each) semisweet baking chocolate

Heat a large saucepan and add the oil. Sauté the onions and garlic until clear. Add the pepper, raisins, and tomatoes and cook for 10 minutes. Remove from the stove and purée in your food processor or blender. Return to the pan and add remaining ingredients, except the chocolate. Simmer for 10 minutes and then add the chocolate, stirring until it melts.

This is to be used over any kind of cooked poultry. For instance, leftover fried chicken takes on a new life when you simmer the chicken for a few minutes in this sauce. Or turkey meat, cooked, has an entirely different flavor when you warm it with this sauce.

CHOCOLATE ELEPHANT

SERVES 12

"The world doesn't need more mousse. We need more elephants!"

—PATTY SMITH, WIFE OF THE AUTHOR

The above remark clearly states the background of this dessert. My wife loves elephants and so, while demonstrating this dish at a chocolate festival at Marshall Field's, Chicago, I decided to name the dish after her favorite pet. Yes, she has always wanted a pet elephant.

This is expensive, very rich, terribly fattening, and it is not good for you. It is also disgustingly delicious. It has all the right attributes for the serious chocolate lover.

12 eggs
1 teaspoon vanilla
½ pound sweet butter
3 tablespoons almond liqueur

1 pound German Sweet Chocolate
4 tablespoons sugar
Whipped cream for topping (optional, very optional)

Separate the eggs. Beat the yolks with the vanilla and butter. When thoroughly blended add the almond liqueur. Melt the chocolate in a double boiler and then allow to cool a bit. Beat the egg whites and sugar until stiff. Blend the chocolate with the butter/yolk mixture, adding the chocolate to the yolks a little at a time. Finally, gently fold the chocolate mixture into the egg whites.

This may be put in small glasses and chilled. Serve

with whipped cream on top if you want to go the whole route.

This will keep covered in the refrigerator for a couple of days. It is best the first day.

HOT CHOCOLATE TO DIE FOR

I cannot believe I am giving you this recipe. It would simply clog up every artery in your body if you were to drink it often. However . . . this stuff is wonderful, now and then.

The recipe was sent to me by a fellow named Smith. Can you believe this? He writes so beautifully that I must quote part of the message that accompanied his recipe.

"You have publicly denounced pasted, powdered, flaked, salted garlic, decried the use of dull, desiccated, prepowdered spices and all of cooking's other irksome pseudo-conveniences, save one.

"All across America each winter millions of cold thoughtful people (one hopes out of innocent misapprehension) put a foul sugary powder in a mug, add hot water and ignorantly dub it 'hot chocolate.' (This stuff rates with microwave pancakes.) I commend this formula to your care."

For each cup, in a double boiler combine:

> **2 to 3 ounces milk chocolate**
> **1 teaspoon butter**
> **¼ teaspoon vanilla**

Stir together until completely melted and smooth. Then add:

**1 cup half-and-half *or*
 cream**

Add the half-and-half slowly, incorporating it gradually as it heats, but do not boil. Serve over a handful of miniature marshmallows and garnish with a dash of nutmeg.

VARIATION Substitute dark (semisweet) chocolate or white chocolate (very elegant). Also try adding liqueurs, Kahlúa (to go with milk chocolate), Cointreau (with dark chocolate), or peppermint schnapps (with white chocolate).

No, I will not give you this man's address. Yes, he has other recipes. No, I do not know how much he weighs. Yes, I will find out.

COCOA CHILI

Another use of cocoa-powder mix with chili. In Cincinnati, chili with meat and beans has a great deal of cocoa in it (page 370). I suggest you add 2 or 3 tablespoons of cocoa powder to your favorite batch of chili con carne and enjoy the results. The kids will think you are crazy at first, but they will enjoy it too.

"From the mountains to the prairies..."

THE HEARTLAND

SWEET POTATO

Every time you go into the supermarket you are misled by a sign in the produce department. They have dark-orange sweet potatoes for sale and they call them yams. The lighter sweet potato is called by its proper name. We do not grow yams in this country; never have. The yam is from Africa and is a member of a tropical herb family. The sweet potato, on the other hand, is ours, coming from the West Indies, and it is a member of the morning-glory family. Now doesn't that bit of news make your day?

Why the common error in names? It is probably due to the fact that the African slaves recognized the American sweet potato as being very close to the common yam of their culture and thus named it accordingly. Incidentally, the word *yam* in many African dialects means "to eat."

The original sweet potatoes that Columbus saw in the West Indies were called *batata,* and they can still be found in Latin American stores. They are very rich and starchy, almost sweet, though white in color. The name was later applied to what we now know as the potato, another food product that had its roots in America.

If you look hard enough in Latin American markets you can find yams that have been shipped in from Cuba, Santo Domingo, Colombia, Puerto Rico, and Costa Rica. Some are even grown in Florida, but most of these go to a very specialized Latin American market. The sweet potato as we know it, including both the light and dark varieties, has been shipped all over the world and is particularly popular in China. The sweet potato is now the third leading vegetable crop in the world. We produce very little of the total world crop in this country since most Americans see the sweet potato as a holiday side dish rather than a daily staple. I hope some of these recipes will change your mind.

SWEET POTATOES, SOUL-STYLE

SERVES 6—8

These are the most delicious sweet potatoes you can imagine. With all of this butter and sugar they should be! Ms. Helen Vallard, "Louisianna born and raised," cooks at a very good soul-food restaurant in Seattle called Southern Comfort. This is her recipe, and when she gave it to me I really thought there was some mistake in terms of the amount of sugar. This will work well, and it is very simple. The dish makes its own syrup and it will be a hit with your family year-round.

6 dark sweet potatoes, medium size (Red Garnet or yams), peeled and cut into ¼-inch slices	½ cup water 5 cups white sugar 1 stick butter

Rinse the potato slices in ample water and drain. Place in a 2-quart covered saucepan and add the water, sugar, and butter. Cover and simmer until very tender, about 30 minutes. Do not stir during the cooking process.

SWEET POTATO PIE

SERVES 8

This pie is truly American. Its roots are in soul cooking and I expect that everyone in your household will love it. The addition of a heavy shot of bourbon, another very American ingredient, gives this pie a very special flavor. Don't worry about the bourbon if you are feeding this to children. The alcohol cooks out completely, but the flavor of the bourbon remains.

2 cups cooked, peeled, and mashed sweet potatoes	1 teaspoon vanilla
	1 teaspoon freshly grated nutmeg
4 tablespoons butter or margarine	1 tablespoon fresh lemon juice
3 eggs, beaten	½ cup bourbon whiskey
1 cup sugar	1 unbaked pie shell

Boil the sweet potatoes until very tender, then peel and mash them well. Mix all ingredients together and place in an unbaked pie shell. Place in a 400° oven and immediately turn the oven to 325°. Bake for about 45 minutes or until the center of the pie is set. Test this by inserting a table knife into the center of the pie. If it comes out clean the pie is finished.

Serve with whipped cream or ice cream on top.

NOTE: Any leftover filling can be baked in a baking dish and served as a pudding.

GAME HENS STUFFED WITH SWEET POTATOES

SERVES 6

In Italy they stuff chickens with potatoes and olives, so I developed this dish just for fun. It turned out to be delicious, and it is a complete meal in one package. Perfect for a family dinner.

3 game hens,
    defrosted
4 sweet potatoes,
    cooked, peeled,
    and mashed
½ cup shelled pecans
2 eggs, beaten

¼ teaspoon grated
    ginger
Pinch of freshly
    grated nutmeg
Salt to taste

Defrost the birds and pat dry with paper towels. Mix all other ingredients together to form a stuffing. Fill each bird and place on an oiled roasting rack. Bake at 375° for about 1 hour. Split the birds down the middle and serve a half to each guest.

These are so delicious and so heavy that I caution you about the rest of the menu. A light salad and perhaps some plain green vegetables would complete the meal.

SWEET POTATO FRENCH FRIES

Now and then it is fun to give only the name of a recipe and leave the rest of it up to you. Just do what the title says, and you will have an unusual and delicious treat. Keep your oil at 375° to prevent them from getting soggy.

GINGERED SWEET POTATO BISQUE

SERVES 6

This one is rich enough to be served as a whole meal or as a first course. I am glad to see that more Americans are beginning really to enjoy the flavor of freshly grated ginger.

4 **medium sweet potatoes, cooked, peeled, and mashed**	1 **clove garlic, peeled and crushed**
5 **cups Chicken Soup Stock (page 29) or canned chicken broth**	2 **tablespoons olive oil**
	2 **teaspoons grated fresh ginger**
	1 **cup whipping cream or half-and-half**
2 **medium yellow onions, peeled and chopped fine**	¼ **cup dry sherry**
	Salt and white pepper to taste
2 **stalks celery, chopped fine**	**Fresh chives, chopped, for garnish**

Boil the sweet potatoes until a table knife can be inserted easily. Peel and either purée in a food processor or mash by hand with 1 cup of the chicken stock.

Sauté the onions, celery, and garlic in the olive oil in a 4-quart pot. When the vegetables are tender, add the remaining stock, sweet potatoes, and ginger. Bring to a boil and simmer ½ hour, stirring often so that the mixture will be smooth. Then add the cream and sherry, and season with salt and white pepper. Heat, sprinkle on chives, and serve at once.

NOTE: If soup is too thick for your taste, you can add more stock, milk, or cream. Check for seasoning if you do this.

SWEET POTATOES IN PRALINE SAUCE

SERVES 8

If you do not like sweet, rich foods on your table, avoid this one. On the other hand, the children will love you for it. The sauce is from New Orleans.

**4 large sweet potatoes, peeled
and halved
Salt**

PRALINE SAUCE

1 cup white sugar	**3 tablespoons butter**
½ cup corn syrup	**¼ teaspoon salt**
¼ cup water	**½ teaspoon vanilla,**
¾ cup chopped pecans	**or to taste**

Boil the potatoes in salted water until not quite tender, about 15 minutes.

Prepare the sauce by melting the sugar in a heavy saucepan over medium heat. In a short time the sugar will begin to turn to a light golden brown. Stir to prevent burning. When light brown syrup is formed, immediately add the corn syrup, followed by the water. Blend thoroughly. Allow to cool for just a moment and then stir in the pecans, butter, salt, and vanilla. If you wind up with a small sugar lump or two, do not worry about it. Simply remove the offending lump.

Place the potatoes in a greased baking dish. Pour some of the sauce over the potatoes and bake at 375° for about 20 minutes.

This sauce is very rich and I expect that you will want to save some of it for ice cream tomorrow.

SWEET POTATOES AND CORN

Try this one on your own. You do not need a recipe for this early-American dish. Simply precook the potatoes a bit, then cool and peel them. Slice and pan-fry with a bit of olive oil and butter, along with some corn kernels. Frozen corn isn't bad with this dish. Keep the frying pan covered as you cook and add some salt and pepper. Very basic but very good.

SWEET POTATOES AND ONIONS

SERVES 6–8

Please understand that sweet potatoes are great for a vegetable *without* sugar. The flavors in the following dish will surprise your family and cause you to cook this vegetable more often.

2 tablespoons *each* olive oil and butter	5 medium sweet potatoes, cooked, peeled, and diced (⅓-inch cubes)
1 large yellow onion, peeled and sliced	¼ cup fresh chopped parsley
Pinch allspice	
⅛ teaspoon cinnamon	

Heat a large frying pan and add the oil, butter, and onion. Sauté for a few minutes until the onion is clear, then add the spices and salt and pepper. Add the diced potatoes and sauté until lightly browned. Toss with the parsley just before serving.

NOTE: A friend, Craig, claims these are great recooked the next morning for breakfast. He cooks them just like hashbrowns.

CHICAGO

Chicago has become a second home for me. I have actually been adopted by the good citizens of the Windy City, and I love it.

The name for the city comes from an old Algonquian Indian word, *Che-cau-gou,* as La Salle, the explorer, spelled the word. The original meaning is a bit obscure but it was probably "great," although most Chicagoans think that it also may have meant "skunk cabbage," "wild onion," or "garlic." It seems that Chicago was actually built upon an enormous onion bog and thus the name. The ground is very soft, and while that poses no problem during the winter when everything is frozen, there are strange occurrences when the thaws come. We lose whole taxicabs in holes in the street!

Chicago has been called the Second City for a long time, due to its place as second in size to New York. Well, let me tell you. My Chicago has the biggest buildings, the biggest fountain, the biggest convention center, and on and on. The first convention held in Chicago took place in 1847, a year before the railroad reached the city. Everyone came by coach or boat, and it started the Windy City on its career as the best convention city in the country.

In 1870 a great flood of immigration occurred and gave the city the wonderful ethnic color that it now enjoys. The Polish community, which is enormous, feeds me regularly, unless I have already had dinner in Greek Town.

There are other interesting things to talk about. The Great Fire of 1871, when Mrs. O'Leary's cow kicked over the lantern in the barn, took an immense toll on the primarily wooden city. Three hundred residents were burned out and the Great Conflagration burned on for over twenty-four hours.

During that same year a fellow by the name of Swift decided that it would be better and cheaper to butcher beef in a central area and ship out the meat rather than the live cow. Thus the meat-packing business was born, in Chicago, of course. The industry is still located near the city, though it is no longer like the accounts by Upton Sinclair in his *Jungle*.

And Prohibition. Chicago had over 150 speakeasy houses and the illegal liquor traffic was run by the likes of Al Capone. Today it is a very sophisticated city with restaurants among the best in the nation. I know. I eat in them often.

One can still see some holdovers from those early days. For instance, Chicago does not have a lot of hamburger stands as do most American cities. Instead, Chicago boasts the largest number of hot-dog stands in the nation. And ribs houses. How Chicagoans love their barbecued baby-back pork ribs. Finally, the deep-dish pizza. We cannot forget the deep-dish pizza.

It is a wonderful city, and terribly middle-American. On behalf of the citizens who have adopted me I invite you to visit this wonderful place. Have a cocktail on the top of the John Hancock tower and look out on the city. Go shopping on Michigan Avenue, "The Magnificent Mile," or go to Greek Town for a wonderful time. If you don't have a great time let me know. That is how confident I am that you will love my "Second City." You stand invited!

HINT: **On Preparing Prechopped Garlic.**
Have garlic ready when you need it without the chemicals that many packers put in the prechopped stuff in the produce section. Clean 40 cloves of garlic and put them in a medium-sized food processor, all at once. Using quick shots of speed cut the garlic to a very fine dice. You don't want mud. Be careful. Place in a 2-cup glass jar with lid. Smooth down the garlic and place 2 tablespoons olive oil over the top. Seal and refrigerate. Now you are ready for garlic at a moment's notice.

Makes 1 cup. Keeps 2 weeks in the refrigerator.

DEEP-DISH PIZZA

Chicago has more pizza joints per capita than any other city in the world. There are two thousand pizza parlors within the city limits of Chicago alone, and who knows how many lurk in the land beyond O'Hare. This wonderful craze goes back many years, too.

Following World War II a local Chicago soldier returned to his city and to a job in a popular bar. The owner wanted something new. "We have to feed these people to keep them coming in!" The soldier, who had just returned from time in Italy, suggested pizza. "It's bread with tomato on it and they give it away in Italy." He began to experiment, and Chicago deep-dish pizza was born. Don't be confused by the fact that you can't buy this in Italy. You never could. This is a Chicago invention, and the bar where it was invented is called Pizzeria Uno.

I have eaten at Pizzeria Uno many times. Nobody in town can quite beat that basic recipe, though many other companies now employ some brilliant cooks who come up with wonderful combinations. Edwardo's serves a "stuffed spinach pizza." I have tried to figure out how it is done at Pizzeria Uno and I think I am very close. I ran the recipe by Mama, a gorgeous black woman who has been cooking the pizza there for *thirty years,* and she smiled and nodded. I think it was a yes. In any case this is great stuff and I suggest you get started as soon as possible. If you are in bed and reading this book as you sip a glass of dry sherry, I shall let you wait until morning.

DEEP-DISH-PIZZA CRUST

This is easy, as you do not have to roll it out. You just push it into place in the pan. No kidding! Please note that there is no sugar or salt in this dough.

2 packages Quick Rise dry yeast	½ cup salad oil
2 cups tepid water (90°)	4 tablespoons olive oil
	½ cup cornmeal
	5½ cups flour

In the bowl of your electric mixer—KitchenAid is perfect for this—dissolve the yeast in the water. Add the oils, cornmeal, and 3 cups of the flour. Beat for 10 minutes with the mixer. Add the dough hook and mix in the additional 2½ cups flour. Knead for several minutes with the machine. It is hard to do this by hand since the dough is very rich and moist.

Pour out the dough on a plastic countertop and cover with a very large metal bowl. Allow to rise until double in bulk. Punch down and allow to rise again. Punch down a second time and you are ready to make pizza!

Oil round cake pans. Put a bit of dough in each and push it out to the edges, using your fingers. (I oil mine with olive oil.) Put in enough dough so that you can run the crust right up the side of the pan. Make it about ⅛ inch thick throughout the pan.

THE FILLING FOR A 9- OR 10-INCH PAN

⅓ pound sliced Mozzarella cheese	2 cloves garlic, peeled and crushed
2 cups canned plum tomatoes, drained and squished	Salt to taste
1 teaspoon basil	3 tablespoons grated Parmesan cheese for topping
1 teaspoon oregano	3 tablespoons olive oil

Place the cheese in tilelike layers on the bottom of the pie. Next put in the tomatoes and the basil, oregano, garlic, and salt, reserving the Parmesan cheese for the top. Drizzle the olive oil over the top of the pie and you are ready to bake.

ADDITIONAL VARIATIONS Before you put on the Parmesan cheese and olive oil drizzle you might like to add any or *all* of the following:

Italian sausage, hot or mild
Yellow onions, peeled and diced
Pepperoni, sliced thin
Mushrooms, sliced
Green sweet bell peppers, cored and sliced thin

Put any or all of these on your pie and then top with the Parmesan and the olive oil.

BAKING THE PIE

Bake the pie in a 475° oven until the top is golden and gooey and the crust a light golden brown. This should take about 35 or 40 minutes.

THE CHICAGO HOT DOG

Don't talk to me about hot dogs in other cities. I have tasted them. The best ones in the country (Oh, New York City, forgive me!) are in Chicago. The Windy City does not have many hamburger stands like most cities do . . . but it does have four thousand hot-dog stands, and there is a certain style to the way it is to be done.

That is more hot-dog stands per capita than any other city in the world! Furthermore, the contest for the best hot dog in town is ever ongoing, and the arguments ever-present. *Chicago* magazine even ran an article in which about thirty outlets were formally critiqued.

One of my favorites is a place called Byron's on Irving Park. Byron boasts, "Eleven Condiments for Your Hot

Dog!" First of all, he starts with all-beef hot dogs. Most Chicago stands do the same. Then he offers you the following selection of goodies to put on the dog. This is Chicago style!

Green sweet bell pepper, diced
Yellow onions, diced
Mustard, of course
Sweet-pickle relish
Dill-pickle chips
Cucumbers, sliced thin
Lettuce, iceberg, shredded
Tomatoes, diced
Hot peppers (peperoncini)
Catsup (By special request only. Everyone will stare at you. I think you need a note from your mother!)
Celery salt (This is the clincher. It is a most delicious addition.)

I have had parties at my home in which I served nothing but Chicago hot dogs with all the condiments. People on the West Coast are surprised by such a wonderful meal. Junk food this is not. It is a hot dog and fine salad on a bun.

STEAK IN A HOT PAN

I do not know what to call this recipe. It is included here to emphasize the fact that Chicago is still a center for fine beef and steak. The city does eat something more than ribs!

This is simple and it will ensure a tender and properly cooked steak every time.

Heat a black frying pan until it is very hot. Rub olive oil, fresh crushed garlic, and a bit of salt on a steak. Throw it into the hot pan and sear one side and then the other. It will take little time and the meat will be sealed and the center rare and delicious.

If you wish to splash some fresh lemon juice on the steak when you serve it, you can enjoy the fresh flavors of both lemon and garlic. Black pepper for me is a must.

CHILI

Most Americans think that the wonderful rich, beefy, and beany dish that we call chili came from some other culture. Mexico, perhaps, or Spain. Not so. I am afraid that both Mexico and Spain refuse to have anything to do with what we call good old American chili. One Mexican dictionary goes so far as to scornfully describe chili as "A detestable food with a false Mexican name sold in the United States from Texas to New York City." Hey, watch that! The rest of the country loves chili, too!

The original dish is truly American, though I have found that a lot of Americans in different locales claim that it was invented in their backyard. After much research (two days) I have come to the following unquestionable decision. Chili was invented in San Antonio, Texas, in 1840. It was a blend of dried beef, beef fat, chili powder and spices, and salt. It was pressed into a brick and it was so potent that it would not spoil quickly. It was then taken by the prospectors to the California gold fields. There it could be reconstituted with water and cooked with beans. It was very much like the pemmican that had been used in earlier times but with spices added. Please note that there is a difference between plain powdered chile and chili powder. Chili powder is a mixture of spices. See hint below.

San Antonio has the distinct privilege in history of laying claim to "Chili Queens." These ladies had little carts and tables and would appear late in the evening and sell chili and whatnot. . . . I expect more whatnot was sold than chili. They were forced to close down in 1943 due to city health regulations of some sort . . . mostly sort.

I would have thought that all of Texas would have been involved in wonderful chili. But in 1890, when chili arrived in McKinney, a town just north of Dallas, all blazes broke loose. It seems that some wayward ministers claimed that chili was "the soup of the devil—food as hot as hell's brimstone." I wonder if these clergy ever bothered to taste a good pot of chili.

This very American dish spread throughout the country and in 1985 the canned chili industry (Lord, only in America) claimed that 240 million pounds had been sold, grossing $254 million. I am repulsed by canned chili and I urge you to make your own. It is not complex and you will become famous in your own dining room.

CHILE PODS: You need to decide what kind of chile pods you wish to use for your own chili. See page 34 for a discussion of the red pods.

PLAIN CHILI POWDER: If a recipe calls for plain chili powder, then you ask the merchant in your Mexican or Latin American shop for just that. You do not want spices in the mixture.

HINT: **On Making Your Own Chili Powder.**
Remember that chile and chili are different. Chile is ground chile pods. Chili is a blend of spices. Commercial chili powders are made of ground chile (see above for your kind), ground cumin, oregano, garlic powder, and salt. Some even contain sugar. I would suggest the following proportions:

12 dried, cored, and seeded chiles (I use 10 pasilla and 2 ancho chiles)
¾ tablespoon freshly ground cumin
1 tablespoon whole oregano leaves
1 teaspoon garlic powder
1 teaspoon salt

Place all in your medium-sized food processor or food blender and grind until fine. Use as you will in your chili recipes. Your version will have a much brighter flavor than commercial chili powder. If you wish to make it hotter, add cayenne pepper to taste. You will have your own blend going in no time.

RED CHILI CON CARNE

SERVES 8 WITHOUT THE BEANS

This recipe comes from the Southwest Indians around Santa Fe, where this kind of chili has been popular for many generations. The title of the dish simply refers to chili cooked with meat. There are no beans about it.

THE CHILI

Prepare a double batch of Blended Red Chile Pods (page 61)

THE MEAT

3 tablespoons cooking oil or shortening	4 tablespoons flour
2 pounds stew beef, cut into ½-inch cubes	2 cans (8 ounces each) tomato sauce (optional)

Heat a Dutch oven or heavy kettle and add the oil or shortening. Brown the meat well. Stir in the flour, being careful to coat the meat well. Add 1½ cups water, stirring carefully until the mixture thickens. Add the Blended Red Chile Pods and the optional tomato sauce. Cover and simmer for 1 hour or until the meat is very tender.

That is the basic dish. It can be served with beans or just as it is. You might try serving this over corn bread for a very delicious meal. If you wish to cook beans in the meat sauce, first soak the beans overnight. Then simmer them until tender. Drain and add to the chili con carne and cook for about 1 hour before serving.

GREEN CHILE STEW WITH PORK AND BEANS

The title may sound a little strange to you, and I will admit that normally beans are not actually cooked in the green chile stew. But, on the other hand, beans in this stew are delicious.

Make a batch of Green Chile Stew with Pork (page 63) and add cooked beans. Simmer for an additional ½ hour and serve. Put some sharp cheese and green onions on top.

HINT: On Preparing Cooked Beans for Chili With Beans.

Chili with beans has a much better flavor if you use dried beans and cook them yourself rather than using canned beans. Simply soak the needed amount of red kidney or other beans in ample water overnight. Then simmer until tender. The beans are then drained and added to the chili. Cook the beans in the chili sauce and simmer for 1 to 1½ more hours.

TEXAS CHILI

SERVES 6, AT LEAST

This old version does not call for dried meat as the original probably did, but it does call for good beef chuck, not fatty hamburger. No, real Texas chili need not have beans at all!

1 tablespoon whole
  cumin seeds
¼ pound bacon, diced
2 pounds beef chuck
  roast, trimmed of
  fat, cut into
  ⅛-inch dice
3 yellow onions,
  peeled and
  chopped
6 cloves garlic, diced
  fine
6 fresh jalapeño
  peppers, seeded
  and chopped

2 teaspoons salt
4 tablespoons plain
  powdered chile, or
  more to taste (Seed
  and grind your own
  chiles in a food
  blender.) or
4 tablespoons
  commercial chili
  powder, or more to
  taste
1 tablespoon whole
  oregano leaves
1 can (28 ounces)
  tomatoes

Place the cumin seeds in a pie pan and toast in a 375°
oven for 10 minutes. Remove and set aside.

Heat a 6-quart kettle and sauté the bacon until clear.
Add the diced meat and brown over high heat along
with the onions, garlic, and jalapeños.

When the meat is brown and the onions clear, add
the remaining ingredients. Mash up the tomatoes with
your hands, but add the juice as well. Simmer for 1
hour and correct the seasoning.

Cooked beans can be added to this, but they are
strictly optional.

EMILY'S CHILI CON CARNE WITH BEANS

SERVES 4–6

My mother, Emily Smith, doesn't even remember
where she picked up this recipe, but she has been making it since I was a child. It is pretty basic American
chili, but you can soup it up with cayenne, Tabasco,
more chili powder, or anything else you can think of.

1 pound lean
  hamburger
2 tablespoons peanut oil
1 large yellow onion,
  peeled and chopped
3 cloves garlic, peeled
  and crushed
3 tablespoons hot
  commercial chili
  powder, or to taste
1 tablespoon whole
  cumin seeds

1 tablespoon
  Worcestershire
  sauce
1 large can (28 ounces)
  tomatoes, puréed in
  a blender
1 green sweet bell
  pepper, seeded and
  chopped
1 pound kidney beans,
  soaked and cooked
  as on page 365 and
  drained
Salt to taste

Brown the beef in the oil, along with the onion, garlic, and chili powder. When the meat is brown and the onion clear, drain the fat and add remaining ingredients, including the beans. Simmer for at least 1½ hours or until all is flavorful and the beans are very tender. This is better the second day.

NOTE: My mother is convinced that cooking the chili powder with the meat is much better than simply putting the chili powder into the total mixture. I am convinced as well!

BLACK BEAN CHILI

This is a great dish! I simply use black beans, sometimes called turtle beans, in place of the kidney beans and use Emily's recipe. The nature of the bean completely changes the chili, and the result is just delightful.

CHILI CON CARNE WITH GINGER AND BEANS

I owe this one to a very fine Chicago chef, Michael Foley. He has several restaurants in the Windy City and I am one of his fans. He adds fresh ginger to a good heavy chili and serves it as a first course.

You do the same by adding 2 or 3 tablespoons of

grated fresh ginger to Emily's recipe above. I also throw in a glass of red wine. This will surprise your most severe chili critic.

LAMB CHILI

SERVES 4–6

There is a very fine young chef by the name of Jimmy Schmidt, who runs a restaurant in Denver called The Rattlesnake Club. (Lord, only in Denver!) He is very skilled and recently served me a chili made with lamb. This is not his recipe, it is mine. But he is certainly the inspiration. You must go to his restaurant.

2 pounds lamb, trimmed of fat and cut into ¼-inch dice
3 tablespoons olive oil
1 yellow onion, peeled and diced
4 cloves garlic, crushed
2 tablespoons plain chili powder (page 363), or more to taste
1 tablespoon whole cumin seeds
1 teaspoon whole oregano leaves

2 jalapeño peppers, seeded and chopped
2 green sweet bell peppers, seeded and chopped
3 ripe tomatoes, diced
1 can (8 ounces) tomato sauce
1 tablespoon Worcestershire sauce
1 pound kidney beans, soaked, cooked, and drained (page 365)
Salt to taste

In a large Dutch oven brown the lamb in the olive oil, along with the onion, garlic, chili powder, and cumin seeds. When the meat is browned and the onion clear, add the remaining ingredients, including the cooked beans. You may need to add a bit of water to cover everything. Cover and simmer for 1½ hours, watching that the dish does not dry out.

At The Rattlesnake Club they serve lamb chili topped with avocado and papaya chunks, along with a dollop of soft goat cheese. Don't ask me. I couldn't figure it out either! But, Lamb Chili is a wonderful dish.

CALIFORNIA CHILI

SERVES 4

This one has to be different. If it came from California, it is unusual and probably has sprouts in it, or at least avocado. Try this. No avocado, but chicken and a very mild chili sauce from a jar. It is really a great dish, although one should not confuse it with the old-line chili cookers' product.

1 pound kidney beans, soaked, cooked, and drained (page 365)
1 chicken, cut up and browned (I do this in a 400° oven.)
3 tablespoons olive oil
4 cloves garlic, sliced
3 yellow onions, peeled and chopped
1 teaspoon whole cumin seeds
2 jalapeño peppers, seeded and chopped
2 cups chili sauce (catsup section of supermarket)
4 tomatoes, chopped
2 green sweet bell peppers, seeded and chopped
1 tablespoon Worcestershire sauce
1 cup red wine
Salt to taste

Cook the beans and brown the chicken. Heat a large frying pan and add the oil. Sauté the garlic, onions, cumin seeds, and jalapeño peppers until the onions are clear. Add *all* to a heavy pot and bring to a simmer. Cook for 1 hour.

CINCINNATI CHILI

SERVES A SMALL NEIGHBORHOOD IF YOU USE THE PASTA
AND CONDIMENTS. FOR YOUR FAMILY IT WILL SERVE 8–10
PERSONS.

This is certainly an interesting dish, though a bit unusual. The story goes that a young chef from Macedonia arrived in Cincinnati and opened a chili stand. He added additional spices, as per his background, and Cincinnati chili was born. Note that this recipe calls for some sweet spices such as cinnamon and allspice, and cocoa. Some recipes also call for nutmeg.

The method of serving is a bit unusual, too. The chili is normally not made with beans. So, when you order Cincinnati chili you get a bowl of meat and spices. When you order it "two way," the sauce comes on a pile of spaghetti. When you order it "three way," you get spaghetti topped with chili and grated Cheddar cheese. A "four way" adds chopped yellow onions and a "five way" adds the fifth ingredient, beans. You can have great fun with this and I expect that your children will think up some additional "ways" of serving this delicious dish.

2 tablespoons peanut
    oil
1 pound lean pork,
    coarsely ground
1 pound hamburger
4 yellow onions, peeled
    and chopped
6 cloves garlic, peeled
    and finely chopped
1 tablespoon whole
    cumin seeds
4 tablespoons hot chili
    powder,
    commercial
3 whole bay leaves
2 teaspoons cinnamon

2 teaspoons allspice
2 teaspoons Tabasco
4 tablespoons cocoa
    powder
2 tablespoons
    Worcestershire
4 tablespoons white
    vinegar
1 can (28 ounces)
    tomatoes, puréed
1 tablespoon oregano
2 pounds kidney
    beans, soaked and
    cooked (page 365)
Salt to taste

Heat a 12-quart heavy stockpot and add the oil. Sauté the pork, hamburger, onions, garlic, cumin seeds, chili powder, and bay leaves until the meat is barely browned and the onions clear. Drain the fat and discard.

Add the remaining ingredients, including the beans, and bring to a simmer. Cook, covered, for 1½ hours or until the beans are very tender. You may need to add water to this dish as it cooks.

Now, you must decide if you are to have it one, two, three, four, or five way. You might even think up a sixth way! The additional condiments that you might wish are cooked spaghetti, grated Cheddar cheese, and chopped yellow onions.

WINSTON'S CHILI

SERVES 4

Fred Winston, a Chicago disc jockey and man about town, makes the basic chili recipe sing with the addition of beer, paprika, jalapeño peppers, Tabasco, red peppers, and brown sugar. Yes, this all goes into the same pot with the normal chili recipe. It is really a very good dish. He even sells the stuff! I am telling you this so that you will gain some nerve in your chili cooking. I have heard of everything going into a chili pot, including peanut butter.

Fred, do you think peanut butter is a bit strange for chili? I didn't think you would.

CHILI IN THE FIREHOUSE

We recently invited firehouse cooks to send in their favorite recipes. We ran a contest and the results can be seen on pages 391–401. The most frequently submitted dish was chili. That makes great sense since firehouse cooks often have to stop cooking right in the middle of the preparation of the dish and then come back to it later. The dish needs to stand up to this kind of treatment. Chili can take it. We have chosen two of the most interesting chili dishes and offer them to you without any explanation. While chili didn't win the contest, we certainly did gain some insight into the meaning of chili.

10–75 CHILI

SERVES 10–12

Robert Vazquez, of Engine Company 212 in Brooklyn, New York, sent in a recipe that caught the eyes of all of us. He offered strange additions that made me think this man is a serious cook; additions such as saffron and shallots. You would not think that these subtle and expensive ingredients would come through, but they do. This is a delicious dish!

I should also tell you that Bob's motto is "You light 'em, we fight 'em!" He is referring to chili?

2 pounds ground round	1 teaspoon oregano
1 pound bulk Italian sausage	1 teaspoon whole cumin seeds
4 cups Basic Brown Soup Stock (page 28) or canned beef broth	½ teaspoon cayenne pepper
	2 tablespoons commercial chili powder
1 teaspoon saffron threads	1 teaspoon salt

3 tablespoons olive oil	Black pepper,
2 cups coarsely chopped shallots	freshly ground, to taste
2 tablespoons finely chopped garlic	1 can (6 ounces) tomato paste
1 can (10 ounces) green chiles, chopped fine	1 can (30 ounces) red kidney beans, drained

In a large, heavy skillet, brown ground meat and sausage. Transfer to a 4-quart pot. In the same skillet add beef stock and bring to a boil. Remove stock from heat. Crumble saffron and add to the stock. Set this aside in a separate bowl. Add olive oil to the skillet and cook the shallots and garlic for 5 minutes, stirring frequently. Remove from heat. Add canned chiles, oregano, cumin seeds, cayenne pepper, chili powder, salt, and a few grindings of black pepper. Stir together, then add tomato paste and beef stock. Mix together thoroughly. Add this to the meat and bring to a boil. Stir. Reduce heat and simmer in half-covered pot for 1½ hours. Add beans 10 minutes before completion.

19-ALARM CHILI

SERVES 18 NORMAL PERSONS OR 4 CHICAGO FIREFIGHTERS

Everybody knows that there is no such thing as a 19-alarm fire. Why, that would mean that babies, lifeguards, bartenders, everyone, would have to show up to fight it! However, Frank Jacobson of the Chicago Fire Department thinks his chili requires 19 alarms. I am ready!

Please note that he makes this in small batches. If you do not know what a #10 can is, figure on just under a gallon.

1 #10 can tomato purée	½ cup commercial chili powder, or more to taste
1 #10 can whole peeled tomatoes, chopped	3 tablespoons whole oregano leaves
6 pounds good ground beef	Salt and pepper to taste
1 large yellow onion, peeled and chopped	1 #10 can red kidney beans, drained

TOPPINGS

Cheddar cheese, grated
Sour cream
Yellow onions, peeled and diced

In a large pot bring the tomato purée and whole tomatoes to a slow boil. While this is heating, brown the ground beef with chopped onion. Add this to the tomato mixture. Add chili powder and simmer for 1 hour. Add oregano, salt, and pepper to taste and simmer 15 minutes. Add kidney beans and simmer 30 minutes.

Serve in a bowl with Cheddar cheese on top and a dollop of sour cream placed in the center. Diced yellow onions complete the garnish.

"Following the meal have Rolaids available."

BARBECUE

No, the term *barbecue* is not strictly an American term, but we barbecue. The rest of the world simply cooks meat over a fire!

The name has disputed backgrounds. Some researchers claim that the word comes from Spanish and Haitian origins and "barbacoa" refers to a framework of sticks set upon posts. On this rack meat was roasted over a fire or simply dried. In the old Caribbean human flesh was supposedly cooked this way. That is not a very appetizing way to discuss the history of barbecue with your children.

Other researchers lean toward the theory based on the French phrase, *barbe à queue,* meaning "from whisker (*barbe*) to tail (*queue*). It refers to roasting a whole animal with a stick through his center, from his beard or chin to his tail. That explanation makes the most sense to me. That is precisely what you see in Old-World communities such as France, Yugoslavia, and Greece. We know that this is the process that was used for outdoor cooking as well as indoor cooking in England and in Colonial America. The word "barbecue" was in use in America by 1709, so I side with the latter interpretation. We also know that Native Americans used this method of outdoor cooking.

In a very short time, by 1733, the name of the cooking process began to take on the name of an event. The process became a party! Barbecue implied a gathering of friends who stood about and drank until the animal was cooked . . . and I think that is pretty much how the barbecue is enjoyed in our time.

Our special addition to this method of cooking over outdoor fires is the sauce. Now be careful here. I was told by a grand old black gentleman from Dallas, "There are two kinds of people in the world. Them that put the sauce on the meat and then cook it, and them that cook the meat and then put the sauce on. I don't talk to those first fools!" That may be putting the case rather strongly, but he does do wonderful barbecue, and he puts the sauce on after the meat is finished. You will have to decide.

HINT: **For a Clean-Smelling Fire.**
Please do not use liquid starters in your barbecue nor use quick-lighting charcoal. I feel that the odor these items leave behind ruins a good barbecue. Make a charcoal quick starter in the following way. Using a "church key" or old-fashioned beer-can opener, punch a series of holes around the outer bottom of a 3-pound coffee can. Then, do the same on the outer edge of the underside of the coffee can. Place the can on some pebbles so that air can get in through both sets of holes. Put in some crumpled newspaper, a few thin kindling sticks, and about 15 charcoal pieces. Light the paper through one of the side holes and allow it to burn until the coals are hot. Using a pair of tongs, put the coals in your barbecue cooker and build the fire around them. The flavor will be much cleaner this way.

HINT: **For Smoked Barbecue Flavor.**
Use wood chips. You can buy them in bags at the market and they are very effective. Or you can gather your own. Use hickory, alder, cherry, whatever you like. If you use small branches you can chop them up in one of those branch choppers and have a whole burlap sack full of chips in no time. Soak them a bit in water and then drain them and sprinkle them over the charcoal fire. Delicious!

PORK SHOULDER BARBECUE

SERVES 8–10

This method of cooking pork is common throughout Virginia and North Carolina. The meat is cooked until it is just about ready to fall apart, and then it is removed from the fire and literally torn apart . . . removed from the bone and shredded. Sauce is added just before serving, and the results are spectacular.

The slow fires are generally made from old scrap hardwoods, and it is not unusual to find a barbecue expert using oak. While I prefer hickory or alder, the oak fire is good, too.

In Greensboro, North Carolina, the meat is shredded and a very light barbecue sauce made of vinegar, crushed red-pepper flakes, and salt is poured on just before serving. I prefer the Richmond, Virginia, style, in which a heavier barbecue sauce is put on as the dish is served. With this method you could have several sauces ready so that your family and guests could choose their own.

The secret here is slow cooking.

> 1 **whole pork shoulder (about**
> **8 pounds), bone-in**
> **Wood chips**
> **Barbecue sauce (optional)**

I prefer the Kamado (page 16) for this but a gas grill or a domed Weber will work well.

Roast, covered, in the barbecue over low heat until the whole roast is terribly tender. Place a meat thermometer in the thickest portion of the shoulder and cook slowly until the device registers between 150° and 155°. The temperature of the barbecue oven should be between 275° and 300°. Now and then, when you are not watching, the temperature will climb to 350°. While this is all right for a few minutes, make every effort to keep the temperature lower.

If you like a true smoked flavor, soak some wood chips and put them on the fire. The instructions for doing this will be found on the package when you buy the chips.

It should take about 4 to 5 hours to properly cook the roast. Remove from the cooker and allow the meat to cool just long enough to handle. Tear it up into shreds and serve with barbecue sauce of your choice. A few recipes for sauce follow in this chapter.

A salad is a must with this, along with some Cooked Greens with Garlic and Tomato (page 126).

BARBECUED SPARERIBS

SERVES 6–7

This is one of the great dishes of our culture. Yes, barbecued pork ribs are very special, and they are ours. Chicago, Kansas City, Dallas, and Houston seem to have the best ribs imaginable, though every major city in America now boasts a few fine ribs houses.

Home cooking of ribs is not difficult at all.

There are several methods. I have heard of people steaming the ribs before barbecuing in order to ensure tenderness . . . but I think there is something heretical about that. Something to do with one's grandmother or the Texas sky. I'm not sure why that steaming suggestion so bothers me. It might just work, but I am not about to waste a good slab of ribs trying to find out.

I have smoked ribs in a garbage-can smoker and then finished them off in the kitchen oven. I discussed that in an earlier book. That works well, but anyone in Kansas City or Dallas would not hear of such a thing.

The old method seems to be the best. Cool fire, slow cooking, sauce on at the end. That is what I want you to try.

At Arthur Bryant's, in Kansas City, the meat is done over a very low fire and offered with the sauce on the side. Their sauce is a bit unusual and I have tried to come close to what they offer. My sauce follows. You must go to Bryant's sometime. Calvin Trillin loves the place and has made it quite famous, although you will be surprised when you walk in. It is simply good barbecue served in a black barbecue house. Paper plates, Formica tabletops, the whole scene.

8 pounds pork
    spareribs
Salt and pepper to
    taste
	Wood chips
	Barbecue sauce
	    (optional)

Salt and pepper the ribs and cook them over a low fire, just as in the pork-shoulder recipe. They should take about 1½ hours to cook. Be sure that you do not put the ribs on top of one another. Give them plenty of room. Control the smoke flavor by the use of the dampened wood chips or sawdust.

Normally the sauce is put on after the ribs are cooked. However, if you like crunchy ribs, baste the ribs when they are finished. Then continue to cook for 15 more minutes. They wouldn't do that in Kansas City, and Edith wouldn't do it in Chicago . . . but sometimes the crunchiness gained from the darkened sugar in the sauce is just great. Don't tell anyone in Kansas City that I told you to do this!

CHICKEN BARBECUED WITH ROSEMARY AND MARSALA

SERVES 2–3

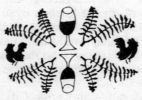

I developed this recipe after having dinner in San Francisco one evening. Harvey Steiman, editor of *Wine*

Spectator magazine, was cooking for me in his backyard and he kept adding rosemary branches to the barbecue. The result was a lamb dish that was heaven. If you do not have fresh rosemary growing in your yard, then you can use whole dried rosemary for this dish. However, look into growing rosemary where you are. It will grow to be the size of a hedge in very little time . . . and it needs little care.

2 whole chickens (each about 3 to 3½ pounds)

MARINADE

4 tablespoons fresh rosemary needles *or* 2 tablespoons dried rosemary needles	**4 cloves garlic, peeled and crushed**
½ cup olive oil	**Juice of 1 lemon**
¼ cup dry Marsala wine	**Salt and pepper to taste**
	Wood chips or sawdust (optional)

Mix everything together for the marinade. Cut the chicken in half and marinate for 2 hours.

Cook over a medium fire in your barbecue. If you are using a dome, the fire should be about 375° to 390°. Cook for about 1 hour or until the chicken is done to your taste. Baste the birds with the remaining marinade now and then. If you are using a covered or lidded barbecue, it will not be necessary to turn the chicken. An open barbecue means the chicken must be turned once. If you wish to have a smoky flavor, put some soaked wood chips or sawdust on your charcoal.

I like this with a Tomato Salad (page 125) and Baked Polenta (page 128).

GRADUATE SCHOOL POT ROAST

SERVES 3–4

Patty and I had great times while in graduate school at Drew, in Madison, New Jersey. Being a Pacific Northwesterner I could not believe the heat of a New Jersey summer, so we took to cooking outside now and then. We developed this recipe because it is inexpensive and very tasty. It can be done on any kind of a charcoal barbecue. Just remember that you don't want the heat too high.

1 **chuck or pot roast (about 3 pounds), 1 inch thick**	1 **teaspoon Colman's dry English mustard**
1 **tablespoon water**	**Freshly ground**
1 **tablespoon salt-free powdered meat tenderizer**	**black pepper**
2 **tablespoons light soy sauce**	1 **large yellow onion, peeled and sliced thin**
2 **tablespoons Kitchen Bouquet**	**Wood chips or sawdust (optional)**

Using a metal pot fork, poke holes in the meat. Sprinkle with 1 tablespoon of water and then one half of the meat tenderizer. Rub it into the meat and then turn the meat over and repeat the process. Let the meat stand for ½ hour. Use a salt-free tenderizer such as Adolf's Salt Free and please understand that there is nothing strange about the contents of this product. It consists of an extract called papain. It is made from the papaya fruit and it is not harmful in any way.

After the meat has sat for ½ hour, mix the soy, Kitchen Bouquet, mustard, and black pepper together and rub this mixture into the meat on both sides. Grill the meat over a low to medium charcoal fire. Turn over the meat after about 45 minutes. Place the sliced onion over the meat and grill about another 45 minutes. Be careful not to dry out the meat or burn it. If you wish a smoky flavor sprinkle water-soaked wood chips or sawdust on the fire during the cooking.

The result will be a tender and flavorful roast that will be a bit crunchy on the outside and pink and lovely on the inside.

This meat is perfect with Barbecued Potatoes (below) and Barbecued Zucchini (page 385).

BARBECUED SHRIMP ON A STICK

This is a simple recipe that you can use to add a bit of color to the barbecue buffet. Purchase large shrimp in the shell and skewer them on bamboo barbecue sticks. Place them in your cooker when everything else is just about finished. They will take only a few minutes to cook and the smoke flavor on the shrimp is just wonderful. Be careful not to overcook this delicacy.

BARBECUED POTATOES

SERVES 6–8

I owe this dish to a friend, Brian. He will put anything in his barbecue except the neighbor's dog. He can eat three meals a day out of his cooker, so I was anxious to respond to his dinner invitation. This recipe was particularly unusual and delicious. It is just too simple to believe.

4 unpeeled potatoes, washed
¾ cup Vinaigrette Dressing
(recipe follows)
Salt and pepper to taste

Bake the potatoes in their skins about 30 minutes at 450°, or until they are just slightly tender. Do not fully cook them as they must be sliced. While still a bit hot, cut the potatoes lengthwise in half and then each half into quarters. Place the pieces in a glass baking dish and cover with the dressing. Let stand 1 hour, turning once. Remove from the dressing and place on the grill. Salt and pepper to taste and grill the pieces until golden brown, about 10 minutes on each side.

VINAIGRETTE DRESSING

MAKES 1½ CUPS DRESSING

This is easy to prepare and keeps for several days in the refrigerator. I prefer to use whole spices and herbs and grind them up when I need them.

½ teaspoon oregano
½ teaspoon rosemary
¼ teaspoon Colman's dry English mustard
½ teaspoon sugar
½ teaspoon salt
¼ teaspoon freshly ground black pepper

1 cup olive oil
⅓ cup white wine vinegar
2 tablespoons water
2 teaspoons fresh lemon juice
2 cloves garlic, peeled and crushed
1 teaspoon Worcestershire sauce

Place the dry ingredients in your food blender or medium-sized food processor. Using the metal blade, grind for a few moments. Add the liquids and whip to an emulsion, or until it is thick. Store in refrigerator for at least 1½ hours before using.

BARBECUED ZUCCHINI

SERVES 6–8

I like vegetables as much as I do meat, perhaps more. There is no reason why you cannot put something into your barbecue cooker other than potatoes and meat. Try this one. Even your children will eat their vegetables.

> **6 medium zucchini**
> **1 cup Italian Salad Dressing**
> **Salt and pepper to taste**

Trim the ends of the squash and cut each lengthwise in half and then each piece into quarters. Marinate in the salad dressing for ½ hour before cooking. Place on the charcoal grill and add salt and pepper to taste. These pieces should cook in very little time, so watch them. Nobody likes soggy zucchini!

GRILLED CORN ON THE COB

SERVES 6

There is nothing new about this one except that you can have it in the winter if you have frozen the corn in the husk. I love to barbecue in the middle of the winter as it helps me to remember that the cold weather will eventually give way to lovely spring days. The smoke of the barbecue will help you maintain your senses, even when there is snow on the ground!

> **6 ears of fresh corn, husk on,**
> ***or* 6 ears of frozen corn,**
> **husk on (page 429)**
> **Butter or garlic olive oil**

Wrap the unopened corn in aluminum foil and place on top of your charcoal grill. Turn every 10 minutes for about ½ hour. Shuck and enjoy. I love garlic olive oil on mine, but butter and salt is more traditional.

If you use the corn that you froze in the husk, be sure and let it defrost completely before cooking.

STOVE-TOP SMOKED TROUT

I am very suspicious of every new gadget that comes along for the "gourmet kitchen." So much junk is sold with the name "gourmet" on it that I am often frustrated over our willingness to buy one thousand gadgets rather than a few that will be truly functional. However, when I saw a stove-top smoker I left my suspicious nature behind and tried it. This is a jewel!

The smoker is called a Camerons Smoker, and since it is made of stainless steel, it is not cheap. The unit will run around $50, but consider the fact that you can smoke on top of your stove and thus give flavor to foods without adding a great deal of salt and fat. I think it is well worth the investment. It also goes into the dishwasher, a bit of frugality that the aluminum version cannot offer.

The principle is simple. Sawdust is placed in the bottom of the pan. A drip pan is then placed over the sawdust and a rack on top of that. Food is placed on the top rack and a tight-fitting lid over the whole. The unit is then placed on the stove top and the smoking sawdust flavors the food while it cooks. It is great! However, please remember that this must be done in a well-ventilated kitchen. One of these kitchen fans that simply recirculates the air will not do.

I put 3 fresh trout in my Camerons and cooked it for about 15 to 20 minutes over medium heat. The result is a very moist and flavorful dish. Nothing else need be added except your own seasoning. I served the trout cold with mayonnaise and capers. Try smoking your own pork chops and then pan-frying them, or smoking salmon steaks, or halibut, or . . . well, you get the idea.

A light dry white wine and a very fresh green salad are all that are needed for this fine fish.

KANSAS CITY BARBECUE SAUCE

MAKES ABOUT 3½ CUPS

I had to guess at this one and it turned out rather well. It is a bit sharper than most sauces due to the turmeric and pepper. There are times when this one will be just the thing for your cooking.

- 1 teaspoon salt
- 3 cups Basic Brown Soup Stock (page 28) or canned beef broth
- ¼ cup white vinegar
- ½ cup Worcestershire sauce
- 1 cup tomato paste
- 1 tablespoon chili powder
- 3 tablespoons paprika
- 1 tablespoon whole sage leaves, rubbed (page 25)
- 1½ teaspoons cayenne pepper
- 1 teaspoon turmeric
- 3 cloves garlic, peeled and crushed

Blend all together in a saucepan and simmer for 30 minutes.

SIMMERED BARBECUE SAUCE

MAKES ABOUT 2 CUPS

Many people like a sauce that is a bit sweet. If you are of that camp, please feel free to add more sugar. I prefer it this way.

1 cup tomato sauce

2 teaspoons commercial chili powder

⅓ cup Worcestershire sauce

2 tablespoons fresh lemon juice

¼ cup chopped onion

1 tablespoon brown sugar

2 cloves garlic, peeled and minced

2 cups Basic Brown Soup Stock (page 28) or canned beef broth

2 tablespoons butter

1 tablespoon paprika

1 teaspoon dry mustard

¼ cup white vinegar

1 cup beer

½ teaspoon Tabasco

2 tablespoons brown sugar (optional)

Blend all ingredients in a saucepan and bring to a boil. Turn down the heat and simmer until reduced by half. This will probably take an hour or more. Stir occasionally.

FIREHOUSE COOKS

I don't get particularly patriotic when the armed forces march by in a parade. I'm sorry that they have such a difficult job to do, though I am glad they do it. Nor does the police drill team get to me, though I am grateful for them, too. But you just watch me when the firefighters bring up the end of the parade with their shiny new truck or their new yellow rescue wagon or their special cardiac-unit truck. I cheer. I holler. I scream and rant. These people are my heroes. I get a lump in my throat just thinking about the number of times I have seen them come to someone's rescue, and they are always so nice about it. It is rare that you meet a fireman who is not a very kind person as well. These people place their lives on the line and they never become arrogant or rude, just supportive.

When my son Channing was tiny he wanted to be a fireman/clown/mailman. There was a little ambiguity there, but I thought, *Why not?* We began visiting engine companies and firehouses and hook-and-ladder companies. Channing knew each piece of equipment and I suddenly realized that he knew just about every fireman in town. He would have me decorate a cake shaped like a firetruck and then he would do the delivery. No wonder these guys were so fond of him. Sometimes, when we were very lucky, we would be in the firehouse and the alarm would sound. Channing would nearly die and I would grab him and hold him in my arms and these wonderful characters would come down the pole, hop onto the truck, the lights would flash and the sirens would scream. And, as they drove off to unknown dangers, they would wave to my little Channing and yell that they were sorry but they would eat the cake when they got back from the fire. My tiny boy could hardly walk. Oh, I tell you, firefighters are great.

I became interested in the daily lives of these civic servants while we were on our visits. I realized that one of the things that they celebrate together is the meal in the firehouse. One is elected to cook and all chip in to pay for the meals. Oh, you thought the city fed the firefighters? Not so. These heroes are confined to the build-

390

ing, so they must cook for themselves, and they also have to pay the bills. Can you imagine cooking for fifteen guys knowing that the alarm will probably go off just as you are about to serve? Well, that is what happens, and firehouse cooks have a great deal to teach us.

We ran a contest and invited firemen from New York, Chicago, Seattle, New Orleans, Los Angeles, San Francisco, and Philadelphia. We had some wonderful chili recipes come through, since chili will stand up during an alarm and can be reheated. The following recipes in this section are winners for taste, ease, creativity, and simplicity, but, most important, they will stand up when your family alarm goes off or Aunt Agnes is late for dinner. Enjoy.

FRITTORTA

SERVES 8 AS A DINNER SIDE DISH, MORE AS A COCKTAIL PARTY APPETIZER

This is an interesting contribution to our firehouse cooking contest. Lieutenant Harry Paretchan of the San Francisco Fire Department combines a couple of Italian cooking methods that are common in the City by the Bay. A *frittata* is a broiled or baked Italian omelet, and a *torta* is a baked sort of cake. He does both with this wonderful dish that is easy to make, inexpensive, and delicious hot or cold.

Normally I do not give you recipes that contain instant food products or dried soup mixes. However, with firehouse cookery you are sometimes up against the wall and may need to fall back on some prepared ingredients. He uses a very fine product from Knorr, and since I have used it as well, I can hardly complain about Mr. Paretchan not cooking from scratch.

1 cup long-grain rice
1 cup Chicken Soup Stock (page 29) or canned chicken broth
1 cup water
1 stick butter, melted (Use microwave.)
1 pint small-curd cottage cheese
1 cup diced (⅛-inch pieces) salami
1 envelope Knorr-Swiss leek soup mix
1 teaspoon *each* garlic salt, onion salt, freshly ground black pepper
12 eggs
1 package (10 ounces) frozen chopped spinach, thawed and well drained
2 tablespoons butter for greasing baking dish
½ cup freshly grated Parmesan or Romano cheese

Cook the rice in the broth and water (page 447). When cooked, place in a large bowl and add the melted butter. Mix well and add the cottage cheese, salami, soup mix, and salts and pepper. Beat 9 eggs and stir into the mixture. Add the drained spinach and mix well.

Grease an 11 × 16 × 1-inch baking dish with the remaining butter. Sprinkle half of the grated cheese on the bottom of the dish. Add the rice mixture and smooth out the top. Beat the remaining 3 eggs and pour over the top of the dish. Sprinkle with the remaining cheese and bake, uncovered, at 325° for 35 to 40 minutes. After cooling a bit, cut into small serving pieces.

The lieutenant claims that the dish sets up better if it is made a day in advance. A quick reheating is no work at all.

ALL HANDS STUFFED CHICKEN BREAST

SERVES 6–8

James Brown, of Engine Company 81 in the Bronx, New York, won the contest with this dish. You can tell just by reading the recipe that this fireman knows his stuff. I can imagine the pleasure that Company 81 gets when this man turns on the fires . . . on his stove.

He calls this dish "All Hands" because the line refers to that difficult situation in a fire when absolutely everyone is needed. I can tell you that all hands will show up when you cook this chicken dish.

Officer Brown gives help to everyday cooks as when he points out that this dish "has the advantage of holding in heat in case of an alarm or they can sit for a while and be reheated." (At about six each evening, doesn't your house sound as if there is about to be a four-alarm fire?)

You will enjoy this and it is not really difficult to make. I am not giving you his proportions, as they might seem a bit large for a family of four. So, cut down. I have already cut it in half!

12 chicken breasts, skin and bones removed	2 cups Italian-flavored bread crumbs
⅛ cup olive oil	Peanut oil for pan-frying or deep-frying
2 cloves garlic, peeled and crushed	2 tablespoons butter
1 pound fresh spinach, carefully washed and chopped	1 cup sliced mushrooms
Salt and freshly ground black pepper to taste	1 tablespoon flour
	1 cup Chicken Soup Stock (page 29) or canned chicken broth
½ pound Feta cheese, crumbled	1 cup dry white wine
½ cup milk	Juice of ½ lemon
4 eggs, beaten	¼ cup chopped parsley, for garnish

Using a heavy water glass or wooden mallet, pound each breast between 2 sheets of plastic (page 18) until about double in area size but not torn.

Heat a large frying pan and add the olive oil and

garlic. Stir for a moment and add the spinach. Sauté the spinach until barely wilted. Add salt and pepper to taste. Cool and drain in a colander.

Lay each chicken portion flat on the counter and salt and pepper to taste. Place 1/12 of spinach in a layer on each piece of chicken and add a bit of the cheese. Roll up and hold together with toothpicks.

Mix the milk with the eggs and dip each piece into the egg wash and then dredge in the bread crumbs. Pan-fry in a bit of peanut oil until golden brown, turning once. Or deep-fry in oil at 375° until golden brown. I really prefer these pan-fried. Remove the pieces to a pan and cover. Bake in a 350° oven for 30 minutes.

In the meantime, prepare the gravy. Drain the fat from the frying pan, leaving the scrapings in the pan. Heat the pan and add the butter and mushrooms. Sauté until tender and then stir in the flour, being careful to keep stirring as it thickens. We don't need lumps! Add the chicken stock, wine, and lemon juice. Cook until thickened, stirring with a wire whip. Check for seasoning of salt and pepper.

Pour the gravy over the chicken rolls and serve with a parsley garnish.

For a winner menu, serve this with Frittorta (page 391) and Corn Oysters (page 441).

RICE WITH BURNED ALMONDS

SERVES 4 AS A SIDE DISH

This is a very nice side dish, though the name that Officer Bill Galvin, from Philadelphia, has given it is somewhat misleading. Maybe it is because he is a fireman! You don't want to burn the almonds. They simply need to be toasted until golden. That makes for wonderful flavor!

The restaurants in Philadelphia are just wonderful, but it looks like the firefighters eat very well at the firehouses. Very well indeed.

⅓ **cup slivered almonds**
3 **tablespoons butter**
2 **cups *cooked* long-grain rice**
   (page 447)

Sauté the almonds in the butter until they are golden. Stir into the rice and taste for salt.

CRAWFISH REGAL

SERVES 8

Just the thought of hanging around a firehouse kitchen in New Orleans sends me into Cajun/Creole fits! These guys have the most wonderful selection of foods and traditions. How hard it must be to jump up from the table and head for a fire when a dish as fine as this one has just been served up. John Alfortish, of the New Orleans fire department, sent us this jewel. The chief has been cooking in a firehouse for twenty years!

8 **puff-pastry shells**
½ **stick butter**
½ **cup flour**
1 **pint whipping cream or half-and-half**
½ **teaspoon thyme**
½ **teaspoon paprika**
1 **clove garlic, minced or grated**
  Cayenne and white pepper to taste

2 **pounds crawfish meat, cooked (page 275)**
1 **bunch green onions, chopped**
  Salt to taste
2 **tablespoons chopped parsley, for garnish**
1 **lemon, cut into 8 wedges, for garnish**

If using frozen puff-pastry shells, bake according to directions and set aside.

Cook the flour and butter together in a 3-quart heavy saucepan to form a roux. Do not brown. Add the cream, stirring constantly until it thickens. Add the thyme, paprika, garlic, and the 2 peppers to taste. Do not salt at this time. Simmer very slowly for 15 minutes.

Add the crawfish and green onions to the sauce. Salt to taste. Simmer 15 minutes. Spoon mixture into the pastry shells and garnish with the parsley and lemon.

A big green salad is a must with this rich dish. I also enjoy Apple and Cabbage (page 325).

NOTE: If you do not wish to use pastry shells, this dish is very good over rice or pasta.

CHICKEN AND SAUSAGE GUMBO

SERVES 6

This is another dish from New Orleans firefighter Gayle Rogers. It is too late for me to learn to be a fireman in New Orleans, but it is certainly not too late to go to New Orleans and eat with this engine company!

I have added a bit of Worcestershire and Tabasco. I hope Gayle is not put out with me.

1 pound sausage, browned (You may use hot links, smoked pork sausage, Italian sausage, or even breakfast sausage.)
½ cup peanut oil
1 chicken, about 3 pounds, cut up
½ cup flour

4 cloves garlic, peeled and chopped fine
2½ quarts Chicken Soup Stock (page 29) or canned chicken broth
2 whole bay leaves
½ teaspoon basil
½ tablespoon poultry seasoning
Pinch of ground cloves

1 large yellow onion,
   peeled and
   chopped
1 bunch green onions,
   chopped
1 green sweet bell
   pepper, cored
   and chopped
2 stalks celery,
   chopped

Pinch of ground
   allspice
1½ tablespoons
   Worcestershire
   sauce
1 teaspoon Tabasco
Salt and freshly
   ground black
   pepper to taste
2 cups raw long-grain
   rice

Brown the sausage in a frying pan with just a small bit of the oil. Remove and set aside.

Add the remaining oil to the pan and fry the chicken until brown. Remove and set aside.

Add the flour to the pan and cook with the oil and pan drippings until you have a dark, rich roux, about the color of peanut butter. Scrape the bottom of the pan with a wooden spatula to ensure no sticking. Add the vegetables and garlic and sauté until limp. Place the vegetable roux in a 6-quart stockpot and add the stock. Stir constantly over medium-high heat until the stock thickens. Add the seasonings and simmer, covered, for 1 hour, stirring occasionally.

In the meantime, cook the rice (page 447).

Add the chicken and sausage to the stockpot and cook until the chicken is tender.

Serve over the cooked rice.

This can be eaten as a main dish as long as you have enough beer.

SHRIMP AND CRAB BISQUE

SERVES 6–8 AS A SOUP COURSE

The firefighters in New Orleans must eat the most delicious food you can imagine. While this next contribution to our firefighters' contest may look a little expensive to make, Officer Gayle Rogers in New Orleans knows the crew will enjoy it and foot the bill. You do know, don't you, that firefighters do not get their meals free with the work? They chip in each week to cover the cost of the groceries. I'll bet that Fireman Rogers's cooking is popular enough to bring about support for any bill!

1 pound raw peeled shrimp

2 tablespoons butter

½ cup *each* butter and flour, cooked together to form a roux (page 25)

4 stalks celery, with leaves, chopped fine

1 large yellow onion, peeled and chopped fine

1 tablespoon Worcestershire sauce

1 can (8 ounces) tomato sauce

1 green sweet bell pepper, cored and cut into 4 pieces

2 whole bay leaves

1 pound crab meat

2 cups Fish Stock (page 31) or Chicken Soup Stock (page 29) or canned fish or chicken broth

2 cups milk

3 chicken bouillon cubes

⅛ teaspoon ground cloves

¼ teaspoon garlic powder (I prefer 2 cloves crushed fresh garlic.)

1 pint whipping cream

White pepper to taste

Tabasco to taste

Dry sherry to taste

2 green onions (green tops only), chopped, for garnish

Heat a medium frying pan and sauté the shrimp in the 2 tablespoons butter just until the shrimp changes color, about 3 minutes. Set aside.

In a 2-quart saucepan cook the butter and flour together to form a roux. Cook to a very light brown. Add the celery and yellow onion and sauté in the roux until soft. Stirring constantly, add the fish or chicken stock and milk. Stir until it thickens a bit. Add Worcestershire sauce, tomato sauce, bell pepper, and bay leaves. Simmer, covered, 1 to 2 hours. Remove the bell pepper pieces and the bay leaves. Add the shrimp and crab meat, along with the cream. Heat the soup again, being careful not to let it come to a boil. Add additional seasonings such as white pepper, Tabasco, and dry sherry. Garnish with the green-onion tops and serve.

CHICKEN BREASTS STUFFED WITH SMOKED MOZZARELLA

SERVES 11

Talk about creative! Just hearing the name of this firefighter, Douglas Bartocci, Engine Company 151, Staten Island, New York, causes me to think of wonderful Italian smells in the firehouse kitchen. This dish takes some doing, but the Italian smells that it will create in your kitchen will be well worth the effort.

This recipe is for eleven people. Does that sound strange? It must be that Fireman Bartocci feeds eleven people regularly. It is easy to adjust this recipe to your crowd.

NOTE: When a recipe calls for a chicken breast, it means just that. Each chicken has two breasts, right?

3 tablespoons olive oil
4 cloves fresh garlic,
   peeled and
   crushed
1 pound fresh
   mushrooms,
   sliced thin
1 pound fresh
   spinach, washed
   and chopped
1 pound smoked
   Mozzarella,
   shredded
1 cup cooked rice
¼ pound prosciutto or
   smoked ham,
   diced
½ cup chopped Italian
   parsley
¼ cup freshly grated
   Parmesan cheese
   Salt and freshly
   ground black
   pepper to taste

11 chicken breasts,
   skinned and boned
2 cups flour
6 eggs, beaten
4 cups Italian-
   flavored bread
   crumbs
1 cup olive oil
5 tablespoons
   chopped shallots
¼ pound (1 stick)
   butter
1 cup dry white wine
2 cans (28 ounces
   each) Italian
   plum tomatoes,
   crushed (Use
   your hands.)
Chopped Italian
   parsley, for
   garnish

Heat a large frying pan and add the olive oil and 2 cloves of the garlic. Sauté the mushrooms in the oil for about 5 minutes. Remove from the pan and set aside.

Blanch the spinach in boiling water for 1 minute. Drain well.

In a large bowl mix together the Mozzarella, rice, prosciutto or smoked ham, parsley, Parmesan cheese, and add salt and pepper to taste.

Pound each chicken breast between 2 sheets of plastic (page 18). I use a wooden mallet or a metal meat pounder for this process. Be gentle and each breast will about double in size. Place each breast flat on the counter and spread ¹⁄₁₁ of the rice mixture on each. Roll each up and tie with 2 pieces of string or secure with a toothpick.

Dust each roll in the flour and then dip in the beaten eggs. Roll in the bread crumbs.

Heat a very large covered frying pan and add the olive oil. When the oil is hot add the rolls and cook over medium-high heat until brown on all sides. Remove and set aside. Leave the olive oil in the pan.

To the hot pan, add the shallots and the remaining 2 cloves of garlic. Sauté for a minute and add the butter, wine, and tomatoes. Return the chicken to the pan, baste with the sauce, and simmer over low heat, covered, for 30 minutes, basting once or twice.

Remove the chicken to a serving platter and cover to keep warm. Test sauce for salt and pepper and then spoon some of it over the chicken. Garnish with chopped parsley.

Rice with Burned Almonds (page 394) is a nice accompaniment, along with a green salad.

"From sea to shining sea..."

COASTAL DELIGHTS

CRABS

Crabs can be found all over the world, so they are not strictly American. However, the crabs that live on both of our coasts have fed us since the very beginning. The West Coast Native American lived on salmon, clams, oysters, and crabs. The East Coast Native American had a similar seafood diet as he enjoyed clams, crabs, lobsters, and oysters. Our crabs are wonderful, though citizens on each coast will still tell you that they prefer their particular local crab over any others. It is all a matter of taste, but I happen to know that the wonderful Dungeness crab of the Pacific Northwest, where I live, is the best crab in the world. (Wow, watch the mail come in on that one!)

The coasts of North America have a greater variety of edible crabs than any other continent, and the creatures have always been important to our cuisine. The animal is of an ancient form in the sea world and I want you to enjoy the delicious flavor of crab from the West Coast or the East Coast as often as you can.

The following recipes should help you get started with my campaign to get us to eat more crab. Yes, I know it is expensive, but it is also rich and there is no waste, so a little goes a long way.

CRAB CAKES MARYLAND

SERVES 4

Baltimore has some wonderful crab houses, and crab cakes are a basic part of the menu. This recipe works well for year-round eating, since crab cakes can be made even with frozen crab. Please do not overcook these rascals!

2 tablespoons chopped fresh parsley	1 pound cooked crab, flaked or broken up
1 teaspoon dry mustard	1 cup fresh bread crumbs *or* ½ cup unsalted cracker crumbs
1 teaspoon Worcestershire *or* dash of Tabasco	
2 eggs, beaten	Salt and pepper to taste
2 tablespoons mayonnaise	Flour for dredging

Mix the parsley, dry mustard, Worcestershire or Tabasco, eggs, and mayonnaise together. Add the crab and crumbs, and season with salt and pepper to taste. Simply taste it and go from there!

Divide the mixture into 8 cakes and dredge in flour. These can be deep-fried at 375° to 380° for 2 to 3 minutes, or until golden brown.

Or you may pan-fry them on both sides in a bit of butter. I prefer the butter-fried cakes.

I serve these with salad. A big salad. Period! You might try some Sweet Potato French Fries (page 349). That would have tickled the early Baltimore folks.

NOTE: Fresh bread crumbs are made by removing the crusts from fresh bread and placing the bread in your food processor. Chop quickly and use the crumbs immediately. They are not to be dry.

FRIED CRAB LEGS

These are so rich and expensive that I hesitate to tell you about them. I have them in Tacoma, my home, every once in a while, since they are made from the shelled leg pieces of the great Dungeness crab. La-Moyne, who runs the Harbor Lights, one of our basic but very good seafood houses on the Tacoma waterfront, simply fries them on a griddle with a bit of butter.

"Nothing more need be done," she says, "as the crab legs speak for themselves." That is good advice for all seafood cooks. Do not overcook. Let the seafood speak for itself.

When you see the price on fresh Dungeness crab legs, you will want them to speak for themselves. You may want them to lecture!

Salad and hash browns come on the plate at La-Moyne's. I think she is right.

STEAMED BLUE CRABS

This is another favorite from the Maryland region. The blue crabs must be fresh. They are brought to you on big trays along with a wooden mallet for cracking. The table is covered with newspaper and the beer flows. This is just wonderful eating!

CRAB AND SHRIMP SEASONING

This is very close to the seasoning used at famous Book-binder's in Philadelphia.

1½ tablespoons celery seed	1 tablespoon paprika
1½ tablespoons salt	1 teaspoon freshly ground black pepper
2 teaspoons cayenne pepper	½ teaspoon dried ground ginger
½ tablespoon dry English mustard (Colman's)	2 whole bay leaves, crushed
½ tablespoon whole thyme	

Grind all ingredients in an electric coffee grinder or in a medium-sized food processor. My KitchenAid food processor is perfect for this. Store in a covered container.

Arrange the fresh blue crabs in a steaming rack. If you have a Chinese bamboo steamer, it will work wonderfully for this or simply put a rack in a large kettle.

Set the rack over cans or cups so that it does not get into the water in the bottom of the kettle. Or you can use a stainless-steel vegetable steamer. Sprinkle some of the Crab and Shrimp Seasoning on each crab, cover the pot, and steam until the crabs are bright orange in color, about 15 minutes.

FRIED SOFT-SHELL CRABS

This is the most simple recipe I can offer you for soft-shell crab . . . and I also think it is the best. These delicate creatures need very little additional flavoring, so I keep a light hand when I do these. And for heaven's sake, if anyone tells you to deep-fry these, turn and run, immediately!

**Soft-shell crabs (I buy
    mine already
    cleaned! If yours are
    not cleaned be sure
    to ask the
    fishmonger how to
    clean them.)
Flour for dredging**

**Salt and pepper
Cayenne
Butter and peanut oil
    for pan-frying
White wine
Fresh lemon juice**

The amounts for this recipe are impossible, since I do not know how many crabs you have managed to acquire.

Season the flour for dredging with salt and pepper, and a bit of cayenne. Do this to your own taste. Dredge each of the soft crabs in this mixture and pan-fry over medium heat in a bit of butter and peanut oil, about 2 tablespoons of each per pan. Fry them 4 or 5 minutes on a side, just till they turn a bit golden. Do not crowd them in the pan.

Deglaze (page 23) the pan with dry white wine and lemon juice when you have finished frying the last batch. Pour the pan juices over the crabs and serve.

A green salad and a bit of plain buttered pasta is all that can be offered to such a rich dish.

CRAB LOUIS SEATTLE

I cannot think of anything that is more typical of a fine lunch in Seattle than a Crab Louis. This is a grand salad, and a properly prepared one is laden with fresh Dungeness crabmeat. You can use other kinds of crabmeat, of course, but I want to stick to my Dungeness.

CRAB LOUIS DRESSING

1 cup mayonnaise	1 egg, hard-boiled and grated
¼ cup chili sauce (catsup style)	1 teaspoon Worcestershire sauce
¼ cup whipping cream or half-and-half	2 teaspoons chopped fresh parsley
1½ tablespoons minced green sweet bell pepper	1 tablespoon fresh lemon juice
3 tablespoons peeled and minced yellow onion	Salt and pepper to taste

Mix all of the above together and chill.

THE SALAD

Whole iceberg-lettuce leaves to form a basket or bowl for each serving	Pitted black olives
	Green sweet bell pepper rings
Shredded iceberg lettuce	Crabmeat, legs included
Sliced hard-boiled eggs	Louis dressing

Arrange a whole leaf of lettuce on each plate. Use a leaf that is large enough to form a sort of bowl. Put a handful of shredded lettuce in each bowl and then a good serving of crabmeat. Top with sliced eggs, olives, and pepper rings. Pass the Louis dressing and allow your guests to add a bit to their salads.

CRAB COCKTAIL

All you need for this one is the crabmeat and a good cocktail sauce. I make mine in the following way. It is very simple.

1 bottle chili sauce
  (catsup section of
  supermarket)
Juice of one lemon
1 tablespoon
  Worcestershire
  sauce

1 tablespoon hot
  prepared
  horseradish
1 tablespoon Dijon
  mustard (Grey
  Poupon is fine.)
Salt and pepper to
  taste

Mix all the ingredients together and chill. Serve the crab in small glasses and allow each guest to add his own sauce. In a restaurant you usually get more sauce than crab. Shame!

JOE'S FLORIDA STONE CRAB MUSTARD SAUCE

SERVES 4

So many kinds of crab to eat in this country and so little time! Joe's Stone Crab Restaurant, in Miami Beach, is a mecca for serious seafood lovers. I have eaten there a couple of times and each time I was terribly happy. The surroundings are nice, the staff terrific, and the stone crab claws are superb. They sell more of this rare delicacy than just about anybody, and they have been doing so since 1913.

The thing that makes the meal is their special mustard

sauce. Jo Ann Sawitz, the charming owner, was kind enough to give us the recipe.

MUSTARD SAUCE

3½ teaspoons dry
    English mustard
    (Colman's)
1 cup mayonnaise
2 teaspoons Lea &
    Perrins
    Worcestershire
    sauce

1 teaspoon A.1. Sauce
⅛ cup light cream or
    half-and-half
⅛ teaspoon salt

Beat the dry mustard and mayonnaise together for 1 minute. Add the remaining ingredients and beat until the mixture reaches a creamy consistency. Chill.

The legs are dipped into this sauce with the fingers and enjoyed. Even your fingers will taste good with this sauce.

CRAB BISQUE

SERVES 8

This is delicious, rich, and expensive. The only way I can call it frugal is to tell you that it is so rich that people are not going to be able to eat much of it. Does that help?

2 tablespoons olive oil
2 stalks celery,
    chopped
2 tablespoons
    chopped parsley
½ cup diced carrots
½ yellow onion, peeled
    and sliced
4 cups Fish Stock
    (page 31) or
    canned fish
    broth, clam
    broth, or Chicken
    Soup Stock (page
    29) or canned
    chicken broth
2 whole cloves
1 whole bay leaf
6 peppercorns
¼ cup butter and ¼
    cup flour for a
    roux (page 25)
3 cups milk
⅛ teaspoon cayenne
    pepper or to taste
Salt and pepper to
    taste
1 pound cooked
    crabmeat, flaked
    or broken up
1 cup hot cream (Do
    not boil.)
¼ cup dry sherry
Minced parsley for
    garnish

Sauté the celery, parsley, carrots, and yellow onion in the oil until the onion is clear. Place in a 4-quart soup pot. Tie the cloves, bay leaf, and peppercorns in a little cheesecloth bag and add to the pot, along with the stock. Simmer the stock, covered, for ½ hour.

In the meantime, use a small frying pan and prepare a roux (page 25) by melting the butter and stirring in the flour. Cook just until the roux begins to turn a very light brown. Heat the milk and, using a wire whip, stir the roux into the hot milk. Continue stirring over medium heat until the milk becomes very thick. Add the cayenne pepper and set aside.

Remove the bag of spices from the stock and purée the vegetables in a food processor or blender, reserving the stock.

Return the puréed vegetables, along with the stock, to the soup pot and add the thickened milk. Bring this mixture to a simmer and add salt and pepper to taste. Stir in the crab, the hot cream, and the sherry. Remove from the heat. Serve immediately with a chopped parsley garnish on each bowl.

CLAMS

This ancient bivalve, the clam, has provided food for men and women since earliest recorded history. The Chinese prized clams four thousand years ago and our Pacific Northwest Native Americans can give us simply no clue as to when they began dining on this versatile creature.

In 1620 the Indians showed the Massachusetts Bay Colony members how to cook clams by burying them, along with corn on the cob, in great pits filled with seaweed and hot rocks. Clambakes are still celebrated in the East in this very manner, though they are becoming less and less frequent. The clam was so important to the life of the New England colonists that the shells were used as a form of currency in trading with the Indians. And in ancient Rome the clam was considered to be great food and an elegant medicine besides!

In our time we can appreciate a food with a grand history and a food that is both versatile and easy to prepare. It is one of the most economical sources of protein and flavor that we can find, and the little creatures are low in fat. So enjoy, the clam has been with us since the very beginning.

STEAMED CLAMS

SERVES 4

Now we are approaching delicate territory. I am a child of the Pacific Northwest, and nobody is allowed to mess

416

with our clams. We like them very close to plain, and that is the way God meant them to be eaten. I know. A very wise old Norwegian told me so.

This is the way that Patty, my wife, likes steamed clams. She is a converted New Yorker, so I now watch her eat them often. Simple to prepare and one of the best seafood dishes I know.

8 pounds steamer clams	**½ cup chopped fresh parsley**
¼ cup olive oil	**1 cup dry white wine**
3 cloves garlic, peeled and sliced thin	**Black pepper to taste (very little)**

Plan on 2 pounds of clams for each person. Wash the clams by stirring them around in a pan in the sink. Keep fresh running water going. Watch for clamshells that are filled with mud. The clam has left home! The mud will ruin your dish. Soak the clams in fresh water for about 1 hour before cooking. They will clean themselves out.

Heat a 12-quart covered soup pot and add the oil and garlic. Cook for a moment and add the remaining ingredients, including the drained clams. Cover and bring to a boil. Stir well once. Cover and simmer for just a few minutes until the clams open. Discard those that do not open. This should take about 8 to 10 minutes.

The stock in the bottom, or nectar, is wonderful. Serve it by the cup with a bit of freshly ground pepper on top.

The clams are eaten from the shell, along with a big green salad, fresh Italian or French bread, and too much beer. This is Seattle/Tacoma heaven.

In my part of the country steamed clams are served with salad and toasted rolls. That's it. If someone orders something in addition to this menu, we know he is from out of town.

VARIATION Try adding ½ tablespoon whole thyme to this dish. Really very good.

FRIED RAZOR CLAMS

I don't know why I am giving you this recipe. It is strictly a Pacific Northwest luxury item and the clam is becoming scarce. It breaks my heart.

The clams are shelled and then dredged in flour seasoned with a bit of salt and pepper. Fry these in a mixture of olive oil and butter, over medium heat, turning once, until they are very lightly browned. This should take about 4 or 5 minutes to a side. In Seattle/Tacoma people who overcook razor clams are put in jail. And they have NO chance of appeal!

Remember that these are very rich and rather sweet. I might add a course of Rice with Cheese and Onions (page 448) and a green salad. Oh, so rich!

GEODUCK STEAK

When you visit the Pike Place Farmer's Market in Seattle you will see these gigantic clams at the fish stalls. The body is cleaned and chopped up for chowder or ground for any of these recipes that call for chopped clam meat. The neck, however, is very large and is first blanched, then peeled. It is then cut open the long way and pounded with a meat tenderizer. My mother used to use the back of a knife. The neck steak is then dredged in seasoned flour and pan-fried in a bit of butter and olive oil. This clam is so ugly that you will not even want to try it . . . but I tell you that this is one delicious seafood steak.

Serve this as you would any very rich piece of meat. Go light on the salad dressing and add Asparagus with Almond Butter (page 494).

PASTA WITH WHITE CLAM SAUCE

SERVES 3–4

It is impossible to have too many variations on white clam sauce. In Seattle/Tacoma we could live on this dish. As a matter of fact, some weeks I *have* lived on clams and pasta. The green pepper adds a new little twist to an old standard. While I will admit that it was the Italian immigrant who taught us how to prepare this, it is nevertheless a very American version. I think Thomas Jefferson would have loved this dish.

4 pounds clams, steamed (page 383) and chopped, *or* 2 cans (6½ ounces each) Gorton's minced clams	½ teaspoon basil
	1 cup clam nectar *or* juice from the canned clams
	3 cloves garlic, peeled and chopped fine
3 tablespoons olive oil	¼ cup dry white wine
1 medium yellow onion, peeled and chopped	1 cup whipping cream
	Salt and pepper to taste
	Dash of Tabasco
2 tablespoons finely chopped green sweet bell pepper	Dash of Worcestershire sauce
2 tablespoons flour	½ tablespoon fresh lemon juice
¼ cup chopped parsley	1 pound spaghetti

If using fresh clams, steam them (page 383) and remove the meat from the shells, reserving the nectar. Chop the meat. Save some of the nectar for this recipe and serve the remaining nectar in a cup with a bit of freshly ground black pepper on top.

Heat a frying pan and add the olive oil. Sauté the yellow onion and green pepper until the onion is clear. Stir in the flour, parsley, and basil and remove to a bowl.

Reheat the frying pan and add the clam juice or nectar, along with the garlic, and reduce (page 25) by half. Add the wine and cream and bring to a simmer. Stir in the vegetables with a whip, stirring as they cook so that the mixture can thicken. Cook over medium heat for a few minutes to further reduce and thicken the sauce. Add the remaining seasonings, including the lemon juice. Stir in the clams and pour over the freshly cooked pasta.

This works well as a first course, and great as a main course along with salad and perhaps Skillet Bread (page 476).

FRIED CLAMS

This dish is great for regular clams, and LaMoyne, from the Harbor Lights Restaurant in Tacoma, Washington, sells these by the plateful. So easy, but please do not overcook them.

    1½ pounds of whole clams
         per person
         Cracker crumbs
         Butter and olive oil

Shuck or shell the clams. Dredge them in the cracker crumbs and pan-fry in ½ butter and ½ oil. Lightly brown on both sides over medium heat. This should not take long.

This is a very rich dish, so serve it with a green salad, a light dry white wine, and lots of good crunchy French bread or Sourdough French Bread (page 459).

Try a salad with the Crab Louis Dressing (page 410) along with these little rascals.

CLAM AND POTATO PANCAKES

MAKES 10 PANCAKES

This dish is one of the few things that I can remember my father cooking. It is really just a Jewish potato latke with clams. Hardly kosher!

1 can (6½ ounces)
   Gorton's minced
   clams, drained
2 cups peeled and
   coarsely grated
   potatoes
½ medium yellow
   onion, peeled and
   coarsely grated

1 egg, beaten
1 teaspoon salt
   Pepper to taste
   Oil for pan-frying (I
   use peanut oil.)

Blend all ingredients together. Don't forget to drain the clams first. Pan-fry until golden brown on both sides and serve hot.

CLAM PANCAKES

These remind me of fall mornings in Seattle. They also remind me of winter dinners in Seattle. We ate a lot of these when I was a child.

Mix a can of minced clams, drained, into your favorite pancake batter. Fry as usual and be ready for a treat. You will be surprised at how good clams and maple syrup taste together.

STUFFED CLAMS

SERVES 6 AS AN APPETIZER

This makes a very elegant first course for dinner or a nice plate for lunch. I developed this recipe years ago for Ivar Haglund and his restaurants—called "Ivar's Acres of Clams." He was an important part of the Seattle restaurant scene when I was a child. He also gave to Seattle our yearly Fourth of July fireworks display and to public television, *Monty Python's Flying Circus*. He was a grand old man...and we miss him. So, as Ivar would say, "Keep eating, and Keep Clam!"

2 cups chopped clam meat; save the shells (about 6 pounds of clams in the shell)	1 tablespoon minced parsley
	½ cup bread crumbs
	¼ cup coarsely grated Swiss cheese
1 teaspoon Worcestershire sauce	1 tablespoon butter, melted
1 tablespoon cooked and diced bacon	2 tablespoons dry white wine
	Salt and pepper to taste

Shuck the clams and save the shells.

Mix all ingredients together and stuff about ⅓ of the shells. Bake in a 375° oven for about 15 minutes or until clams are barely brown on top.

TURNER'S BOSTON CLAM CHOWDER

SERVES 10

Boston has so many truly fine seafood restaurants that trying to decide where to go for dinner is frustrating. Turner's offers good food and fine chowder and claims to have won several Boston contests with this recipe. It is very basic Boston chowder. Bostonians don't want you messing around with good basic chowder. I have adapted this recipe to use regular clams.

Clams on the West Coast have a bit stronger flavor than those in the East. While I prefer the western clam, some of my eastern friends say that my favorite is too strong for them. You can adjust this recipe to your liking.

8 pounds of clams,
steamed (Check
Steamed Clams
recipe, page 416,
for ingredients.)
2 cloves garlic, peeled
and crushed
1 stick butter
1 medium yellow
onion, peeled and
minced
1 rib celery, minced
½ teaspoon white
pepper
1 bay leaf

¼ teaspoon whole
thyme leaves
½ cup flour
5½ cups clam nectar
and milk (Use the
nectar from
steaming and
make up the
quantity needed
by the addition of
milk.)
1 large potato, peeled
and cut into
¼-inch dice
1 pint whipping cream

Wash clams and steam (page 416) in a 12-quart heavy stockpot. Reserve the broth. Remove the clams from their shells and chop coarsely. Cover both items and set aside.

In the same pot sauté the garlic in the butter for about 3 minutes. Add the onion, celery, pepper, bay leaf, and thyme. Sauté until the onions are clear. Add the flour to make a roux (page 25), stirring constantly. Cook over low heat for 5 minutes (don't brown). Slowly add the clam nectar, stirring constantly to avoid lumps. Simmer for 10 minutes (the soup will be thick at this point so be careful that it does not burn). Add the potato and cook until tender. Add the cream and clams and bring back to a boil. Correct the seasoning (page 23).

CLAM AND MACARONI SALAD

Try this one for a nice summer change. Add chopped Steamed Clams (page 416) to your favorite macaroni salad. Very tasty!

CLAMS WITH VEGETABLES AND BALSAMIC VINEGAR

SERVES 2–3 AS A MAIN COURSE, 6–8 AS AN APPETIZER

Don't be put off by the thought of light vinegar in your clams. This is a bit unusual, I will admit, but it is very delicious.

6 **pounds clams in the shell, prepared for steaming (Clean according to recipe on page 416)**
1 **thick slice bacon, or 2 thin slices, diced**
½ **yellow onion, peeled and chopped**
1 **large clove garlic, peeled and crushed**

1 **tablespoon chopped green sweet bell pepper**
2 **ribs celery, chopped**
¼ **cup** *each* **balsamic vinegar and red wine vinegar**
Juice of ½ lemon
Freshly ground black pepper to taste

Wash the clams in fresh water and then soak them in fresh water for 1 hour. Check to be sure none are simply full of mud.

In a 12-quart stockpot, sauté the chopped bacon until clear. Add the onion, garlic, green pepper, and celery and sauté for 5 minutes. Add the clams and the vinegars. Cover the pot and cook over medium high heat until all the shells are open. Add the lemon juice and toss. Discard those clams that do not open.

This is generally served as an appetizer, but it holds up well along with a Corn Pudding (page 433).

"For amber waves of grain..."

THE GRAINS

CORN

Our national motto should not be "In God We Trust."
I wish that we did! Our national motto should be "Two
kernels on the outside and a dead fish in the hole in the
middle." That is what saved us from starvation during
the very early Colonial times. Corn! It was a gift to us
from the Native Americans who met us on the shores,
and they taught us how to grow and eat and enjoy this
native grain, "maize," as they called it.

We now use corn in a thousand ways, and we have
shipped it to hundreds of other places, including China.
We have yellow corn, blue corn, Indian corn, popcorn,
red corn, hominy, cornmeal, corn syrup, cornstarch,
corn oil, and many more products. It is impossible to
think of contemporary American eating habits without
corn. And don't forget cornflakes, a product invented
by Dr. John Harvey Kellogg in 1907.

The American Indians who originally shared corn
with us knew that corn was so important to life in this
country that it was called Sacred Mother. The early
colonists became so dependent upon the grain that they
used it as money in paying rent, taxes, and so on. Today
it is America's premier crop, with corn going to the
products I mentioned above and to feed livestock and
poultry. We are now manufacturing alcohol from corn,
and automobile fuel cannot be far away.

A friend challenged my claim that corn is strictly
American. She reminded me that corn is mentioned in
the Bible, and she is right. However, she is referring
to an English translation and in Great Britain the term
corn was used in earlier times to refer to any kind of
grain at all. So, when the English Bible mentions corn
it is talking about grains that were common in biblical
times and not about corn as we know it. Corn is ours,
it is American, and we have used it since the beginning.

HINT: **On Freezing Corn on the Cob.**
I love corn on the cob and I like to have it
year-round. I have had very good luck with
this freezing method.

Buy the freshest corn possible and *do not*
remove any of the husk. Cover each ear in
plastic wrap and then in aluminum foil. Freeze
it immediately and it seems to keep very well
until the next season.

Do not unwrap until the ear is defrosted.
Then, cook as usual.

CORN WITH GARLIC AND OLIVE OIL

I know that most of us believe that corn on the cob
cries out for fresh butter. But, in order to cut down on
the cholesterol, try this: Heat some olive oil in a frying
pan and add a bit of crushed garlic. Do not let the garlic
brown, but let it cook a tiny bit. Brush that on your
corn and you won't miss the butter at all. In fact, I think
that you will prefer the garlic oil.

FRIED CORNMEAL MUSH

I remember my father making this dish when I was a
boy. He had eaten it often as a child, and I could not
understand why he would be cooking something that
marked difficult times in his youth. I asked him why
and he replied, "Because I can." There is something
very important about choosing to eat foods from times
in which you had few or no choices at all. Dad's younger
brother, Dale, told me that he remembers Thanksgiving
dinners at which fried cornmeal mush was served . . .
and nothing else.

I enjoy the dish very much. Make it for your kids
now and then. I think they will get a kick out of history
on the table for breakfast.

Make a batch of Hasty Pudding (page 431) and add 4 tablespoons of flour to the mixture. Whip it in, in a hurry. Pour the mush into an oiled loaf pan and chill overnight. In the morning slice the cold mush ¼ inch thick and fry in oil, butter, bacon fat, or a mixture of same. Fry it slowly until it takes on a golden and crunchy crust. This will take some time, about 15 minutes on each side. No, this is not an instant breakfast!

My friend Beatrice, in St. Paul, tells me that I should always flour the slices before frying. She's right. They brown evenly and taste wonderful.

Serve with butter and maple syrup.

CORN BREAD

SERVES 6

This is another use of cornmeal that is terribly versatile. One New England lady told me that she does not remember a dinner in her childhood without corn bread. And for breakfast it was served broken up in a bowl, with milk and sugar or maple syrup.

I love it just baked and on the table for dinner.

¾ cup flour	2 eggs, beaten
1½ cups cornmeal	1¼ cups milk
4 teaspoons baking powder	¼ cup salad oil
1 teaspoon salt	

Place all of the dry ingredients in a mixing bowl and mix up with an electric mixer. Add the liquids and mix until smooth.

Place in a greased 8 × 12-inch pan, and bake in a hot oven (400°) for about 30 minutes.

This same recipe can be used for cornmeal muffins or for corn sticks, baked in a heavy black iron mold.

HASTY PUDDING
Cornmeal Mush

SERVES 4–5 AS A SIDE DISH

This dish was an absolute staple in Colonial times. It was called hasty because it takes only about 40 minutes to make . . . and in terms of early cooking techniques that was a very short time. It could be prepared quickly and served just with gravy. That was often the whole meal. Or it could be served as a side vegetable dish. Or the colonists would sprinkle it with sugar and top with milk for dessert . . . or breakfast. Finally, it could be fried. Hasty pudding saved many a family in earlier times.

> **6 cups boiling water**
> **1 teaspoon salt**
> **1 cup yellow cornmeal**

Bring the water to a rapid boil in a heavy covered pot. Add the salt and slowly add the meal to the boiling water, stirring all the time. I use a wire whisk for this. Continue stirring until the cornmeal thickens, about 5 minutes. Turn the heat down low and cover the pot. Continue to simmer lightly, stirring the pudding several times, for 30 minutes more.

JOHNNYCAKE

Johnnycake is just corn bread with a bit of sugar added. The name comes from the practice of offering sweet corn bread to people in the midst of a journey. In New

England the word *journey* is pronounced "johnny."
Now you know!

Add 2 or 3 tablespoons of sugar to the Corn Bread
recipe (page 430) and you will have Johnnycake.

CORN FRITTERS, PAN-FRIED

When a gracious New Hampshire woman told me she
remembered "cawn frittahs" from her childhood, I told
her I did not know what "cawn" was. "Why," she replied, "don't you have cawn frittahs in Tacomar?" She
had dropped the *r* in *corn*, a very unfrugal thing for a
Yankee to do. But she wasted nothing. She saved the
dropped *r* and added it onto a word later in the sentence
. . . thus my city of Tacoma became "Tacomar." She
ate cawn frittahs throughout her childhood.

Thin down a bit of the Corn Bread batter (page 430)
with a little additional milk and fry it like pancakes.
Wonderful with dinner! Some people like to add a little
fresh hulled corn to the batter. I have even tried it with
frozen corn kernels and the results are just fine.

CORN FRITTERS, DEEP-FRIED

I have eaten both pan-fried and deep-fried corn fritters,
and I like them both. I will not become involved in the
argument as to which is more authentic. I think it simply
depends on what your mother used to make.

Use the Corn Bread batter (page 430) and drop wal-
nut-sized balls of same into deep fat. Have the fat at
375° and cook the fritters until they are very light golden
brown. Drain on paper towels and serve with honey for
dinner. If the fat is hot, you should not produce greasy
fritters.

CORN PANCAKES WITH CHEESE
Aropas

While corn is ours alone, we have shipped it all over
the world. Everyone has discovered a special way of

eating this glorious grain, and I think this one, *aropas,* from South America, is an absolute winner.

Prepare Corn Fritters (page 432) or pancakes, but make them a bit thinner than usual. Simply stir in an additional ¼ cup milk. Place sliced Jack cheese in between two cooked pancakes and refry in the pan, using a bit of additional butter or oil. Fry them on both sides until the cheese melts.

This will stop traffic at a luncheon or a party for your children. Boy, will you appear to be clever!

HOECAKE

This sounds very strange, I know. But in the old days, when farmers were working in the fields, it was not uncommon to cook Corn Fritters (page 432) on the back of a hoe. I actually tried this and it worked very well. Let your fire burn down to coals and make pancakes on the hot hoe. You must remember that these things are going to stick unless you use some Pam spray. How did they do it in the old days?

CORN PUDDING

SERVES 6 AS A VEGETABLE DISH

In New Orleans this is a great dish, but a seasonal one. I have tried to make it with frozen corn so that I can have it more often, and the results are not bad. Of course, fresh corn is the best.

1¾ cups milk
1 stick butter, melted
4 eggs, beaten
1 bag (20 ounces)
    frozen corn
    kernels *or* 2½
    cups fresh corn
    kernels

2 tablespoons sugar
2 teaspoons salt
½ teaspoon freshly
    ground black
    pepper
Dash Tabasco

In a saucepan, heat the milk and gently melt the butter. Allow this to cool for a bit while you beat the eggs and chop up the corn a bit in a food processor or by hand. Don't purée it, as you want a rough texture. If using frozen corn, allow it to melt first in a colander. Mix all the ingredients together and place in a buttered 2-quart baking dish. Bake at 325° for 1¼ hours. The top should be lightly browned.

BAKED CREAMED CORN

SERVES 4

I had never tasted this dish, nor had I ever even heard of it, until one of my staff in Chicago, Mark Blank, told me about his summer days on his grandfather's farm in Indiana. This was one of his favorite dishes and he even brought me the device that his grandfather had made for this special dish. You need a corn scraper in order to do this properly, and it can be done only with fresh corn. I just bought an "original" Lees corn cutter and creamer (page 16) and it seems to work quite well.

When Mark was sitting in a corner of the studio scraping, he said, "You know, this won't taste right. You have to have bees flying about your head while you scrape corn in the Indiana sun. We have no bees!" The dish is quite delicious, nevertheless. You will think that there is actually cream in this dish, but there is none.

6 ears fresh corn
3 tablespoons butter, melted
Salt and pepper to taste

Scrape the corn from the cob and cream it, using a corn cutter/creamer. Place the mixture in a greased baking dish and pour the melted butter on top. Bake uncovered at 375° for about 30 minutes, or until the top lightly browns.

MISACQUETASH

This is another gift from the Indians, a gift we now call succotash. In the early days, however, red beans were used rather than lima beans. Soak and cook the beans first, drain them, and place them in a casserole with fresh-cut corn kernels (or frozen), a bit of butter, salt, and pepper, and a very small amount of water. Cover and simmer on the top of the stove for a few minutes, until the corn is tender.

In the old days this dish was made with bear grease rather than butter. If you are out of butter or bear grease, try olive oil. It is very good!

INDIAN PUDDING

SERVES 8–10

Cornmeal was originally called Indian meal, since it was a gift from the Indians. The early recipes for this dish do not call for spices, of course, but this old New England version is very delicious. I like the addition of the cinnamon and nutmeg.

1 cup yellow cornmeal	2 eggs, beaten
½ cup black molasses	½ teaspoon cinnamon
¼ cup sugar	¼ teaspoon freshly grated nutmeg
¼ cup butter	6 cups hot milk
¼ teaspoon salt	Vanilla ice cream for topping
¼ teaspoon baking soda	

Mix the cornmeal with the molasses, sugar, butter, salt, baking soda, eggs, and spices. Add 3 cups of the hot milk, stirring carefully. Place in a 2-quart bean pot or other covered pot and bake in a 400° oven until all comes to a boil. Then stir in the remaining hot milk and bake, covered, at 275° for 4 to 6 hours, or until all is absorbed. Stir every half hour.

Serve hot in little bowls with a bit of vanilla ice cream on top.

CORN CHOWDER WITH CRAWFISH

SERVES 8–10

Although this delicious soup is just perfect for a cold winter evening, I made it one day in July and enjoyed it even in the summer heat. It seems that we are getting back to making soup, a food product that our forefathers and foremothers practically lived on.

2 quarts Chicken Soup Stock (page 29) or canned chicken broth
1 medium yellow onion, peeled and diced
4 tablespoons butter or olive oil
4 tablespoons flour
2 cups unpeeled diced (¼-inch pieces) potatoes
1 bay leaf
2 cups half-and-half
8 ears fresh corn, scraped from the cob (page 16) *or* 1 bag (20 ounces) frozen corn kernels and 1 can (17 ounces) creamed corn
Salt and freshly ground black pepper to taste
1 pound crawfish tail meat, cooked (page 275)
4 tablespoons chopped parsley for garnish
3 hard-boiled eggs, peeled and sliced

Place the chicken stock in a 6-quart kettle and put it on to heat.

In a small frying pan sauté the onion in the butter or oil just until clear. Stir in the flour and cook for a moment, thus making a roux. Stir the roux into the hot soup stock, stirring until the soup thickens a bit.

Add the potatoes and bay leaf and cook until the potatoes are tender. Remove the bay leaf.

Add the half-and-half and the corn. Bring to a simmer and season to taste with salt and pepper. I like a bit of extra pepper in this dish. Finally, add the crawfish meat and heat for just a moment. Serve, garnished with the parsley and sliced eggs.

CORN CHOWDER WITH SHRIMP

Use the recipe on page 436, substituting cooked and peeled shrimp for the crawfish.

CORN CHOWDER WITH CLAMS AND CHICKEN

This is terrific, and very typical of early dishes in the colonies. Prepare the Corn Chowder with Crawfish, omitting the crawfish. Add 2 cups of diced cooked clams along with 1 cup of their nectar. Add 2 cups of diced cooked chicken and proceed with serving. You will get raves on this one.

CREAMED CORNMEAL TIMBALES

SERVES 12

This is a blend of several dishes from our past, and a little European influence through Thomas Jefferson as well. I developed this dish one day on a corn binge, and when I tasted it I immediately became depressed. No, I was not depressed because it was not an interesting dish. This dish is so good I became depressed over the fact that I could not serve it to Mr. Jefferson. Such is the plight of the historical cook. What fun!

1 **quart water**	1 **cup freshly grated**
1 **teaspoon salt**	**Parmesan or**
1 **cup cornmeal**	**Romano cheese**
1 **cup cream**	**Black pepper, freshly**
5 **eggs, beaten**	**ground, to taste**

Bring the water and salt to a full boil in a 2-quart saucepan. Slowly stir in the cornmeal. I use a wire or wooden whip for this. Using a wooden spoon, continue to stir the mixture on medium heat until it is thick, about 6 minutes. Lower the heat and simmer, stirring occasionally, for 15 minutes more. Remove from the heat and allow to cool a bit.

Mix the cream with the eggs and stir into the cornmeal mush. Add the cheese and pepper to taste.

Oil or butter 12 timbale molds or custard cups. Fill each with the mixture and place in an oven-proof pan. Add water up to ½ inch on the sides of the molds. Bake at 350°, uncovered, until the custard sets and a table knife inserted in the center of the cup comes out clean. This will take about 50 minutes.

Allow the timbales to cool a bit, then unmold them and serve as a side dish. They can be served as they are or with a fresh light tomato-sauce topping.

HOMINY

This dried-corn dish goes back to the original white settlers. The Indians taught us to do wonderful things with corn, and this is one of the most interesting.

Hominy consists of dried corn kernels that have been treated with lime or lye so that the germs and hulls are removed. It is ground by Indians in the Southwest for making tortillas and it is cooked whole by the Indians in the Great Lakes and New England regions. Southwest Indians also cook it with meats in a wonderful stew (page 65). Long Islanders claim their own version of broken hominy, called Samp.

You can find this very American food product in some specialty supermarkets, in Latin American markets, and in some health-food stores. I dislike the canned variety, preferring to cook my own from the dried-corn product. Canned hominy tastes like a can. What else can I say?

To cook hominy, soak the dried product overnight in ample water. Then simmer, covered, for 3 hours, maybe more, until it is greatly puffed and tender. You will have to keep checking on the water content throughout this process. More water will need to be added. You may wish to add some salt to the water when cooking.

Hominy can be served as a side dish with gravy or in many other ways. Plan on 1/3 cup uncooked hominy for each serving. Cooked the day before and refrigerated, it becomes an easy dish to warm.

HOMINY AND EGGS

This is common in the South and is really quite good. Cooked hominy (page 438) is prepared with scrambled eggs and served for breakfast or a Sunday evening meal.

CREAMED HOMINY ON TOAST

The recipe is exactly what you think it is. Cooked hominy is warmed in a good cream sauce and served over hot toast. I like lots of black pepper on mine and I serve it over a toasted English muffin. Terrific!

HINT: **On Cream Sauce in the Microwave.**
Cream sauce in your microwave is easy. Use the ingredients for Creamed Chipped Beef on Toast (page 303), omitting the beef.

In a 1-quart glass mixing bowl, heat the butter at medium-high setting for 1½ minutes. Add the chopped onions and cook for 30 seconds more at the same temperature setting. Add the flour and mix to form a paste or roux. Cook at medium for 1 minute. Add the milk and blend thoroughly with a wire whip. Add the paprika, pepper, and Tabasco. Blend again and return to microwave for an additional 6 minutes at medium-high setting. Whip once more halfway through the final cooking process. Repeat this if necessary until the sauce is thickened and hot. Stir in the sherry. Taste for salt.

HOMINY BAKED WITH CHEESE

SERVES 6 AS A DINNER SIDE DISH

This is quick and delicious (quick providing you have cooked the hominy the day before). It is a nice dish from the South.

3 cups cooked Hominy (1 cup dried) (page 438)	2 large yellow onions, peeled and sliced thin
Salt and freshly ground black pepper to taste	1 cup sour cream
2 tablespoons butter	1 cup coarsely grated sharp Cheddar cheese

Place half of the hominy in a greased baking dish. Season to taste with salt and pepper. Heat a frying pan, add the butter, and sauté the onions until clear. Mix the onions and sour cream and place half of this mixture over the hominy. Top with half of the cheese and repeat for the second layer, topping the whole dish with the remaining cheese.

Bake uncovered at 350° for 40 minutes or until all is hot and bubbly.

CORN RELISH

SERVES 6

This is a lovely way to serve a cold corn dish, in summer or winter. Frozen corn works fine with this.

1 bag (20 ounces) frozen corn kernels
1 green sweet bell pepper, cored and diced
1 red sweet bell pepper, cored and diced

1 cup Vinaigrette Dressing (page 384)
¼ cup chopped parsley
Salt and pepper to taste

Melt the frozen corn in a large bowl of hot water from the tap. When melted, drain the corn very well. Mix all ingredients together and refrigerate for 1 hour before serving.

Serve as a cold side dish or salad.

CORN OYSTERS

MAKES 12

This one has you stumped, doesn't it? I first heard about this dish from a fellow who works on the airlines. I told

him about the show I was working on at the time, the
Corn Show, and he told me I had to have a corn oyster.
A young chef, I believe he is in Boston, has done much
research into real American cooking and now serves
this dish. I had to do some real digging before I could
find his source, which I will tell you now was *The New
England Yankee Cookbook,* published in 1939, the year
I was born. The book is now out of print, but some
enterprising used-bookstore person might be able to
find you a copy. It is a delight. In any case, these are
delightful, though rich.

A corn oyster is simply a deep-fried corn fritter
shaped like an oyster. So there! However, you should
know that the Shaker community (page 151) is given
credit for this simple and unusually good dish.

½ cup flour	1 egg, well beaten
½ teaspoon baking powder	2 tablespoons butter, melted
½ teaspoon salt	1 tablespoon milk
1 cup frozen corn kernels, defrosted	1 cup peanut oil

Mix the dry ingredients together in your electric mixer
bowl. Mix them well. Put the corn in your food processor with the metal blade and give it a few whirls.
We want the corn chopped fine but not mushy. Mix the
corn with the remaining ingredients, except the peanut
oil, and mix into the flour mixture. You should have a
thick batter.

Heat the oil in a large black frying pan to about 375°.
Drop spoonfuls of the batter into the fat and cook until
golden brown, turning once. They should be about the
size of, and look like, a small oyster. Serve as a bread
course with dinner.

NOTE: You may also wish to deep-fry these little jewels.

FRIED CORN WITH GREEN CHILE
(Southwest Indians)

SERVES 4–5

This is very quick and offers a most unusual combination of American flavors. You need not just serve this with Mexican dinners, as it will go well with many main courses.

3 cups fresh corn off
    the cob or frozen
    kernels, defrosted
½ cup peeled and
    diced yellow
    onion
3 tablespoons butter
    or olive oil

1 can (4 ounces) diced
    green chiles (I like
    Ortega brand best.)
Salt and pepper to
    taste

In a large frying pan sauté the corn and onions in the butter until tender. Add the chiles and check for salt and pepper.

RICE

The cultivation of rice originated in China some six thousand years ago and it has been the most important food item there ever since. Evidence for this is found in the fact that the terms for *food* and *rice,* in Chinese and most other Southeast Asian languages, are synonymous. The image of rice has been used in religious festivals and has always represented long life, abundance, and happiness. That is why we throw rice at weddings in our time!

Rice was not known in Europe until it was introduced into northern Italy in the 1400s. It is still very popular there as one can see from just a few meals in wonderful Milan. *Risotto Milanese* is one of the most delightful dishes that you could ever imagine. It is even more popular in Milan than pasta.

Rice finally arrived in England but the English were not really keen on the grain. Nevertheless, the American colonists brought rice with them to the New World and began planting it as early as 1622. Rice grew poorly in most regions but very well in South Carolina, and it became a major food item for the South. During the American Revolution the British captured Charleston and the Redcoats shipped the entire rice crop home to England, leaving no seed behind. It was Thomas Jefferson who smuggled some rice seed out of Italy at a time when such treasonous action meant death if the smuggler was caught. Yes, we are talking about the author of the Declaration of Independence. He brought back to the colonies a new strain of rice that he stole from Italy, and in a very short time South Carolina was back in business with the grain.

Today we produce rice in many southern states and in California. Rice became a major crop in California during the building of the great railroads and the Chinese rail workers looked to rice for their normal diet.

We did have a form of rice in this land prior to the

importation of the seed from the East. We have an
Indian rice, or wild rice, but it was expensive to harvest
in the old days since it grows in lakes and very deep
marshes. It is still expensive but it is a very American
product. Other rices common in America now include
long-grain, pearl (short-grained Japanese rice), converted, brown long- and short-grain, arborio from Italy,
basmati from India, and sticky sweet rice from the Ori-
ent.

Rice is basic to fully one half of the world's peoples,
and consumption in the Far East runs about 300 pounds
per person per year. In the rest of the world the per
capita consumption is about 143 pounds per person, but
in America it is much less than that. And much of what
we do eat is in a terrible form called instant rice. Ugh!
Rice is easy to cook, good for you, and very versatile.
I think we should serve it much more often than we do.

STEAMED RICE

Let's begin at the beginning. Cooking rice is so simple
that I cannot understand why so many people claim to
have trouble with it. Nor can I understand how people
can buy that instant stuff that tastes like the cardboard
box in which it comes. Maybe the box tastes better!

Instructions for cooking perfect rice are simple. Use
a heavy covered saucepan. For size, figure 1-quart ca-
pacity for each cup of rice: 1 cup of rice takes a 1-quart
pot; 4 cups, a 4-quart pot. Add 2 cups of water and
¼ teaspoon salt for each cup of rice. Bring to a boil
with the lid off and keep it off for about 3 minutes. Put
the lid on the pot and turn the heat to very low. Let it
cook for 15 minutes and then turn off the heat. Do not
open the lid during this process, and let the pot stand

on the burner for another 5 or 6 minutes. You are now ready to serve.

HINT: **On Cooking Rice.**
When cooking rice use a heavy saucepan. If your pans are light stainless steel use a heat diffuser (page 14). It will help keep the heat even on thin pans.

Remember, rice doubles in bulk so 1 cup will give you 2, or 4 servings of a normal side dish.

RICE WITH CHEESE AND ONIONS

SERVES 6

This is a very simple but flavorful dish. It will help you break the habit of eating normal starches such as potatoes. This will take little time to prepare, since it will cook while you prepare the rest of the meal.

1½ cups converted rice
3 tablespoons olive oil
1 large yellow onion, peeled and sliced
2 tablespoons butter
3 cups Chicken Soup Stock (page 29) or canned chicken broth

½ teaspoon salt
½ cup coarsely grated Swiss cheese
⅛ cup freshly grated Parmesan cheese
Black pepper to taste

Put the olive oil in a hot frying pan and add the rice. Cook for a few minutes over medium heat until the rice begins to lightly brown. Remove from the pan to a 2-quart covered saucepan.

Place the butter in the heated frying pan and sauté the onions until they begin to lightly brown. Place the onions, broth, and salt in the pan with the rice and bring to a boil. After the pot boils for 3 minutes, cover with the lid and turn the heat to low. After 15 minutes turn off the heat. Do not remove the lid for 5 more minutes. Stir in the cheeses and pepper. Serve as a side dish with just about any meal.

EMILY'S SPANISH RICE

SERVES 4 AS A MAIN DISH

Funny how the memory of a dish can stick with you for decades. When I was a child, my mother had a very limited food budget. It was during World War II and she made this dish often. I liked it, so I thought she was cooking this just to be nice to us. Now I realize that it is a great way to feed 4 people on ½ pound of hamburger. I don't make the dish often anymore but I still think about it now and then. This dish will not win any cooking contests but it will tickle your children . . . and perhaps give them some good memories.

1 tablespoon olive oil
½ pound hamburger
1 yellow onion, peeled and coarsely chopped
1 green pepper, cored and coarsely chopped
½ teaspoon commercial chili powder (I like extra hot.)
1½ cups water
½ cup tomato sauce
1 tablespoon butter
1 cup converted rice
2 tablespoons Worcestershire sauce
¼ teaspoon Tabasco
¼ teaspoon whole thyme leaves
Salt and pepper to taste

Heat a 2-quart Dutch oven and add the oil, hamburger, and onions. Sauté until the meat browns and falls apart and the onions are clear. Remove excess fat from pan and add the green pepper and chili powder. Sauté an additional 5 minutes. Add all remaining ingredients and bring to a boil. Cover the pan and cook over low heat for 25 minutes, or until the rice is tender.

Mom used to serve this with canned corn and white bread. I know you can do better than that.

OLD-FASHIONED RICE PUDDING

SERVES 6–8

We know that this was popular with the likes of Thomas Jefferson and other forefathers and foremothers. People don't seem to be making it much anymore and that saddens me. It is little work and just delicious, cold, in the middle of the night.

1½ cups milk
Pinch of salt
5 tablespoons sugar
1 tablespoon butter, melted
1 teaspoon vanilla
5 eggs, beaten
¼ cup brandy
2 cups *cooked* long-grain rice
1 tablespoon fresh lemon juice
Cinnamon for topping

Mix all ingredients except the rice and lemon juice and cinnamon. Mix them well and then add the rice and lemon juice. Sprinkle a bit of cinnamon on top. Place in a 8×10-inch greased baking dish and bake at 325° for 50 minutes, or until it is lightly browned and the custard is set. Test with a table knife. Stick it in the center of the dish, and if it comes out clean the dish is baked.

In earlier times maple syrup was served on top of this pudding. Milk is enjoyed as well.

RICE FOR BREAKFAST

Use leftover rice for an Early American breakfast. Heat it, covered, in the microwave and serve with hot milk, cinnamon, and sugar.

WILD RICE WITH MUSHROOMS AND ONIONS

SERVES 8–10

I have used this dish as a side dish, a main course, a stuffing for fowl, and a filler for stuffed vegetables such as tomatoes or green peppers. Wild rice takes longer to cook and requires more water because the grain triples, while regular rice only doubles.

2 teaspoons salt	3 tablespoons butter
1 cup wild rice	or olive oil
1 cup converted rice	½ pound mushrooms,
1 yellow onion, peeled	sliced
and cut into ¼-inch	½ teaspoon freshly
dice	ground black
	pepper

In a 3-quart heavy-lidded saucepan bring 6 cups of water to a boil. Add the salt and the wild rice. Cover and simmer over low heat for 30 minutes. Add the converted rice to the pot without stirring. Cover and continue cooking another 15 minutes. Do not remove the lid. Let the rice sit for 5 minutes after finishing the cooking.

In the meantime, sauté the onion in the butter or oil. When the onion becomes clear, add the mushrooms and sauté for 5 or 6 minutes.

When the rice is finished, stir in the mushrooms, onions, and black pepper.

Correct the seasoning. Serve hot.

FRIED RICE WITH SEAFOOD

SERVES 6–8, DEPENDING UPON HOW MUCH SEAFOOD YOU PUT IN THE PAN

This is not a Chinese dish though I am going to use my wok. A regular heavy frying pan will work almost as well. This is one of those dishes that has a thousand variations, so don't be reluctant to change my recipe completely.

1½ cups raw converted or long-grain rice, cooked and chilled (3 cups cooked)
2 tablespoons olive oil
3 cloves garlic, peeled and crushed
1 yellow onion, peeled and cut into large dice
1 medium-sized tomato, cut into ¼-inch dice
½ green sweet bell pepper, cut into ¼-inch dice

½ pound cooked seafood (shrimp, crab, clams, fish, etc.)
Tabasco to taste
Salt and freshly ground black pepper to taste
2 tablespoons rice wine vinegar (optional)
Green onions, chopped, for garnish

Cook the rice (page 447) and allow it to cool. I do this the day before so that the rice will fall apart easily when I prepare this dish.

Heat a wok or a large frying pan and add the oil. Sauté the garlic and yellow onion until the onion is clear. Add the remaining ingredients and stir-fry (page

22) until all is hot. Use any kind of cooked seafood you wish. Even leftover lobster will do. (I'm sorry. I just could not help saying that!)

I like to add a green vegetable such as green beans. This is a rich dish and really needs very little support.

WILD RICE WITH SPARERIBS

SERVES 4–5

This is a recipe sent me by a viewer. It was good in her version, but we decided to zip it up a bit with a few additions. I hope that Gertrude will not be angry with me. This is a whole meal when served with bread and a very crisp salad.

¾ cup wild rice
4 pounds spareribs, cut into 3- or 4-rib servings
2 cups tomato juice
½ teaspoon salt
1 teaspoon freshly ground black pepper
1 teaspoon sugar
1 tablespoon Worcestershire sauce

Dash of Tabasco, or to taste
½ teaspoon thyme
2 cloves garlic, peeled and crushed
1 tablespoon Dijon mustard (Grey Poupon is fine.)
Salt and pepper to season the ribs
1 large yellow onion, peeled and sliced thin

Place the rice in a large bowl and cover with 6 cups boiling water. Allow to soak for 4 hours. Drain, discarding the water.

Cut the ribs into 3- to 4-rib serving pieces and place on an oven broiling rack. Bake at 450° for about 15 minutes, or until lightly browned.

Mix all other ingredients, except the onion slices and the seasoning of salt and pepper for the ribs.

Choose a large, lidded oven-proof casserole and place ⅓ of the rice on the bottom. Top with ⅓ of the browned ribs; season the meat with salt and pepper and top with ⅓ of the onion slices. Repeat the layer of rice, ribs, and onions as before. Continue until you have 3 complete layers.

Pour the tomato mixture over the pan contents and cover. Bake in a 350° oven for about 2 hours, or until the bones are loose from the meat.

You should stir this mixture twice while it is in the oven.

This is one of those "jump in" dishes, so I hesitate to add too much to the menu. You need a salad, a lot of beer, many napkins, and certainly people whom you like at the table. It is messy!

BEEF AND RICE "OLIVES"

SERVES 8–10

This dish comes from a cookbook that is about 200 years old. I cannot quite figure out the background of the name but we have seen the dish many times since those early days. It is obviously a way of stretching meat using rice. I have added some seasoning and the dish is baked, so it is easy to prepare.

2 pounds ground beef (lean)	1 teaspoon salt
	½ teaspoon pepper
2 cups cooked converted rice	1 egg, beaten
1 teaspoon oregano	

Mix all together and form into 1-inch balls. Place on a baking sheet and bake for about 20 minutes at 375°, or until they are done to your taste.

If you make these small enough, they are terrific as party snacks. Larger sizes fit the dinner table well, along with a green salad, rolls, and perhaps some Cabbage and Salt Pork (page 114).

SOURDOUGH

Sourdough is probably the oldest form of "raised" or "leavened" bread that we know. While the Egyptians are generally given credit for baking the first raised bread, we must also remember that their claim to this fame occurred just after the Jews had fled Egypt, leaving their leavening behind. They were taught to bake unleavened loaves of bread in the desert. I am convinced by the historical evidence that it was the Jews who brought a wild leavening from the desert, a sourdough, into Egypt, and the Hebrew slaves taught the Egyptians how to bake raised bread in the first place!

In any case we are all familiar with the biblical lines about a little leaven leavening the whole. The Bible is referring to sourdough, and we have been using these wild yeast forms ever since. There is some evidence that Columbus brought a sourdough starter with him on the ships when he set out for the New World. In the time of Columbus, sourdough was the only kind of yeast available. It was used in this country from the very beginning.

When commercial yeasts were developed, it was no longer necessary to use the old, but sometimes unsure, sourdough method. However, the pioneers continued to use the leavening as they attacked each new frontier. The prospectors of the Yukon during the Alaskan Gold Rush of the 1890s were probably the most colorful of this camp. They used sourdough so constantly that the name was associated not only with the bread but with the prospectors themselves. Later, by extension, it became associated with all of the "Old Alaska" crowd. My grandfather on my mother's side was one of these colorful characters.

Since many of the prospectors set out by boat from San Francisco, sourdough bread is often associated with that city, and it is still a San Francisco specialty. There are some fascinating stories about the old San Francisco sourdough bakers. My favorite claims that the old basement bakeries that produced this bread had the sourdough bug literally living in the damp humidity there. One old baker, who was loved by the whole of the city, used to bake without a shirt on of any kind. After rolling a loaf he would flop the dough on his chest and then onto the baking rack. He knew that his body chemistry and that of the sourdough was just right, and the bread he produced was prized in "Baghdad by the Bay." The city health department closed him down only a few years ago. I like to think that the story is true since I have many San Francisco friends who claim that the bread is not as good since they put him out of business. Don't look for the old man but the Boudin Bakeries of San Francisco are shipping the mother sponge to other cities, where they have had great success, Chicago being a perfect example.

Most lovers of sourdough claim that the older the starter is the better it is. Some Alaskan sourdoughs claim to be using starters that are fifty years old.

BASIC SOURDOUGH STARTER

Sourdough starters can be purchased commercially or they can be started on your own. Your own might be more fun. One cup of water is mixed with 1 tablespoon sugar, 1 cup flour, and 4 tablespoons commercial buttermilk. Mix all of this together and place it in a glass or stainless-steel bowl. Do not use aluminum. Cover this with a towel and allow to stand in a warm place for a few days, or until it has begun to ferment and has a wonderful sour smell. You might keep this on the top of the water heater or in your oven and leave the light on all the time. The starter should be the consistency of pancake batter and it can be covered and stored in the refrigerator. Use this as your starter in any of the recipes that follow.

The old-timers claim that you can get a sourdough starter going by just mixing flour and water together and allowing it to sit in a warm place for several days. This may work, but it is not terribly reliable.

> HINT: **On Storing Sourdough Starter.**
> When storing sourdough starter in the refrig-
> erator, remember that it should be kept at
> around 42°. If it is too cold, it will take a long
> time to come around again, to come back to
> life. Your refrigerator is probably colder than
> this, so perhaps you may want to store the
> starter in a very cool place.

SOURDOUGH BATTER

This must be made about 12 hours before you are going
to begin the bread-making process. Just do it at night
before you go to bed. It takes only a minute.

Remove the starter from the refrigerator and allow
it to come to room temperature. Measure out 1½ cups
of starter and put it into a 2-quart mixing bowl. Add
1½ cups flour and 1 cup tepid water (85°). Mix this well,
cover, and allow to sit overnight, unrefrigerated. This
is called "proofing," and when the batter is ready, the
natural yeast will have spread throughout the dough
and it will be bubbly and offer a strong sourdough odor.

When ready to bake, measure out the amount of
batter called for in the recipe and return the remaining
batter to your starter bowl in the refrigerator. Remember that you must replenish your starter by adding back
what you take out. Return the same amount of water
and flour that you have removed. Just whip it up and
stir it into the starter bowl.

SOURDOUGH FRENCH BREAD

This loaf has a wonderful flavor, and it uses both normal yeast and sourdough. It is simple to do and the odor of this stuff baking will bring the kids in from the yard— I promise.

2 cups proofed Sourdough Batter (See page 458. Make this the night before.)	1 package dry yeast 1 cup tepid water (85°) 3 teaspoons sugar 1 teaspoon salt 6 cups all-purpose flour

Make your batter the night before. Cover and let it sit out. Dissolve the yeast in the water. Mix with the Sourdough Batter and then stir in the sugar and salt. Finally, stir in the flour. I use my KitchenAid dough hook so there is no pain to this method. Knead with a machine or by hand until the dough is very smooth and elastic.

Place the dough on a plastic tabletop and cover with a large metal bowl. Allow to double in bulk, about 1½ hours.

Punch the dough down, knead it a bit, and divide it into 2 pieces. Shape each into a loaf and place on a baking sheet that has been sprinkled with cornmeal. Using a pastry brush, dab a little water on the top of each loaf. Allow the loaves to rise until double in bulk and bake in a 375° oven for about 30 minutes, or until the crust is brown and the loaf sounds hollow when you tap the bottom with your knuckle.

GREEN CHILE ROLLS

This is an unusual bread product using good old American chiles. I love the flavor and the rolls do add a new dimension to a normal meal. No, they are not hot!

Make the dough as above, adding two 4-ounce cans of Ortega-brand diced green chiles. Mix the chiles into the batter just before you add the 6 cups of flour. Allow to rise and punch down, just as with the bread, but shape into 24 small rolls rather than 2 loaves.

Bake as you would the bread, remembering that rolls take less time in the oven.

SOURDOUGH BISCUITS

These are light and sour. What more could you want of a biscuit than that?

2 cups proofed Sourdough Batter (page 458)	½ teaspoon baking soda
	½ teaspoon salt
	¼ cup butter or Crisco
2¼ cups flour	½ cup milk or buttermilk
1 tablespoon baking powder	
1 teaspoon sugar	

Prepare your batter the night before. Mix the dry ingredients together in a bowl and cut in the butter using a pastry blender (page 17). The flour mixture should resemble a grainy mix, something like cornmeal. Mix the milk with the batter and stir into the dry ingredients. Knead on a board for about 30 seconds. Roll the dough out about ½ inch thick and cut into circles with a glass or biscuit cutter.

Place on a greased cookie sheet, giving the biscuits room to rise. Allow to rise for 30 minutes to 1 hour.

Brush tops of biscuits with melted butter or milk and bake at 400° for 15 minutes or until they are puffed and golden brown.

SOURDOUGH CORN FRITTERS

MAKES 4 DOZEN FRITTERS

These are wonderful. Mix 1 cup cornmeal along with 1 cup defrosted corn kernels with the Sourdough Pancake batter on page 461. Allow the mixture to sit for 1 hour before cooking.

Drop balls of batter about the size of a walnut into fat that is heated to 375°. Cook until they float and are golden brown. Turn each one several times. Do not put too many into the fat at once.

SOURDOUGH CLAM FRITTERS

MAKES 4 DOZEN FRITTERS

Prepare as the Sourdough Corn Fritter recipe on page 460, but add one 6½-ounce can of Gorton's chopped clams along with the corn and cornmeal.

Corn and clams together produce a flavor that is as old as Plymouth Rock . . . at least!

SOURDOUGH PANCAKES

SERVES 4–5

I remember having breakfast with David and Glenn Mann when I was a boy. We were in Boy Scouts together and their German mother, Lucille, served sourdough pancakes almost every morning for years. It was great fun to spend the night with the Manns and then arise to the smell of sourdough pancakes cooked in bacon grease. My memory tells me each pancake was 1 inch thick . . . but I'm sure they couldn't have been. They were wonderful, in any case.

2 cups proofed
    Sourdough Batter
    (page 458)
1½ cups flour
1 tablespoon sugar
¼ teaspoon salt
½ teaspoon baking
    soda

1 tablespoon baking
    powder
1 cup milk
3 eggs, beaten
¼ cup melted butter

Prepare the Sourdough Batter the night before. Mix the dry ingredients together. Add the milk and eggs to the batter. Mix with the dry ingredients and let rest for 15 minutes. Gently stir in the melted butter.

Noodles, Dumplings, Biscuits, and Scones

Just the name of this section should bring to your mind the wonderful smell of the homemade biscuits you had when you were a child. At least, I hope you had that kind of a childhood. Actually, I did not. My mother rarely made biscuits, but her noodles or dumplings were wonderful.

The following few recipes are just to get you started ... or perhaps back to doing something that you used to love to do: making biscuits, something very simple to do.

HARRIET'S SOUTHERN BISCUITS

MAKES 6–8 BISCUITS

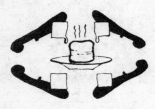

Harriet Fields is a dear friend and a fine cook. She comes from Texas and her husband, Ron, comes from Arkansas. Ron's mother taught Harriet to make these biscuits, but now Ron claims that Harriet's biscuits are better than his mother's. Boy, if Mrs. Fields sees this book, I'll bet we are all going to be in trouble.

One of the secrets to these little jewels is a very hot, oiled, black frying pan. I had never seen this prior to my instruction from Harriet, but now I can do these quite well myself.

1 cup plus 2
  tablespoons flour
1 teaspoon baking
  powder
½ teaspoon salt
¼ teaspoon baking
  soda

2 tablespoons Crisco
½ cup buttermilk
1 tablespoon Crisco
  for frying pan

Mix the dry ingredients together in a mixing bowl. Blend in the Crisco until the mixture is coarse and grainy. Harriet uses a fork, but I have better luck with a pastry blender (page 17). Then, using a fork, stir in the buttermilk. Do not overmix. Put out on a floured board or marble pastry board and knead just a few times. Pat out the dough to about ½ inch thick. Cut with a biscuit cutter or a glass. (Flour the cutter.) Do not handle the dough too much or it will get tough.

Use a heavy black iron frying pan. Place the 1 tablespoon of Crisco in the frying pan and put the frying pan in the oven for about 7 minutes. Remove the pan from the oven and place the biscuits in the pan. Turn each once in the oil and bake the biscuits at 500° for 10 minutes, or until light brown.

NETTIE SMITH'S CHICKEN AND NOODLES

SERVES 8–10

Nettie Smith was my paternal grandmother, and she was a grand woman indeed. She looked and thought like Eleanor Roosevelt, and she would be very flattered that I should say this about her here. She was a Democratic member of the Washington state legislature and a "Wobbly," an early union organizer in the Pacific Northwest. And she was tough. The old girl had a pistol that she used to use for shooting rattlers when the children were being raised in Montana. She was bright and charming, too. Oh Lord, how I miss her.

While she was a wonderful and exciting person, Grandma Smith was not a cook. I know it's a terrible thing to say about your grandmother, but she was an awful cook. She used to cremate a turkey each Christmas . . . and the whole family had to attend the service. However, the following dish was hers, and she did it well. She could feed her whole family, eight people in all, with one chicken, just by using this recipe.

I have worked on this dish until it tasted like my childhood. I think that you will find it delicious, too.

NOODLES

4 cups all-purpose flour
6 eggs
½ teaspoon salt
2 tablespoons water

CHICKEN

2 chickens (about 3½ pounds each), cut in half
Chopped parsley for garnish

STOCK

3 pounds chicken backs and necks
3 carrots, cut up (Don't bother to peel.)
1 yellow onion, peeled and chopped
4 stalks celery, chopped
2 whole bay leaves
1 teaspoon whole thyme leaves
1 teaspoon whole sage leaves
10 whole peppercorns
Salt to taste

Prepare the noodles: Place the flour in a large bowl and add the eggs and salt. With your fingers, pinch the flour into the eggs and then stir with a wooden fork until grainy. Add the water and knead into a heavy dough. Knead on a marble board until smooth. Cover and let rest 30 minutes.

Divide the dough into 4 equal balls. Roll each out to about 12 inches in diameter. Use plenty of flour. Leave each circle to dry on the counter for ½ hour.

Place the stock ingredients in a 20-quart kettle and cover with 5 quarts of water. Bring to a boil and simmer, covered, for ½ hour.

Place the chicken halves in the stockpot and cover. Simmer for 45 minutes and then remove the chicken halves to cool. Separate the bones and skin from the meat and return the bones and skin to the pot. Keep the meat covered in a separate container. Continue cooking the stock for another 45 minutes.

Place 1 of the noodle circles on top of another and roll up tightly like a jelly roll. Repeat with remaining circles. Slice into ⅓-inch-wide rolls and then separate into noodles. Sprinkle more flour on the noodles and allow them to dry on the counter for at least 1 hour before cooking. You can allow them to sit there up to a whole day before cooking.

NOTE: You can also roll the noodles using an Italian pasta machine. Separate the dough into 6 snakes and run them through the machine to the thickness you like. Use plenty of flour when cutting into noodles. This method is much easier than the hand-rolled method.

Drain the stock from the pot and discard all else. Remove the fat from the stock and return the stock to the kettle. You should have about 4 quarts. If not, add water to make up the difference. Bring the stock to a rapid boil. Shake the excess flour off the noodles and add to the kettle. Boil gently until the noodles are tender, about 11 minutes. Add the deboned chicken meat to the noodles and bring to a simmer again. Check seasoning and add salt and pepper if required. Serve in a large bowl with a chopped parsley garnish. This dish will be very thick and rich.

Be sure that you think some old left-wing thoughts when serving Nettie's noodles!

This is a whole meal, and I mean whole. Add a salad and some green vegetables.

RAISIN SCONES

MAKES 12 SCONES

I remember these from the Puyallup County Fair when I was a kid. Just as soon as I had seen the baby pigs I ran to get in line for a scone, a triangular biscuit served hot, filled with butter and raspberry jam. The smell of the hay, the horses, the carnival midway, and the taste of the raspberry jam that stuck to my fingers combined to form a sensuous memory that I doubt I shall ever lose.

This is as close as I can come to that American biscuit product, the scone. I do think that you need a horse standing around in order to get the full effect.

2 cups flour	½ cup raisins, soaked
½ teaspoon salt	in hot water for
3 teaspoons baking	½ hour, drained
powder	½ cup half-and-half or
2 tablespoons sugar	cream
¼ cup cold butter	1 egg, beaten

Sift the dry ingredients together. Cut the butter into the dry ingredients, using a pastry blender (page 17). Add the drained raisins to the flour mixture. Mix the half-and-half with the beaten egg and stir into the flour mixture. Use a fork and do not overmix. It should take only a few turns to get a dough.

Divide the dough into 3 balls and pat each out into a ½-inch-thick circle. Cut each into 4 triangular scones. Bake on an ungreased baking sheet at 450° for about 12 minutes, or until golden brown.

Serve with butter and raspberry jam.

DUMPLINGS

MAKES 12 DUMPLINGS

Dumplings were with us in the colonies, they were with us when we moved to the Midwest, they were with us on the Oregon Trail, and they were with us when we hit the West Coast, the "Last Frontier." If it is possible to remember things prior to your actual appearance, prior to your physical birth, my primordial memory is of dumplings. I love them! These are so easy they should be a regular part of your cooking repertoire.

2½ cups flour	3 tablespoons Crisco
3 teaspoons baking powder	2 tablespoons chopped parsley
1 teaspoon salt	1¼ cups milk

Mix dry ingredients and cut in Crisco, using a pastry blender (page 17), until the mixture is coarse and grainy. Add chopped parsley and, using a wooden fork, stir in the milk. Do not overmix. It should only take a few turns to get a dough.

Drop by large spoonfuls on top of simmering stew or very thick soup. Simmer 5 minutes with the lid off the pot and then cover and simmer 15–20 minutes longer.

Serve immediately.

"From purple mountain majesties..."

THE FRONTIER

OREGON TRAIL

I think Americans still believe that somewhere a great chance, a wonderful opportunity, is waiting just for them. There is no other way I can possibly explain the popularity of the television game shows or the fascination we have with state lottery games. We believe that the American frontier, the place where everything was new and open and filled with glittering chances, now is a matter of gambler's luck. I see a similar connection between the old American belief in the western frontier as the land of golden opportunity and the reality that it was a simple gamble whether you were going to live long enough on the trail to reach it.

The hardships on the trails to California, to Utah, to Oregon, were just horrible. Why would you leave the comforts of Boston or Virginia to climb in a wagon and spend six months covering a distance of several thousand miles? The estimated cost for the trip was $800 to $1,200, at a time when wages were less than $1.50 a day. For most who took the gamble, western expansion meant free and untamed land for farming and homesteads. Everyone who went west had to be highly motivated, much like the early English colonists who came to the New World.

One of the major problems to solve on the trip was, of course, food. The basics that most emigrants lived on during the journey were flour, cornmeal, beans, rice, bacon, and dried fruits and vegetables. Some people were wealthy enough to bring along sugar, clarified butter, coffee, spices, and dried beef. On the trail, certain supplements to a rather bland diet could be found. In buffalo country, things looked brighter. The meat was eaten fresh, and much was dried and made into pemmican to eat later. When buffalo meat was plentiful, it was consumed at every meal. It was boiled, fried, roasted, and dried. One woman wrote in her journal that she was very happy with the buffalo diet, and as long as she had her buffalo meat she had no other wants and would be happy indeed. After two months of the same diet she was beside herself, and her writings concerning the great bison were considerably less affectionate.

Cooking posed numerous problems. Firewood was scarce or nonexistent, so buffalo chips and sagebrush took its place. And since the cooking had to be done over open fires or in pits, the rains and heavy winds made things difficult. Sand and mosquitoes would blow into the bread dough and stay there. Nevertheless, bread baked in this difficult manner was often the only food that the travelers had to eat.

The final leg of the journey was the most treacherous. Supplies had run low and the mountains still had to be crossed, causing the death of many who had almost completed the trip. Starvation was so common at this point that anyone who did not complain of hunger was suspected of being ill.

But they did it. They moved to the West and settled communities, which still thrive and seldom think about the hardships suffered by those first pioneers.

BACON CORN BREAD

SERVES 6

Bacon was one meat that would keep fairly well during the long trip on the trail, providing you kept it in bags surrounded by bran. The bran would help prevent the bacon fat from melting under the heat of the prairie sun. This dish offers a new flavor, which must have been truly delicious after a day in that wagon!

½ cup pan-fried bacon,   1 batch of Corn Bread
    about 5 thick slices   (page 430)
    (Save the fat!)

Cook the bacon until crisp. Reserve the fat. Chop the bacon and stir it into the corn bread batter. Use bacon fat instead of shortening, if you wish, to make the batter.

Grease the pan with a good bit of the bacon fat and bake the corn bread as directed.

SODA BREAD OR SKILLET BREAD

SERVES 6

The black frying pan went on the trail as one of the main pieces of cooking equipment. It worked well over the fire for regular cooking, and, since you did not have an oven, it also had to act as a baking device. The pan was filled with dough, then it was moved about the fire and angled in such a way that the bread finally baked.

You and I can do this easy recipe in an oven. But don't serve it without remembering how hard times were on the Oregon Trail.

3¼ cups flour	2 tablespoons butter
1 teaspoon salt	or Crisco
1 teaspoon baking	1¼ cups buttermilk or
powder	sour milk
1 teaspoon baking	Shortening for
soda	greasing the pan

Mix all the dry ingredients together and then cut in the shortening. On the trail, they would have used a fork to do this, but I prefer to use a pastry blender (page 17). Cut in the shortening until the mixture has a fine, grainy appearance. Stir in the milk. Knead the dough a few times and push it into a greased black frying pan. Bake in a 400° oven for about 35 minutes, or until the loaf is browned and light in weight.

FRIED CREAMED SALT PORK

SERVES 4

I am sure that no matter how much you like a dish it can become tiring after many repeats. It must have been that way on the trail. Salt pork was a common commodity, and when milk was available this dish would appear . . . probably again and again. I like it very much and suggest you try it.

1 pound salt pork, cut into ⅓-inch-thick strips	2½ cups milk
⅓ cup flour	Salt and freshly ground black pepper to taste

Bring 2 quarts of water to a boil and throw in the salt pork. Cook for about 5 minutes, then remove from the heat and drain.

Using a large black frying pan, fry the salt pork until lightly browned. Remove it from the pan, reserving the fat. Measure about ¼ cup of the fat and return to the pan. Stir in the flour and cook for just a moment. Add the milk to the pan, stirring all the time to avoid lumps until the mixture thickens. Return the salt pork to the pan.

This is great poured over hot biscuits or served with any dried vegetable, such as beans or hominy.

BUFFALO STEW

SERVES 6–8

It was necessary for the emigrants to supplement their diet with whatever could be found along the trail. When buffalo meat was available, it was eaten boiled, fried, roasted, and dried. It proved to be a lifesaver in desperate times, and it was quite good besides.

The great move to the frontier practically wiped out the buffalo. However, the animals have been saved from extinction and are now being farm-raised for food. Isn't that an interesting turn of events?

The following stew recipe is quite delicious. It was given to me by Lorraine Czimer, of Czimer's Meat outside Chicago. They carry buffalo and a terrific assortment of other specialty meats, including bear. If you can track down a buffalo, you will like this dish. It is a bit more elaborate than would have been possible on the trail. The meat tastes a bit sweet and it is very good.

3 pounds of buffalo, cut up for stew
Salt and freshly ground black pepper to taste
¼ cup peanut oil for browning
3 cloves garlic, peeled and sliced

1 large yellow onion, peeled and chopped
2 bay leaves
½ cup dry red wine
¼ cup catsup
Kitchen Bouquet to taste
1 cup mushrooms, sliced and sautéed

Lightly salt and pepper the meat. Heat a large Dutch oven and add the oil. In two different batches, brown the meat on all sides. Add the remaining ingredients to the pan and stir well. Cook slowly, covered, over low heat.

A good gravy should form in this dish. If you wish more gravy, Lorraine suggests you add a bit of water and some water-flour mixture for thickening. If the color of the gravy is too light, add some Kitchen Bouquet to taste.

Cover the meat and bake at 325° for 1½ hours, or until tender.

Serve this with Bacon Corn Bread (page 475) and Creamed Cornmeal Timbales (page 437). They wouldn't have had timbales on the trail, but they sure are good with this stew.

BUFFALO JERKY

This was a method of preserving buffalo meat on the trail, a method taught us by the Indians. The meat was dried in the sun, and then could be kept for weeks in the wagon. It was later reconstituted in the form of a soup or stew, or it was eaten just as it was.

You can prepare your own jerky with very little trouble.

Trim the meat of all fat. Slice the buffalo (or beef) into strips 1 inch wide and ⅛ inch thick. "Jerk" or pull them a bit and place them on a baking rack. The meat can be dried in a home food drier or it can be placed in your oven overnight. Leave the oven door open and set the thermostat to as low a temperature as possible. You may need to experiment with your oven, as you do not want the heat to rise above 145° to 150°. My large gas oven is perfect for this, as the pilot light is on all the time and the resulting temperature is just right. If you have such an oven, you can do this process in 12 hours.

If you wish some additional flavor in your meat, you can soak the slices in a bit of soy sauce before drying them.

Jerky will keep for 3 months in an airtight container; for longer if frozen.

CHICKEN-FRIED STEAK WITH CREAM GRAVY

SERVES 4

I have no evidence that buffalo was served in this way on the trail. Since the guides and wagon leaders were of the old-cowboy camp, I am sure that they knew this method of cooking. In any case, if I were on the trail I would appreciate this method of changing the normal flavor of the meat. This method is just great with a beef cube steak; it was served this way during the Depression.

4 cube steaks, about 5 ounces each, *or* 4 pieces of round steak, of the same size, pounded	Salt and freshly ground black pepper to taste
1 cup flour	1 egg, lightly beaten
	1½ cups milk
	¼ cup peanut oil

If using round steak, pound the meat with a wooden or metal meat tenderizer.

Season the flour with salt and pepper. Dredge the meat in the flour mixture. Mix the egg with ½ cup milk. Dip the floured meat into the milk mixture and then back into the flour again.

Pan-fry meat in a large black frying pan with the oil. Brown on both sides and remove from the pan to drain on paper towels. Keep warm on a serving platter in the oven.

Drain all the remaining fat from the pan except 2 tablespoons. Stir in 2 tablespoons of the flour mixture and scrape the bottom of the pan carefully so that you remove the brown goodness left over from the frying.

Using a whisk, stir in the rest of the milk and stir over medium heat until the gravy thickens. If the gravy becomes too thick for your taste, you can add some additional milk. Check the cream gravy for salt and pepper; I like lots of pepper in mine. Serve the gravy over the meat.

You have to have creamy mashed potatoes, a green salad, and Cranberry Orange Relish (page 203) with this dish.

PACIFIC NORTHWEST

Food in the Pacific Northwest is the current topic of articles in every food magazine in the country. The reasons for this interest are not at all complex. The great Puget Sound region offers some of the best seafood you can imagine, and you can eat it in restaurants on the waterfront. Fish in the Northwest is not expensive. I can afford to eat fresh salmon until I can hardly move. Produce is superb, and our wines, both from Washington State and from Oregon, are becoming internationally known. The Pike Place Farmer's Market in Seattle provides the city with the freshest and best of everything. Restaurants in Seattle and Portland are awardwinners. We are also just a few hours away from the fascinating ethnic communities in Vancouver, British Columbia.

The influences on the cuisine of the region are interesting. Native Americans here were living on wonderful salmon, clams, and oysters, which were simply gathered on the beaches. While it is not that simple anymore, the Pacific Northwest tribes taught all of us to eat from the sea and truly enjoy it. You can read a discussion of an Indian salmon bake on page 70. Native American contributions to our cuisine are very important.

Another major influence came with the Chinese. They were brought to America to work on the railroads, a main line of which was to terminate in Seattle. When the railroad was finished, there was a large Chinese community here in Seattle. They began opening restaurants and local public services such as laundries, and a thriving Chinatown developed. I really do believe that the Chinese are the best cooks in the world, and it was logical that they should become involved in the restaurants of Seattle. James Beard, a child of the Pacific Northwest, claims that during the 1930s in Seattle every good restaurant had a Chinese kitchen staff. These won-

derful cooks have done things with the local seafood
and vegetables that others would never have thought
of. Just one plate of our famous geoduck clams,
poached, at the Sea Garden restaurant in Seattle's
Chinatown will make my point.

Early in the history of the region, the Scandinavians
came to the waters of Puget Sound. The water and the
mountains, and the wonderful seafood that is regularly
available, reminded them of the old countries. Their
understanding of seafood has been another major influence in the Pacific Northwest.

The Italians came and added their own special color
to the restaurants. And the Japanese community, which
is of considerable size in Seattle, provided its profound
and quiet insights. Finally, since we are the home of
several very large military installations, there has been
an influx of people from Korea, Vietnam, and Thailand.
Each group has helped us better understand creative
uses for the bounty of the area.

We must also thank the World's Fair of 1962. Prior
to that time our restaurants had served fairly decent
food, but since then Seattle has become one of the great
restaurant cities of America. When young chefs come
to Seattle, I send them to the Pike Place Market on the
very first day they are in town. They become so excited
with the possibilities that they begin creating on the
spot. And I listen and taste and smile. Hey, I've got to
watch out for myself!

PICKLED SALMON

SERVES 12 AS AN APPETIZER

This dish is a regular and beloved treat in the Northwest. The background of the recipe is more Scandinavian or Jewish than it is Northwest Indian. The
Indians would often dry or smoke salmon, but this
method of preservation is popular throughout the area.

One thing to remember: Solly, my friend at the Pure
Food Fish Company in the Pike Place Farmer's Market

in Seattle, has taught me an interesting fact about salmon. The fat is found in the skin and next to the bones. Since it is fat that gives a rancid flavor to the fish, you must be careful to remove both the fat and the bones if you are to have a truly sweet-tasting pickled salmon.

2 pounds fresh salmon fillet, skinless and boneless	**1 tablespoon brown sugar**
3 tablespoons salt	**½ tablespoon mixed pickling spices**
⅓ cup white vinegar (I like Heinz.)	**6 thin lemon slices**
	½ yellow onion, peeled and sliced thin

Sprinkle the salmon on both sides with the salt. Rub it in a bit. Cover and refrigerate overnight.

Wash the salt from the salmon and place in a solution of vinegar and brown sugar. Cover and refrigerate for 3 days. Then, add the remaining ingredients, cover, and return to the refrigerator for an additional 3 days.

Slice salmon thin, across the grain, before serving.

This is great as a first course or appetizer served on thin-sliced dark bread or on rye crackers.

SALMON BARBECUE

SERVES 8

I love to have people from the Midwest come to my house for dinner. Generally they have had little salmon in their time, and very little that was truly fresh. I do not buy a salmon at my fish market unless the creature winks at me! People who have never tasted such a fish are always startled by its wonderful flavor and texture.

My wife, Patty, was born and raised in Brooklyn, New York. When we went to our first United Methodist Church parish here, a member of the board delivered a fish to Patty while I was out calling. He opened the trunk of his car and displayed a twenty-five-pound king salmon, which he had just caught. "This is for you!" "What is it?" asked my bride. When Ed told her, Patty almost died. Her only memory of salmon was of the canned kind, mixed into a disgusting salmon loaf and passed off as food at Brooklyn Public School 139. She knew she could never enjoy that big fish. I stuffed it with vegetables and baked it in the oven. She was the quickest convert I have ever made!

This recipe is simple and even better than the baked version.

1 whole fresh salmon, about 6 pounds, cleaned	3 bunches parsley, washed
1 cup olive oil	Alder-wood chips or sawdust for barbecuing
4 cloves garlic, peeled and crushed	

Pat the salmon dry with paper towels. Mix the olive oil and garlic together and brush the outside and inside of the fish with the oil. Place the parsley in the stomach cavity of the fish and set it on a large piece of heavy-duty aluminum foil. Roll up the sides of the foil so that you have a very shallow pan around the fish.

Have your barbecue fire ready. I prefer to do this in a Kamado (page 16) or a covered cooker, such as a Weber. Have the fire at about 375° and place the wood chips on the coals. Soak them first so that they will just smoke rather than ignite. If using sawdust, put it in an old pie pan or aluminum-foil pan and set it on the coals. Place the fish in the cooker and close the lid. Watch the temperature carefully, and in 25 minutes test the fish. The meat should just begin to flake, but still be moist. Remove to a platter and pull the skin off the top side.

You will need no sauce to go with this, as the fish is wonderfully flavored by the smoke and parsley and garlic.

Serve with a great deal of French bread and a large Tomato Salad (page 125). Barbecued Zucchini (page 385) would be delicious.

SMOKED OYSTERS

If you have never had a freshly smoked oyster, you have a great treat coming in this dish. Get your barbecue going and full of good smoke, just as in the Smoked Black Cod recipe on page 490. Open the oysters and cook them on the half-shell in your covered barbecue until done to your liking. This should take a very few minutes. I did this in my stovetop smoker (page 15) and had great results!

OVEN-BROILED SALMON STEAKS WITH HAZELNUTS

SERVES 6

Salmon and hazelnuts, or filberts, belong to the Pacific Northwest. The two flavors together bring me images from my childhood, though when I was a little one, we had hazelnuts in cookies, not on salmon. We have learned a lot since then.

¼ cup dry white wine
¼ cup olive oil
1 teaspoon dried dill
   Juice of 1 lemon
   Black pepper,
      freshly ground, to
      taste (very little)

¾ cup coarsely ground
   hazelnuts
6 salmon steaks
   (about 6 ounces
   each)
Chopped chives for
   garnish

Mix the wine, oil, dill, lemon juice, and pepper together using a wire whip so that the liquid thickens a bit. In a shallow dish marinate the fish in the liquid for 1 hour. Remove fish from the marinade, place on a broiling rack, and broil under full heat for about 4 minutes, or until the fish barely begins to brown. Brush with the marinade and turn the fish. Brush again with the marinade and broil for 3 minutes. Top with the ground hazelnuts. (I grind the nuts in a medium-sized food processor. Keep them coarse!) Return fish to the broiler and broil for 1 more minute or until the fish begins to flake slightly and the nuts are a light brown.

Watch this so you do not overcook the fish or burn the nuts.

Garnish with the chopped chives and serve immediately.

Serve this along with a Frittorta (page 391) and Asparagus with Almond Butter (page 494).

PINK SCALLOPS

This sounds like a decorator's recipe, but it is not. There is a beautiful pink-shelled scallop that lives in the waters of Puget Sound, that inland body of salt water near which Seattle and Tacoma are situated. The pink scallop has a bright taste that is not as sweet as that of the eastern, or bay scallop . . . it is more like the wonderful brininess that one associates with a good oyster or clam.

This special pink creature is sometimes called a "singing" or "scooter" scallop because he lives on top of the sand under water, and snaps his shell shut, thus forcing water out of the shell. The scallop can jet propel himself about the sea bottom in this way.

I doubt you are going to be able to taste this bivalve unless you come to Seattle. The scallops must be very fresh, and they do not take well to travel, unless they do it on their own. If you do find some Pacific Northwest pink scallops, cook them just as I do my Steamed Clams (page 416). The whole creature is edible and just delicious.

SMOKED BLACK COD

This dish is so delicious that I am getting hungry for lunch even as I tell you about it. Black cod is oily and rich, and it takes beautifully to smoking. This can be done in your barbecue, so you might want to read the section on smoking with wood chips in your barbecue (page 377).

Buy fresh black cod steaks (in the East, this fish is called sable), as the whole fish is hard to work with. Place them in your covered barbecue at about 375° and place alder or hickory chips or sawdust on the coals. Cook just until the fish begins to flake, a very few minutes. Do not turn.

You will have great success with this dish if you do it in a stovetop smoker (page 15). Cook and smoke for no more than 13 minutes, maybe 14.

Serve plain with lemon and a chopped-chive garnish. That's it. Please don't do anything more to this great fish!

A large green salad and rolls, along with a Frittorta (page 391) will complete the menu.

NOTE: For real success in this dish you must have your barbecue smoking like mad before you put the fish in the cooker.

CLAMS AND WHITE WINE SAUCE

SERVES 4–5 AS AN APPETIZER; 2–3 AS A MAIN COURSE

Clams are available most of the year in the Pacific Northwest. When I was a child, we used to go digging for them ourselves, but I leave that task to the professionals these days. That reminds me. I have never taken my boys clamming. That is a must, and I'll have to bring their grandmother along to show them how it is done.

This dish is simple and rich. The resulting sauce is better than the clams themselves.

4 pounds fresh clams	½ cup dry white wine
¼ cup olive oil	1/16 teaspoon freshly
3 cloves garlic, peeled	ground black
and sliced thin	pepper or to
2 green onions,	taste
chopped	2 tablespoons *each*
½ cup chopped celery	butter and flour,
tops	cooked together
3 tablespoons	to form a roux
chopped parsley	(page 31)

Be sure the clams are all tightly closed when you purchase them. Wash the clams and soak them in fresh water for about 1 hour. Drain. Heat a 12-quart kettle and add the olive oil. Sauté the garlic and green onions for just a few moments. Put the drained clams in the pot along with the remaining ingredients except the roux. Cover and cook at medium-high heat until the shells are all opened wide. Discard those that do not open. Remove the clams from the pot, leaving the nectar behind. Using a wire whip, stir the roux into the nectar and continue to stir until the sauce thickens. Pour the sauce over the clams and serve.

I like to serve this dish along with Macaroni Pie (page 130) so that the sauce can mix with the pasta.

SHRIMP WITH TEAR-SHAPED PASTA

SERVES 6, OR MORE AS AN APPETIZER

One of my favorite restaurants in Seattle is located near my office. What luck! It is called Place Pigalle and the owner, Bill Frank, is a fine cook in his own right. He and his chef, Hugh Kohl, developed a dish that I believe is typical of the great things going on in the Pacific Northwest. The use of mustard seed here is very creative and delicious. You can also see the influence of the many ethnic groups that have come to Seattle, especially the Chinese and Thai influences. You simply must go to the restaurant and try this dish.

PASTA

1 pound raw orzo or
    melon-seed
    pasta, cooked al
    dente and well
    drained
1 stick butter
2½ tablespoons fresh
    ginger, cut into
    fine julienne
1½ tablespoons yellow
    mustard seed

⅓ cup dry-roasted
    cashews
    (unsalted)
1½ tablespoons
    coconut,
    shredded fine
⅓ cup chopped
    cilantro (page
    37)

SHRIMP SAUTÉ

¼ cup olive oil
1½ tablespoons fresh
    ginger, cut into
    fine julienne
1 pound (16–20 per
    pound) raw
    shrimp, peeled
    and deveined

⅓ cup chopped
    scallions
2½ tablespoons fresh
    lime juice
Salt and pepper to
    taste
Lime wedges and
    cilantro leaves
    for garnish

FOR THE PASTA

Heat a large frying pan and add the butter, ginger, mustard seed, and cashews, and sauté for about 2 minutes. Add the precooked pasta, coconut, and cilantro, and cook over medium heat. Toss or sauté this mixture until all ingredients are hot. Set aside, covered, to keep warm.

FOR THE SHRIMP SAUTÉ

Heat another large frying pan and add the oil and ginger. Sauté for 30 seconds. Add the shrimp, scallions, and lime juice, and cook over medium-high heat until the shrimp just changes color (a few minutes). Add salt and pepper. Serve over the hot pasta and garnish with lime segments and cilantro leaves.

This is a great main course if you serve it with a green salad and a fresh-fruit tray.

SHRIMP CHOWED WITH GARLIC

SERVES 6 AS PART OF A LARGER MEAL

You can cook this recipe in a frying pan rather than in a wok, of course, but I have included it in the Pacific Northwest section of the book to show how vast the influence of the Chinese on the food of the Puget Sound region has been. They are the ones who have always told us not to cook seafood and vegetables so long, and I believe they are right.

While shrimp do not generally live in the cold waters of Puget Sound, we do import a lot of them from Louisiana and Mexico. And I have learned to cook them from the Chinese!

1½ pounds large
    shrimp, peeled
    and deveined
3 tablespoons peanut
    oil
1 teaspoon salt
5 cloves garlic, peeled
    and sliced thin

3 green onions,
    chopped
2 teaspoons sesame
    oil (page 33)
1 tablespoon dry
    sherry

Have everything prepared before you start this dish. Clean the shrimp and pat dry on paper towels.

Heat a wok or large heavy frying pan over highest heat. Add the oil, salt, and garlic, and toss for just a few seconds. The garlic should change color right away. Add the shrimp and toss constantly until they all change to a bright orange color. Throw in the green onions and the sesame oil, and toss for a few seconds. Add the sherry and cover the pan. Turn off the heat and serve immediately.

I serve this with Rice with Cheese and Onions (page 448) and Peas and Salt Pork (page 122).

ASPARAGUS WITH ALMOND BUTTER

SERVES 4–6

When the local asparagus season starts in Seattle, the Pike Place Farmer's Market goes crazy. Asparagus is everywhere and we eat ourselves into an asparagus frenzy.

This quick dish is very tasty. Remember, don't over-cook the asparagus. It should be bright green and a bit crunchy.

2 pounds asparagus spears, cleaned (See HINT page 495.)	3 tablespoons butter
	4 tablespoons sliced almonds
4 tablespoons olive oil	Juice of ½ lemon
1 clove garlic, peeled and crushed	

Cut the spears into 1-inch-long pieces and set aside. Bring 2 quarts of water to a boil and add 2 tablespoons of the olive oil. Throw in the asparagus and cook for 2 minutes. Drain and rinse with cold water immediately. This can be done up to an hour before dinner if you wish. Keep the blanched asparagus in cold water.

Heat a large frying pan and add the remaining olive oil and garlic. Add the drained asparagus and cook only until it is hot. Remove from the pan to a serving dish. Add the butter and sliced almonds to the pan. Stir about until the almonds are toasty brown. Add the lemon juice and immediately pour the sauce over the asparagus. Serve right away.

> **HINT: On Cleaning Asparagus.**
> Some people go to the work of peeling the ends of the asparagus shoots. I do not bother. Hold the spear in both hands and break it off at the most tender point of the bottom of the stem. Just bend it and it will break where it should. The top part is for dinner and the bottom part is to be saved for asparagus soup.

PASTA WITH FRESH ASPARAGUS AND SCALLOPS

SERVES 6 AS A FIRST COURSE

Please don't put any cheese on pasta if it contains seafood. I want the gentle flavor of the seafood to stand on its own, and cheese will get in the way. It is amazing to see what people will do to seafood.

This uses three of my favorite foods. How can I lose?

1 pound asparagus, cleaned (See HINT above.)
3 tablespoons olive oil
3 cloves garlic, peeled and crushed
2 green onions, chopped

1 cup cream or half-and-half
½ pound scallops
Salt and freshly ground black pepper to taste
1 pound pasta

Clean and slice the asparagus into ⅛-inch slices, cut on a 45° angle. Set aside.

Heat a large kettle of water and put the pasta on to cook until just al dente.

Heat a large frying pan or wok and add the olive oil

and garlic. Toss for a moment and add the asparagus. Cook over high heat, stirring all the time, just until the asparagus becomes the least bit tender, about 2 minutes. Add the green onions and toss. Add the cream and bring to a quick simmer. Add the scallops and turn off the heat.

Drain the pasta and place on a platter. Strain the asparagus and scallops from the cream and put on top of the pasta. Reduce (page 25) the cream by one third over medium-high heat. Add salt and pepper to taste and pour over the pasta. Serve immediately.

SEAFOOD SALAD

SERVES 8

This sort of dish is popular with everyone in our region. It is not very fattening and you can keep the level of salt down by using fresh lemon juice. And besides, since the seafood is all fresh, it is delicious.

2 pounds clams, cleaned and steamed (page 416)

2 pounds mussels, cleaned and steamed like the clams (I cook them together in the same pot.)

1½ cups celery, sliced thin

1 large yellow onion, peeled and sliced very thin

⅔ cup olive oil

½ cup white wine vinegar

2 teaspoons oregano, crushed

1 pound halibut or cod fillet, skinless and boneless

½ pound large shrimp, peeled and deveined

½ pound scallops

1 cup chopped parsley

Black pepper, freshly ground, to taste

Lemon wedges for garnish

Cook the clams and mussels in one pot as per the instructions for Steamed Clams (page 416). The only variation is that you must pull the little beard off the mussels before steaming them. This is a mossy growth with which the mussel attaches himself to a rock. Cook as directed, and drain the nectar and reserve. Allow the clams and mussels to cool a bit and remove them from their shells, discarding the shells. Cover and set aside.

Place the fish fillet in the nectar and bring to a simmer. Be sure that the fillet has no bones. Simmer for 6 minutes and then add the shrimp and scallops. Bring to a simmer again and turn off the heat.

Combine all the remaining ingredients in a bowl, except the lemon wedges. Stir well to thicken. Drain the shrimp and scallops, saving the nectar for a later use (like a midnight snack with a bit of beer!) and add all the fish products to the dressing. Chill for 1 hour before serving. Garnish with lemon wedges.

This can be served either as a main course or as an appetizer.

OYSTER STEW

SERVES 4–5

We are talking camps here. Everyone seems to have their own version of oyster stew, but I claim that if anyone is going to cook an oyster for me (I prefer them raw) then that person had better cook the creature in cream. That is all there is to it!

You must not cook oysters. They should be warmed, and just that alone. This is what God intended or the oyster would not have been made to be so delicate. So, be gentle. In New York, at the wonderful Grand Central Oyster Bar, they cook each dish of oyster stew to order . . . right in front of you, in steam jacket pans that they have had for years. Lovely! We do the same thing in the Pacific Northwest. This dish is very rich.

4 tablespoons butter
1 tablespoon finely
   chopped onion
2 cups half-and-half
½ teaspoon salt
   Pinch of white
   pepper

3 cups oysters,
   shucked, with
   their juice
2 tablespoons
   chopped parsley
   for garnish

I think that you should use a heat diffuser (page 14) for this one, as we do not want to overcook the oysters.

In a 2-quart saucepan melt the butter and quickly sauté the onion. Add the half-and-half, along with the salt and pepper, and bring to a light simmer. Add the oysters and juice, and heat just until everything is hot.

Place in bowls and serve immediately with the parsley garnish.

SMOKED SALMON TARTARE

SERVES 6–8

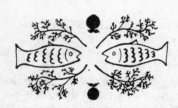

This is a wonderful snack or cocktail party dish. It is typical of the cuisine of the Pacific Northwest, but you must understand that by smoked salmon I do not mean that dry stuff, which is nothing but grainy strings. The salmon that I use for this dish is almost cold-smoked . . . in the East you would probably call it lox.

1 pound light smoked
 salmon, raw
 salmon, or
 combination of
 both
½ can (2 ounces) flat
 anchovies (from
 Portugal or Italy)
1 egg, raw
1 tablespoon Dijon-
 style mustard
 (Grey Poupon is
 fine.)

Dash of
 Worcestershire
 sauce or to taste
3 tablespoons finely
 chopped yellow
 onion
⅛ teaspoon freshly
 ground black
 pepper
1 tablespoon chopped
 capers
2 tablespoons olive oil
Thin rye crackers

Be sure the salmon is skinless and boneless. I like a mixture of two kinds, raw and light-smoked. Chop the salmon and anchovies in a medium-sized food processor for just a few seconds. We don't want a paste but a coarse chop. Place the mixture in a bowl. Mix all other ingredients together and blend with the fish. Chill before serving.

Spread on thin rye crackers as a first course.

"Crown thy good with brotherhood..."

EPILOGUE

The Future

I have offered you this book as an effort at digesting American history. I have had wonderful fun researching the material and now I am convinced, more than ever before, that we have a grand cuisine and we have been, for the most part, good providers. What of the future?

If you have enjoyed reading and tasting this material, then I want you to send some food or money to your local food bank. Not all Americans are enjoying their place in our culture, and you and I are obligated to do something about it. Talk it over with your family and decide what you can do to make all Americans proud of our age of abundance.

Second, we must all look to, encourage, and support efforts at food research. We can continue to help in feeding the world, and I believe it is our responsibility to do so.

I became interested in food as a theological issue while a seminary student. One of our professors, Dr. Franz Hildebrant, was a very pious old German. We loved him dearly and invited him to eat with us at all student gatherings and often in our homes. I always asked this famous churchman to offer the blessing. It seemed to be the only thing to do, and Papa Franz would always say the same thing: "Bless us Lord Jesus, and bless our meal. And we pray thee, keep us mindful of those who starve. Amen." He always turned the direction of the meal away from ourselves.

The Bible is filled with stories of feasts to which the downcast and the poor were invited. This might be the very day in which to open your own table to those who are hungry, not only for food but for companionship and affection.

I bid you peace.

INDEX

Permissions

Recipe for Was-nah Corn and Cherry Snack from *Sam Arnold's Fryingpans West* (Arnold and Company, 1985), used with permission of the publisher.

Recipes for Berry Soup and Indian Blueberry Pudding from *Early American Cooking* (Peter Pauper Press, 1986), used with permission of the publisher.

Recipe for Syllabub from *The Williamsburg Art of Cookery,* by Helen Bullock (Colonial Williamsburg, Inc., 1938), used with permission of The Colonial Williamsburg Foundation.

Sally Lunn Bread; 1,2,3,4 Cake; and Lane Cake reprinted by permission of Grosset and Dunlap, Inc., from *Southern Cooking,* by S. R. Dull, copyright 1941 by Mrs. S. R. Dull, copyright © 1968 by Grosset and Dunlap, Inc.

Recipes for Oyster Sauce for Virginia Ham, Carrot Pudding, Fricassee of Rabbit (or Chicken), Mushroom Catsup, and Rich Cake from *The Art of Cooking,* by Hannah Glasse (Prospect Books Limited, 1983).

Recipe for Skillet Cranberries for a Slack Oven from *The Thirteen Colonies Cookbook,* by Mary Donovan, Amy Hatrak, Frances Mills, and Elizabeth Shull (Praeger Publishers, 1975).

Recipes for Maple Mashed Sweet Potatoes and Virginia Spoon Bread from *America's Cook Book,* compiled by the Herald Tribune Home Institute, copyright 1937 by Charles Scribner's Sons; copyright renewed© 1965 by New York Herald Tribune. Reprinted with the permission of Charles Scribner's Sons, a division of Macmillan, Inc.

Recipes for Huguenot Torte and Pickled Peaches from *Charleston Receipts,* collected by The Junior League of Charleston, 1950.

Recipes for Jefferson Fried Chicken, Baked Polenta, Fish with Potatoes, Cheese Curd Pudding, Apple Pudding, and Philadelphia Rice Pudding from *Thomas Jefferson's Cook Book,* by Marie Kimball (University Press of Virginia, 1976), used with permission of the publisher.

Recipes for Baked-Bean Soup, Oyster and Ham Pie, and Cranberry Bread reprinted with permission of the Macmillan Publishing Com-

Recipes for Salt Pork, Beans and Hominy, Schnitz und Knepp, and Shoofly Pie from the *Pennsylvania Dutch Cook Book* (Leonard S. Davidow, 1934).